"The book fills a gap in the literature on extradition and judicial co-operation in Europe. It is unique in providing a comprehensive and topical multi-disciplinary analysis of the challenges arising from the application of the political offence exception in extradition law. The book is required reading for audiences with expertise in law, international relations and political science and will be of interest to scholars, students and practitioners alike. Sibel Top has emerged as a leading critical voice in the field."

Professor Valsamis Mitsilegas, *Dean of the School of Law and Social Justice & Professor of European and Global Law, University of Liverpool, United Kingdom*

"Sibel Top's book comes some 50 years after I wrote my own PhD on the same subject. When I started studying it, the political offence exception was still generally accepted. At the same time, the process of its erosion was getting in full motion as I was writing, against the backdrop of a multitude of terrorist attacks in the 1970s and 80s. Today, this erosion seems to be complete, especially in Europe, with the advent, shortly after 9/11, of the European Arrest Warrant (EAW). But, as Sibel Top shows, times are changing again. Recent events indicate a decline in democracies around the world and in Europe and are resuscitating the need for a political offence exception. A case in point is the Catalan crisis, in which prominent Catalan leaders have been seeking protection against Spanish EAWs in various European States. None of them has been surrendered. We may, as Sibel Top suggests, be witnessing the rise of a potential 'ghost political offence exception'. The blind mutual confidence between EU States is no longer obvious. One can only hope that there will be no further decline in democracies, but recent developments in parts of Europe and the rest of the world do not augur well. New 'ghost exceptions' may be needed to reset the balance. This book is an excellent study for both academics and practitioners interested in this fascinating and ever-challenging field of the law."

Judge C. Van den Wyngaert, *International Court of Justice (2000–2002), International Criminal Tribunal for the former Yugoslavia (2003–2009), International Criminal Court (2009–2018), and Professor at the University of Antwerp, Belgium*

Extradition and Political Crimes

This book examines the evolution and current application of the political offence exception clause to extradition in Europe.

The long-standing academic exploration of terrorism has recently given way to renewed interest in the political offence exception to extradition, prompted by recent events that signal a democratic downturn globally. Despite the significant curtailment – and, in some cases, the complete abolition – of the political offence exception to extradition in Europe, certain European states continue to quietly implement this exception to deny extradition requests. This work studies the development of the political offence exception in Europe by narrowing its focus from an international perspective to the European context, specifically examining the Council of Europe and the European Union, before zeroing in on the Catalan independence crisis, which offers a particularly valuable case for analysing the application of the political offence exception in the European context.

By providing a detailed examination of the evolving protections for political offenders within European legal frameworks, the text updates the long overdue academic knowledge on the matter. It is therefore an essential resource for anyone interested in European criminal law and extradition, in particular. It will also be of interest to researchers, academics, and policy-makers working in the areas of criminal law, human rights law, legal theory, criminology, and political science.

Sibel Top is a postdoctoral researcher and the managing director of the Fundamental Rights Research Center of the Vrije Universiteit Brussel. She is also an affiliated researcher of the Center for Migration, Diversity and Justice of the Brussels School of Governance of the Vrije Universiteit Brussel, Belgium.

Transnational Criminal Justice
Series Editor
Saskia Hufnagel
Queen Mary University of London, UK

The concept of 'transnational criminal justice' has frequently been interpreted in the academic literature as 'international criminal justice' or 'global criminal justice'. Many publications that use the term 'transnational' therefore discuss international criminal justice and international legal frameworks. Another form of studies that has developed under the umbrella of transnationality in the field of criminal law is comparative. There has hence been a move from the terminology of 'international', 'global' and 'comparative' criminal justice towards 'transnational' criminal justice.

This series considers these developments, but focuses primarily on publications that adhere to a more literal interpretation of the term 'transnational'. The aim of the series is to provide a forum for discussion of bilateral and multilateral relationships between nations in the field of criminal justice. International law influences these relationships, but is not the focus here. Equally, to explain transnational relationships, comparative analyses are required. While incorporating comparative studies in this series, their aim is the explanation of challenges to criminal justice cooperation in bilateral or multilateral relationships.

Titles in this series:

The Transnational Crime of Human Trafficking
A Human Security Approach
Maria O'Neill

Cultural Property Crime and the Law
Legal Approaches to Protection, Repatriation, and Countering Illicit Trade
Michelle Fabiani, Kate Melody Burmon and Saskia Hufnagel

Extradition and Political Crimes
The Use of the Political Offence Exception in Europe
Sibel Top

For more information about this series, please visit: https://www.routledge.com/Transnational-Criminal-Justice/book-series/TRANSCJ

Extradition and Political Crimes

The Use of the Political Offence Exception in Europe

Sibel Top

Routledge
Taylor & Francis Group
LONDON AND NEW YORK

First published 2025

by Routledge
4 Park Square, Milton Park, Abingdon, Oxon OX14 4RN

and by Routledge
605 Third Avenue, New York, NY 10158

Routledge is an imprint of the Taylor & Francis Group, an informa business

British Library Cataloguing-in-Publication Data
A catalogue record for this book is available from the British Library

Library of Congress Cataloging-in-Publication Data
Names: Top, Sibel, author.
Title: Extradition and political crimes : the use of the political offence exception in Europe / Sibel Top.
Description: Abingdon, Oxon [UK] ; New York, NY : Routledge, 2025. | Series: Transnational criminal justice | Includes bibliographical references and index.
Identifiers: LCCN 2024046283 (print) | LCCN 2024046284 (ebook) | ISBN 9781032546230 (hardback) | ISBN 9781032546254 (paperback) | ISBN 9781003425847 (ebook)
Subjects: LCSH: Extradition—Europe. | Political crimes and offenses—Law and legislation—Europe.
Classification: LCC KJC9570 .T67 2025 (print) | LCC KJC9570 (ebook) | DDC 345.24/052—dc23/eng/20241008
LC record available at https://lccn.loc.gov/2024046283
LC ebook record available at https://lccn.loc.gov/2024046284

ISBN: 978-1-032-54623-0 (hbk)
ISBN: 978-1-032-54625-4 (pbk)
ISBN: 978-1-003-42584-7 (ebk)

DOI: 10.4324/9781003425847

Typeset in Galliard
by Apex CoVantage, LLC

Contents

Acknowledgements

Writing a monograph is like running a marathon. Enthusiasm, self-doubt, determination, and ending up squeezed like a lemon, are all part of the process. I could not have crossed the finish line, however, without the crucial support of people around me. To paraphrase the Village People, *no one does it all by themselves!*

Central to completing the PhD dissertation on which this book is based were my thesis supervisors, Paul De Hert and Florian Trauner. They not only gave me the trust and freedom to grow in my own way and find my identity as a researcher, but they also guided me in the process by emboldening me to use my interdisciplinary background as my added value and continuously pushed me to defend my project and do so with confidence. Crucially, their support and words of encouragement at the most critical moments of the redaction enabled me to finish this project.

My research led me, in 2019, to Queen Mary University, London, where I met Valsamis Mitsilegas who became part of my supervisory committee. It did not matter that I was merely a visiting scholar; Valsamis treated me as one of his own and provided me incredible support and guidance for the whole year. I was extremely lucky to be surrounded by a team of professors who showed me continuous support and always worked in my best interest.

I am forever indebted to Paul Bekaert, Christophe Marchand, Paul Rietjens, Claude Debrulle, and Olivier Peter for kindly accepting to give me interviews on their experience at the Belgian Ministry of Foreign Affairs at the moment of the adoption of tools discussed in this book or on their defence of Catalan exiles. Their crucial insights were simply essential to this work as they provided information that was nowhere else to be found.

Receiving outstanding supervision is one thing, being in a well-meaning and supportive environment with amazing colleagues is another. Life as a researcher at the Vrije Universiteit Brussel is definitely made better thanks to the incredible team at the Fundamental Rights Center that make our research group a beacon of support and benevolence.

It would be widely misconstrued, however, to think that academic support alone gets one across the finish line. A special and heartfelt thank-you goes to my parents, who have been nothing but supportive since I know myself. I have been so lucky to be surrounded in life by people who wanted nothing but the best for me. My incredible friends have played an enormous role in that. Finally, my core. My husband, daughter, and newly born son. I dedicate this book to you.

Credits

This book is based on a PhD thesis, defended on 20 November 2022 at the Vrije Universiteit Brussel, which was funded by the Flemish Research Foundation (Fonds Wetenschappelijk Onderzoek – FWO).

1 Reviving the political offence exception in Europe

Reigniting interest in research on the political offence exception to extradition

Traditionally, political crimes have enjoyed a distinctive protection within the criminal law of European states, and later within European criminal law more broadly. This special status dates back to the French Revolution and the subsequent liberation movements across Europe in the late 18th and early 19th centuries.[1] At the time, it was largely admitted that if leaders of movements fighting tyranny and despotism fled, it would be unthinkable to treat them as criminals and surrender them back to their oppressors, who would not be able to provide them a fair trial.[2] However, as explored in the following chapters, the evolution of shared ideals, levels of democracy, the rule of law, and respect for human rights among European countries fostered increased trust in each other's judicial systems. This trust facilitated the adoption of stringent anti-terrorism legislation and policies. The fight against terrorism took a sharp turn between 1970 and 1990 and, later, in the post-2001 period and greatly impacted the protection of political offenders.[3] Despite their fundamentally different moral implications,[4] political crimes and terrorism share a common denominator that often complicates their distinction in practice. While the political offence exception clause still exists within the Council of Europe (CoE) framework, albeit substantially weakened, it was completely abolished in the European Union as part of the European Union's counterterrorism efforts. Given these developments, why examine this issue now?

This topic has gained renewed relevance due to increasing evidence that threats to democratic principles are proliferating across the European political

1 J. Jansson, *Terrorism, Criminal Law and Politics: The Decline of the Political Offence Exception to Extradition* (Routledge, Abingdon, New York 2020) 71–75.

2 I. Stanbrook and C. Stanbrook, *Extradition: Law and Practice* (Oxford University Press, Oxford 2000) 5.

3 The terms *political offences* and *political crimes* are used interchangeably in this work.

4 C. Van den Wijngaert, *The Political Offence Exception to Extradition: The Delicate Problem of Balancing the Rights of the Individual and the International Public Order* (Kluwer, The Netherlands 1980) 29.

DOI: 10.4324/9781003425847-1

landscape. Some of these threats have developed gradually, initially appearing relatively benign, but they have accumulated to exert a harmful impact on the core principles of democracy, the rule of law, and human rights upheld in Europe.[5] For example, as a result of a long process of democratic decline, no less than 11 out of the 47 member states of the Council of Europe – that is over a fifth of CoE member states – were on the Parliamentary Assembly Monitoring list in 2021 for persistently violating the rule of law, democratic principles, and human rights.[6] Being included on that list requires persistent and continuous violations of the organisation's principles. These violations must occur over an extended period and be recurrent, reflecting a genuine and serious decline in democratic standards.[7] In March 2022, Russia was even expulsed from the Council of Europe following its invasion of Ukraine and ceased to be a contracting party to the European Convention on Human Rights on 16 September 2022.[8]

At the EU level, the Court of Justice of the European Union (CJEU) issued resounding rulings in 2016 underlining that the trust among EU member states was not to be blind. It also reminded the member states of their responsibility to ensure that their counterparts respect human rights before cooperating with them in criminal matters. In the now famous *Aranyosi* and *Căldăraru*,[9] as well as *Bob-Dogi*,[10] cases, the CJEU backtracked from the idea that cooperation in the European arrest warrant framework should be automatic. The very next year, the European Union triggered article 7 of the Treaty on the European Union against Poland,[11] and Hungary followed suit in 2018.[12] Meanwhile, and as a result of all these events, mutual trust among EU member states has continued to dwindle, which the CJEU periodically reminds in its powerful rulings, more recently in its ruling on the *LM* case, which openly questioned the mutual trust

5 Council of Europe, 'Values' (Council of Europe) <https://www.coe.int/en/web/about-us/values> accessed 21 February 2024.

6 Parliamentary Assembly, Resolution of 25 January 2021 on 'Progress of the Assembly's Monitoring Procedure (January-December 2020)' (Resolution 2357) 2021.

7 Parliamentary Assembly of the Council of Europe (Committee on the Honouring of Obligations and Commitments by Member States of the Council of Europe - Monitoring Committee), The Monitoring Procedure of the Parliamentary Assembly' AS/Mon/Inf(2017)03rev (2017).

8 Council of Europe Newsroom, 'Russia Ceases to be a Party to the European Convention on Human Rights on 16 September 2022' (Council of Europe 2022) <https://www.coe.int/en/web/portal/-/russia-ceases-to-be-party-to-the-european-convention-on-human-rights> accessed 21 February 2024.

9 Pál Aranyosi et Robert Căldăraru [5 April 2016] Joined cases C-404/15 and C-659/15 PPU. EU:C:2016:198.

10 Niculaie Aurel Bob-Dogi [1 June 2016] case C-241/15. EU:C:2016:385.

11 European Commission, 'Rule of Law: European Commission Acts to Defend Judicial Independence in Poland' (European Commission 2017) <https://ec.europa.eu/commission/presscorner/detail/en/IP_17_5367> accessed 21 February 2024.

12 European Parliament Resolution of 12 September 2018 on a Proposal Calling on the Council to Determine, pursuant to Article 7(1) of the Treaty on European Union, the Existence of a Clear Risk of a Serious Breach by Hungary of the Values on Which the Union is Founded (2017/2131(INL)) P8_TA(2018)0340 [2018].

principle.[13] In 2019, the European Union started producing rule of law reports, assessing the rule of law situation in EU member states, and in January 2021, the European Union's conditionality regulation entered into force[14] – tying EU funds to the respect of rule of law, which can only be construed as an EU attempt to call some of its member states to order.

It is against this general backdrop that the Catalan crisis has unfolded since 2017, with several leaders of the Catalan independence referendum fleeing into self-imposed exile. Despite numerous attempts by Spanish judicial authorities to secure their return, these leaders have remained abroad for years.[15] This referendum raised multiple questions, including the legitimacy of such actions in contemporary Europe and the level of trust among EU and CoE member states, even toward countries like Spain, whose democratic standards are generally not questioned. The violent repression of the referendum by Spanish police only exacerbated tensions and raised further concerns about whether Catalan exiles should receive protection.[16] The already challenging position of the EU countries where the exiles sought refuge was further complicated by the erratic handling of European arrest warrants by Spain – warrants that were issued, withdrawn, and re-issued – raising suspicions over their misuse by Spanish judicial authorities.[17] Conversely, Switzerland, not being an EU member state, explicitly declared on two occasions that it would not extradite Catalan exiles because it considered the crimes committed by separatist leaders to be political.[18] The Catalan crisis thus truly put the question of the political

13 Minister for Justice and Equality v. LM [25 August 2018] Case C-216/18 PPU. EU:C:2018:586.

14 Regulation (EU, Euratom) 2020/2092 of the European Parliament and of the Council of 16 December 2020 on a General Regime of Conditionality for the Protection of the Union Budget [2020] OJ L 433/1

15 A. Willems, 'The Extradition Saga Continues: Is the Latest Ruling a Win for Puigdemont, Spain, or for Mutual Trust?' (EUROPP blog - LSE 2018) <http://blogs.lse.ac.uk/europpblog/2018/07/18/the-extradition-saga-continues-is-the-latest-ruling-a-win-for-puigdemont-spain-or-for-mutual-trust/> accessed 21 February 2024.

16 Human Rights Watch, 'Spain: Police Used Excessive Force in Catalonia' (Human Rights Watch 2017) <https://www.hrw.org/news/2017/10/12/spain-police-used-excessive-force-catalonia> accessed 21 February 2024.

17 Ramon Tremosa i Balcells (ALDE), Josep-Maria Terricabras (Verts/ALE), Jordi Solé (Verts/ALE), Martina Anderson (GUE/NGL), José Bové (Verts/ALE), Bodil Valero (Verts/ALE), Igor Šoltes (Verts/ALE), Izaskun Bilbao Barandica (ALDE), Josu Juaristi Abaunz (GUE/NGL), Jill Evans (Verts/ALE), António Marinho e Pinto (ALDE), Bart Staes (Verts/ALE), Barbara Spinelli (GUE/NGL), Maria Lidia Senra Rodríguez (GUE/NGL) and Rolandas Paksas (EFDD) 1145474.EN, PE 617.651 Question for Written Answer E-000746/2018 to the Commission. Subject: Misuse of the European Arrest Warrant by Spain [2018].

18 CPE-N Commissions de Politique Extérieure, 'Communiqué de Presse – La Protection des Intérêts Économiques Extérieurs de la Suisse à l'Ordre du Jour' (L'Assemblée Fédérale – le Parlement Suisse 2018) <https://www.parlament.ch/press-releases/Pages/mm-apk-n-2018-04-17.aspx> accessed 21 February 2024; A. Harari, 'La Suisse N'Expulsera pas l'Indépendantiste Catalane Anna Gabriel' (Le Temps 2018) <https://www.letemps.ch/suisse/suisse-nexpulsera-lindependantiste-catalane-anna-gabriel> accessed 21 February 2024.

offence exception back on the table more than any other event and serve as a focal point for this book that argues that European countries who received extradition requests by Spain applied an unspoken form of the political offence exception to the cases of Catalan exiles.

Structure of book

What this book does is thus revisit the long-forgotten political offence exception clause to extradition and discuss its newfound relevance through a recent event in the European context. What it does not do is discuss the desirability of the clause or try to define the concepts of political offences and terrorism. Numerous and more seasoned scholars have attempted to define political offence or terrorist crimes before and draw a moral line between them. This work bypasses the contentious debates over definitions, which risk derailing rather than clarifying the research. Instead, it focuses on the evolution of legal protections for political offenders, irrespective of the lack of precise definitions for political crimes or terrorism. In doing so, it aims to update academic knowledge on the political offence exception clause and recontextualise it within modern times.

The book is divided into seven chapters, funnelling down from the international context to the more specific Catalan question. Chapter 2 outlines the difficulties of defining political crimes and explores the main theories applied in extradition law to determine the political nature of a crime. These theories include the Anglo-Saxon incidence test, the French injured rights theory, and the Swiss proportionality test. The chapter shows that the Swiss proportionality test is the most widely accepted assessment and has been adopted as the benchmark in various international forums.

Despite existing theories for determining the political nature of an offence, the fight against terrorism has led to a de facto 'negative' definition of political crimes. Successive counterterrorism conventions have progressively excluded certain crimes from the protection afforded to political offenders. The third chapter examines changes in the protection of political offenders at the CoE level through a chronological approach. It begins with the protection offered under the 1957 European Convention on Extradition, the first multilateral tool for criminal cooperation in Europe, and traces how subsequent counterterrorism measures have increasingly eroded this protection.

Chapter 4 outlines how the trend to diminish the protection of political offenders persisted and was further entrenched at the EU level, culminating in the abolition of the political offence exception clause. It shows how, within the European Union, cooperation in criminal matters became a measure of member states' commitment to shared European values such as democracy, human rights, and the rule of law. One member state in particular, Spain, played a pivotal role in shaping the European Union's mechanisms for extradition and counterterrorism. Confronted with Basque terrorism and frustrated by decades of insufficient cooperation on the extradition of ETA members,[19] Spanish authorities advocated for years for, and eventually achieved, the development of the EU counterterrorism framework. This framework encompassed increased automatism in extradition, the abolition of the political offence exception, the removal of the right to political asylum for EU citizens, and a repoliticisation of the definition of terrorism. When Catalan independence leaders feld in self-imposed exile following the Catalan independence referendum Spain was thus expected to have all the necessary tools for their swift return. However, the process did not unfold as seamlessly as Spanish judicial authorities had anticipated.

Zooming in on the Spanish context and focusing on the Catalan independence crisis, Chapter 5 begins by outlining the perspective of Catalan separatists, who characterise Spain as a post-Francoist state from which they seek to secede to establish what they believe would be a true democracy. While it is acknowledged that Catalan separatists do not form a homogeneous group, their arguments are presented together in this book. The first reason for this pertains to the limits of this work, which does not seek to map the Catalan political scene in greater detail than necessary for the point made here. The second one relates to the fact that separatists across the political spectrum joined forces in the independence process. In a second phase, the chapter discusses the initial reaction of Spanish (political and judicial) authorities who responded with police violence and a full judicialisation of the process. This response was characterised by severe prosecutions, including charges such as rebellion, which could result in sentences of up to 30 years in prison. The chapter further explains how this reaction was all the stronger that the Partido Popular, the party in power at the time of the referendum, is a party with a traditionally strong anti-devolution stance in the Spanish political landscape. When it was replaced by the Partido Socialista Obrero Español at the head of the country, the approach of central authorities became much more compromising.

Chapter 6 looks at the response of the judicial authorities of EU member states and Swiss authorities on the Catalan question. It shows how Catalan exiles internationalised the crisis by fleeing abroad and seeking refuge in other European countries. Despite the near-automatic nature of extradition within the European Union, no EU member state's judicial authority was comfortable enough to surrender Catalan exiles. Although Germany did agree to extradite Puigdemont, it was only for the non-political charge of embezzlement. The German court, reminding that criminal law should be used as restrictively as possible in political cases, refused to extradite Puigdemont on the rebellion charge by applying an exceptionally high standard for the dual criminality requirement. The chapter further outlines how, in light of the Catalan argumentation and the Spanish reaction to the Catalan independence referendum,

19 The ETA, Euskadi Ta Askatasuna, is a Basque separatist organisation whose paramilitary wing committed attacks to gain independence. E.-P. Guittet, 'Political Identity and Democratic Solidarity After 9/11: The Spanish Case' [2004] *Altern. Global Local Polit.* 441, 443.

the lawyers of Catalan exiles made the case for a political trial, where the fundamental rights of Catalan exiles would be jeopardised. It also details how the Belgian Court, the only other EU member state judicial authority to issue a ruling at the time of writing, followed the arguments of the Catalan exiles' lawyers and declined to execute the European arrest warrant issued by Spanish authorities, citing concerns over the right to a fair trial for the Catalan leaders. Based on these developments and statements from Swiss authorities regarding the political nature of the crimes and prosecutions, this chapter argues that the judicial authorities of EU member states who received European arrest warrants for Catalan exiles applied a form of 'ghost political offence exception' to this case. To that end, they invoked different sets of arguments to refuse the surrenders, reflecting concerns that the exiles might not receive a fair trial if returned to Spain.

Chapter 7 finally concludes by integrating the content of all previous chapters. It advances that the evolution of the CoE and EU criminal law frameworks especially, based on mutual trust and recognition among states who share ideals of democracy, rule of law, and fundamental rights, are no longer designed to accommodate safeguards, such as the political offence exception clause, that frustrate its goals of enhanced cooperation. Yet, EU member states and Switzerland directly or indirectly applied such a clause to the case of Catalan exiles after arguments of political persecution of these leaders in Spain were raised. The chapter finally discusses how all this points to the limits of judicial cooperation in criminal matters in the areas of freedom, security, and justice in the EU.

Bibliography

Legislation, official publications, parliamentarian questions

European Union

European Parliament Resolution of 12 September 2018 on a Proposal Calling on the Council to Determine, pursuant to Article 7(1) of the Treaty on European Union, the Existence of a Clear Risk of a Serious Breach by Hungary of the Values on Which the Union is Founded (2017/2131(INL)) P8_TA(2018)0340 [2018].

Ramon Tremosa i Balcells (ALDE), Josep-Maria Terricabras (Verts/ALE), Jordi Solé (Verts/ALE), Martina Anderson (GUE/NGL), José Bové (Verts/ALE), Bodil Valero (Verts/ALE), Igor Šoltes (Verts/ALE), Izaskun Bilbao Barandica (ALDE), Josu Juaristi Abaunz (GUE/NGL), Jill Evans (Verts/ALE), António Marinho e Pinto (ALDE), Bart Staes (Verts/ALE), Barbara Spinelli (GUE/NGL), Maria Lidia Senra Rodríguez (GUE/NGL) and Rolandas Paksas (EFDD) 1145474.EN, PE 617.651 Question for Written Answer E-000746/2018 to the Commission. Subject: Misuse of the European Arrest Warrant by Spain [2018].

Regulation (EU, Euratom) 2020/2092 of the European Parliament and of the Council of 16 December 2020 on a General Regime of Conditionality for the Protection of the Union Budget [2020] OJ L 433/1.

Council of Europe

Parliamentary Assembly, Resolution of 25 January 2021 on 'Progress of the Assembly's Monitoring Procedure (January-December 2020)' (Resolution 2357) 2021.

Parliamentary Assembly of the Council of Europe (Committee on the Honouring of Obligations and Commitments by Member States of the Council of Europe - Monitoring Committee), The Monitoring Procedure of the Parliamentary Assembly' AS/Mon/Inf(2017)03rev (2017).

CJEU cases

Minister for Justice and Equality v. LM [25 August 2018] Case C-216/18 PPU. EU:C:2018:586.

Niculaie Aurel Bob-Dogi [1 June 2016] case C-241/15. EU:C:2016:385.

Pál Aranyosi et Robert Căldăraru [5 April 2016] Joined cases C-404/15 and C-659/15 PPU. EU:C:2016:198.

Books

Jansson J., *Terrorism, Criminal Law and Politics: The Decline of the Political Offence Exception to Extradition* (Routledge, Abingdon, New York 2020).

Stanbrook I. and Stanbrook C., *Extradition: Law and Practice* (Oxford University Press, Oxford 2000).

Van den Wijngaert C., *The Political Offence Exception to Extradition: The Delicate Problem of Balancing the Rights of the Individual and the International Public Order* (Kluwer, The Netherlands 1980).

Journal articles

Guittet E.-P., 'Political Identity and Democratic Solidarity After 9/11: The Spanish Case' [2004] *Altern. Global Local Polit.* 441.

Online resources

Council of Europe, 'Values' (Council of Europe) <https://www.coe.int/en/web/about-us/values> accessed 21 February 2024.

Council of Europe Newsroom, 'Russia Ceases to be a Party to the European Convention on Human Rights on 16 September 2022' (Council of Europe 2022) <https://www.coe.int/en/web/portal/-/russia-ceases-to-be-party-to-the-european-convention-on-human-rights> accessed 21 February 2024.

European Commission, 'Rule of Law: European Commission Acts to Defend Judicial Independence in Poland' (European Commission 2017) <https://ec.europa.eu/commission/presscorner/detail/en/IP_17_5367> accessed 21 February 2024.

Human Rights Watch, 'Spain: Police Used Excessive Force in Catalonia' (Human Rights Watch 2017) <https://www.hrw.org/news/2017/10/12/spain-police-used-excessive-force-catalonia> accessed 21 February 2024.

Willems A., 'The Extradition Saga Continues: Is the Latest Ruling a Win for Puigdemont, Spain, or for Mutual Trust?' (EUROPP blog - LSE 2018) <http://blogs.lse.ac.uk/europpblog/2018/07/18/the-extradition-saga-continues-is-the-latest-ruling-a-win-for-puigdemont-spain-or-for-mutual-trust/>accessed21February 2024.

Newspaper articles

CPE-N Commissions de Politique Extérieure, 'Communiqué de Presse – La Protection des Intérêts Économiques Extérieurs de la Suisse à l'Ordre du Jour' (L'Assemblée Fédérale – le Parlement Suisse 2018) <https://www.parlament.ch/press-releases/Pages/mm-apk-n-2018-04-17.aspx> accessed 21 February 2024.

Harari A., 'La Suisse N'Expulsera pas l'Indépendantiste Catalane Anna Gabriel' (Le Temps 2018) <https://www.letemps.ch/suisse/suisse-nexpulsera-lindependantiste-catalane-anna-gabriel> accessed 21 February 2024.

2 The concept of the political offence exception to extradition and existing tests to determine the political nature of an offence

The emergence of the political offence exception to extradition

The political offence exception is a relatively recent development in extradition law, emerging around the time of the French Revolution. Prior to this, concepts such as political offence and political asylum were largely absent from national legal systems, in contrast to the more ancient practice of asylum. Extradition itself, which contradicted the traditional hospitality afforded by asylum, evolved much later and was initially considered more of a diplomatic courtesy between sovereigns rather than a formalised procedure. Because extradition was initially so exceptional, it only concerned serious crimes – those challenging the authority of the sovereign or public order. Public prosecution of common criminals was typically not pursued and often resolved privately. Offenders generally avoided exile, as foreigners were poorly treated abroad and lacked the rights afforded to citizens. For those who did go into exile, prosecution was usually not pursued, as exile was considered to be punishment enough.[1] Perpetrators of crimes against the sovereign or public order, however, faced severe punishments. Public authorities were highly motivated to bring such offenders to justice, even if they had fled into exile.[2] The willingness to bring political offenders back to land for prosecution was in fact so important that, in some cases, sovereigns threatened to go to war to ensure their return from the requested state.[3] In practice, the closer the ties between two countries were, the greater was the inclination to collaborate.[4] The religious wars following the Reformation in the 16th century further prompted European states to grant shelter to members of the same religious community,

1 C. Van den Wijngaert, *The Political Offence Exception to Extradition: The Delicate Problem of Balancing the Rights of the Individual and the International Public Order* (Kluwer, The Netherlands 1980) 4–5.

2 C. Bassiouni, *International Extradition: United States Law and Practice* (6th edn, Oxford University Press, Oxford 2014) 5.

3 P. Papadatos, *Le Délit Politique: Contribution à l'Étude des Crimes contre l'État* (Librairie E. Droz, Geneva 1955) 60.

4 C. Bassiouni (n 2) 6.

DOI: 10.4324/9781003425847-2

while collaboration with rival states became even scarcer.[5] In that same period, however, legal philosopher Jean Bodin introduced the idea of extradition as a means of international cooperation to suppress criminality. The notion of extradition as a tool of cooperation for the protection of common social interests was further developed by thinkers such as Hugo Grotius and Charles Dumoulin. However, it only gained significant traction in the 17th and 18th centuries.[6]

During the 18th century, the idea of extradition as a tool to foster peaceful relations and cooperation in Europe flourished under the impetus of philosophers of the Age of Enlightenment,[7] who took notice of the benefits of collaboration for the general social order, even during religious wars.[8] Extradition treaties multiplied and, contrary to the previous practice, mainly concerned common criminals whose mobility became increasingly perceived as a problem of international commerce and traffic. Conversely, (non-political) asylum started being viewed as a way to escape criminal prosecution and became gradually more restricted.[9] While extradition developed into a standard practice, the rise of revolutionary ideology, culminating with the French Revolution, simultaneously carved the idea that those fighting oppression should be protected from prosecution.[10] Although it met initial resistance in practice, the idea of protecting political offenders quickly spread around Europe. Liberal democracies, often themselves forged through revolutions, came to view the protection of political offenders as a matter of paramount importance.[11] The political offence exception to extradition was codified for the first time in an extradition act in the Belgian Extradition Act of 1 October 1833 and has become a customary practice of extradition law since then.[12] Today, the political offence exception clause to extradition finds its place in most bilateral extradition treaties[13] and in a wide number of international and regional extradition agreements and treaties, including, but not limited to, the UN Model Treaty on Extradition,[14] the European Convention on Extradition,[15] the Inter-American Convention on Extradition,[16] the Extradition Agreement between the Mercosur countries and the Republic of Bolivia and the Republic

5 P. Papadatos (n 3) 61.
6 C. Bassiouni (n 2) 5.
7 C. Bassiouni (n 2) 6.
8 P. Papadatos (n 3) 61.
9 C. Van den Wijngaert (n 1) 7–8.
10 C. Van den Wijngaert (n 1) 9.
11 C. Van den Wijngaert (n 1) 11.
12 C. Van den Wijngaert (n 1) 12.
13 J. Jansson, *Terrorism, Criminal Law and Politics: The Decline of the Political Offence Exception to Extradition* (Routledge, Abingdon, New York 2020) 77–85.
14 Model Treaty on Extradition (Adopted by General Assembly Resolution 45/116) 1990 (Art. 3).
15 European Convention on Extradition (ETS 24) 1957 (Art. 3).
16 Inter-American Convention on Extradition, 1981 (Art. 5).

of Chile,[17] the Arab League Extradition Agreement,[18] the Riyadh Arab Agreement for Judicial Cooperation,[19] the Commonwealth Extradition Scheme,[20] or the Economic Community of West African States Convention on Extradition (ECOWAS) Convention on Extradition.[21] Despite the widespread incorporation of the political offence exception clause in extradition treaties, however, the term *political offence* is not explicitly defined in these agreements.

The difficulty of defining political crimes

To this day, *political offence* has not been properly defined, and the relationship of the political offence exception to various forms of political activism and objectives remains a debated question. The difficulty in defining political crimes arises from the fact that the political component of a crime is not a substance but that it is a quality that can essentially clothe any action.[22] In this sense, virtually any crime can be considered political as long as it has a political motive and/or consequence. Certain authors thus consider that crimes that have recourse to excessive levels of violence or that traumatise the collective conscience should not qualify as political.[23] It is indeed widely accepted that the political justification of an act does not exceed all forms of violence and that a balance between the political goal and the means used should be respected. Regardless of theoretical debates on the essence and constitutive elements of political crimes, however, legal and judicial practice has given political crimes a functional meaning in their application of the political offence exception without truly helping to provide a harmonised working definition. Christine Van Den Wijngaert notes in this respect that political crimes are subject to the principle of unilateral characterisation, which means that the determination of the political nature of a crime is made unilaterally by requested authorities.[24] In their decision, requested authorities will often choose to define crimes as political based on the conclusion they pursue on the extraditability of a particular case rather than on the crime itself.[25] All of this leads to a multiplicity of definitions that make the prospect of having a common working definition relatively out of reach.

17 Acuerdo Sobre Extradición entre el Mercosur, la República de Bolivia y la República de Chile (CMC 15/98) 1998 (Art. 5).
18 The Arab States and the Arab League Extradition Agreement, 1952 (Art. 4).
19 Riyadh Arab Agreement for Judicial Cooperation, 1983 (Art. 41).
20 The London Scheme for Extradition within the Commonwealth, Incorporating the Amendments agreed at Kingstown in November 2002 (Art. 12).
21 ECOWAS Convention on Extradition (A/PI/8/94) 1994 (Art. 4).
22 P. Papadatos (n 3) 70.
23 H. Lévy-Bruhl, 'Les Délits Politiques. Recherche d'une Définition' [1964] *Rev. Fr. Sociol.* 131, 137.
24 C. Van den Wijngaert (n 1) 103.
25 C. Van den Wijngaert (n 1) 97.

Extradition treaties themselves also add another layer of complexity to the definition of political crimes as they usually make a distinction between 'pure' and 'related' political offences. The former refers to crimes that are solely directed at the state or political organisation without injuring any other private party and that are not accompanied by common crimes in the course of their commission.[26] The most commonly cited crimes in that respect are crimes of treason, espionage, conspiracy, and the like that all require active participation. However, active involvement in the commission of the crime is not a defining criterion for pure political offences. Acts of passive dissent, such as opposing the prevailing ideology, can equally be classified as pure political crimes.[27] Related political offences, by comparison, are common crimes that are classified as political offences due to their purpose, consequence, or the political context in which they are committed. This broad categorisation means that almost any crime could potentially be considered a related political offence. In assessing whether a crime qualifies as a related political offence, three main approaches have been developed.[28] The 'political incidence theory', commonly applied in countries with an Anglo-Saxon legal tradition, typically determines the political nature of a crime by examining the (political) context in which the offence occurred. This approach contrasts with the French 'injured rights theory', which defines the political nature of a crime based on the nature of the rights injured (*e.g.* an attack on a parliamentary institution). A third approach, the Swiss proportionality test, considers a range of factors to evaluate the political nature of a crime, offering a more nuanced assessment.

The 'political incidence' theory

The British approach to the political incidence theory

The British approach to defining political crimes is based on the general definition of political crimes provided by John Stuart Mill, which was complemented by Judge James Fitzjames Stephen and later more precisely developed in case law. Mill defined political crimes as crimes committed in the course of a civil war or other types of political unrest, to which Judge Stephen added that the crimes in question would need to be 'incidental to' and 'form part of' the political commotion to qualify as political (hence the name 'political incidence' theory).[29] The objectiveness of this approach thus stems from contextual cues to determine the political nature of an offence rather than intentional ones.

This definition found its first application in the *Castioni* case in 1890, when Swiss authorities requested the extradition of Angelo Castioni, a Swiss national, convicted for the wilful murder of Luigi Rossi, a public official, in the course

26 C. Van den Wijngaert (n 1) 106.
27 C. Van den Wijngaert (n 1) 107.
28 C. Van den Wijngaert (n 1) 108.
29 I. A. Shearer, *Extradition in International Law* (Manchester University Press, Manchester 1971) 169.

of an armed uprising. In the case at hand, the judges (one of them being Stephen) considered that the crime for which Castioni was requested was political because it was incidental to and formed part of the political disturbance.[30] It was more specifically considered that Mill's understanding of an action having to take place 'in the course of' a political turmoil should be understood as meaning that the crime was committed 'in the furtherance of' a political rising, as fears arose that Mill's definition would open the door to any crime to be considered political, even those without a link to the political situation as long as they took place during its course. In this case, the judges considered that Castioni's action was clearly aimed at advancing a political project. The fact that Castioni did not personally know Rossi and that no spite or ill will existed between the two finished convincing them of the political nature of the case.[31]

This approach was later supplemented in the *Meunier* case of 1894 in which French authorities requested the extradition of an anarchist, Meunier, for having organised two explosions that killed two persons. The judges in charge of the case contemplated that the political offence exception could not apply here as they considered that for an offence to qualify as political and benefit from the exemption to extradition, there should, first, be two or more parties fighting to impose the government they desire to see in power and, second, that the crime in question be committed by one of the sides pursuing their political objective. In their view, anarchist crimes did not fall under this category, as they considered that the anarchist party was the enemy of all governments and that its actions did not so much target political power as they did the general body of citizens.[32]

The British approach to defining political crimes as laid out by Mills and Stephen and later specified in the *Castioni* and the *Meunier* rulings remained unchanged until 1954, when the *Kolczynski* case introduced a new margin of appreciation to the requested state. The case concerned seven Polish seamen who revolted on a trawler in British territorial waters. Fearing that another member of the crew, who was a political representative of the Communist Party, had overheard and recorded their political discussions in view of preparing a case against them for their arrest upon their return to Poland, the seven seamen took charge of the trawler and brought it to an English port to lodge asylum requests. When Poland requested the extradition of these men, the United Kingdom refused the extradition based on the political offence exception. However, as the reasoning behind *Castioni* and *Meunier* could not be used to refuse the extradition requests because there was neither an active opposition to the Communist Party nor a political uprising in Poland to which the offence could be considered incidental, the British judges adapted the incidence test to fit this case. Arguing that the notion of political offence should

30 In re Castioni (1891) 1 QB 149.
31 In re Castioni (1891) 1 QB 149.
32 In re Meunier (1894) 2 QB 415.

be apprehended in the context within which the offence occurred and that the political context of the *Kolczynski* case was very different to the one of *Castioni* and *Meunier* in that it was not considered treason at the time of the *Castioni* and *Meunier* cases to leave one's country to start a new life in another, J. Cassels, one of the judges in charge of the case, contemplated that the mutiny on the ship that was under political supervision was the only way available to the seamen to revolt. He therefore argued that they committed an offence of a political character and that, should they be returned to Poland, they would be punished for a political crime. To that Lord C.J. Goddard added that the offence should be considered political because the revolt of the seamen was made to prevent their prosecution for a political offence. It was thus considered necessary, in this case, to give a wider meaning to the term *political offence* to adapt to changing times and changing political regimes. As a result, the extradition of Kolczynski and the other crew members to Poland was refused on account of the political offence exception to extradition,[33] despite the fact that revolt was listed among extraditable offences in the extradition treaty between the two countries.[34] According to Green, the *Kolczynski* case preserved the fiction that it was the type of offence that motivated the refusal to extradite (by loosely qualifying the non-political offence of mutiny as a political one), while it in fact introduced the idea that specific individuals with acceptable political leanings could be protected from prosecution.[35]

Commentators of the case have argued that, in the *Kolczynski* decision, the British approach actually remained very loyal to the essential *raison d'être* of the political offence exception, that is the protection of political dissidents against the punitive power of the state.[36] This finding was confirmed in the *Schtraks* case, which concerned an extradition request issued by Israel for Nachman Schtraks, who refused to return his grandson, Joseph Schuchmacher, to his parents because he feared they would not provide him with an orthodox education. The case sparked great political debate in Israel among proponents of the left-wing liberals and the right-wing orthodox. Schtraks used the political debates surrounding the case to argue that he should not be surrendered on grounds of the political offence exception to extradition. The Queen's Bench Division refused the argument, contending that the political controversy arose only after Schtraks's actions, which meant that the *Castioni* criterion of his actions taking place amidst political turmoil could not be fulfilled. On appeal, the House of Lords further emphasised that the Israeli government had remained neutral in this conflict and that there was therefore no

33 Regina v. Governor of Brixton Prison, Ex Parte Kolczynski and others (1955) 2 QB 540.
34 J. Jansson (n 13) 58.
35 L. C. Green, 'Political Offences, War Crimes and Extradition' [1962] *ICLQ.* 329, 331; V. Epps, 'The Validity of the Political Offender Exception in Extradition Treaties in Anglo-American Jurisprudence' [1979] *Harv. Int'l. Law J.* 61, 68.
36 C. Van den Wijngaert (n 1) 113.

struggle between the state and the fugitive that would qualify the offence to be considered political. The extradition was consequently refused.[37] Van Den Wijngaert noted here that while, in the *Kolczynski* case, the extradition was refused on the basis of the political offence exception to protect the seamen from a retaliatory trial of the state for the men's political opinions, the absence of such a risk in the *Schtraks* case led the Court to consider the crimes were not political and were therefore extraditable.[38]

In 1973, a new case arose that further developed the British approach to the incidence test. It concerned an extradition request issued by the United States of America for Tzu-Tsai Cheng, a Taiwanese national living in the United States, for the attempted murder of the vice-president of Taiwan during the latter's visit to the United States. Cheng was part of a political movement, the World United for Formosan Independence (WUFI) that contested the ruling regime in Taiwan, the Chinese Nationalist government, for being oppressive and corrupt. The WUFI also denounced the United States' support to the ruling party and sought to change the United States' policy towards Taiwan. Cheng was convicted in the United States, failed to surrender to his bail and fled to Sweden. Sweden in turn accepted the extradition request issued by the United States and undertook to return him. However, Cheng fell ill in the course of his journey and landed in London, where he was taken to a prison hospital. When the United States sent an extradition request, Cheng opposed his surrender, arguing that he had committed a political offence. Both the Queen's Bench Division and the House of Lords refused Cheng's argument of a political offence because Cheng's crime did not target the U.S. government. The fact that one of the WUFI's objectives was to change the American policy towards the Chinese Nationalist government was therefore not considered relevant in this respect, as the Court noted that Cheng was not at odds with the U.S. government and that this was what mattered in this case.[39] The idea elaborated in the *Cheng* case that for an offence to qualify as political, it should be specifically targeting the requesting state failed to convince commentators of the case, who suggested that this decision was motivated by policy reasons,[40] and that it did not respect the wording of the British Extradition Act or the interpretation of the term *political offence* applied in other countries.[41]

The years of the Irish conflict later begot several cases that, within a strict application of the incidence theory, should have given rise to their qualification as political crimes. However, to proceed with the extraditions in those cases, British courts turned away from a rigid interpretation of the incidence

37 Schtraks v. Government of Israel and Others (1964) AC 556, (1962) 3 All ER 529, (1962) 3 WLR 1013.

38 C. Van den Wijngaert (n 1) 113–114.

39 Tzu-Tsai Cheng v. Governor of Pentonville Prison (1973) 2 All ER 204.

40 P. O'Higgins, 'Extradition. Offence of a Political Character. Terrorism' [1973] *CLJ*. 181, 181–182.

41 C. Van den Wijngaert (n 1) 114.

theory and favoured the criterion developed in *Schtraks*, whereby the criminal whose extradition is requested should be at odds with the requesting state. The courts also paid greater consideration to subjective elements, that is, the intention of the perpetrator.[42] Van Den Wijngaert advances that these new points of attention were especially visible in the *Taylor*, *Keane*, and *Littlejohn* cases. In the *Taylor* case, the Court considered that the murder of two young people, one of whom was a member of the Irish Republican Army (IRA), was not a political offence because the defendant was neither 'at odds' with the Irish Republic requesting his extradition nor was he at risk of undergoing an unfair trial in Ireland.[43] Van Den Wijngaert explains the same rationale underpinned the *Keane* case, where both the Queen's Bench Division and the House of Lords refused to recognise the killing of an Irish policeman and involvement in an armed robbery as political crimes.[44] In the *Littlejohn* case, she says, attention was rather paid to subjective elements to grant the extradition. The case concerned an armed bank robbery committed by Littlejohn for the benefit of the IRA. Littlejohn sought to oppose his extradition by contending his crime was political, to which the Queen's Bench Division retorted that the fact that the crime was committed to provide financial support to the IRA was not enough to deem the offence political, further reminding that the intention of the offender was of paramount importance in the determination of the political nature of a crime. Littlejohn was extradited to Ireland where he was sentenced by a special criminal court dealing with crimes against the state. In 1974, Littlejohn escaped and fled to Northern Ireland, which prompted Irish authorities to request his extradition once again. In its second decision, the Queen's Bench Division confirmed its first verdict and further added that his conviction by a special criminal court – which Littlejohn argued attested to the political nature of his crime – did not affect this conclusion.[45] With these cases, British courts reaffirmed their commitment to adapting their approach to the incidence test to meet changing needs. These decisions also confirmed the 'at odds' criteria previously developed in the *Schtraks* and *Cheng* cases to the British application of the incidence theory and introduced considerations on intentionality that added an extra layer to the incidence test normally only concerned with contextual elements.

Equally deviating from a strict interpretation of the incidence test was the *T v. Secretary of State for the Home Department* case that introduced a certain element of proportionality to the British approach. The case concerned the application for refugee status of an Algerian citizen who was part of an illegal political organisation, the Front Islamique du Salut (the Islamic Salvation Front (FIS)), whose aim was to overthrow the Algerian government by any means possible, including the bombing of Algiers Airport (which led to the

42 C. Van den Wijngaert (n 1) 114–115.
43 C. Van den Wijngaert (n 1) 115.
44 C. Van den Wijngaert (n 1) 115.
45 C. Van den Wijngaert (n 1) 115.

killing of ten people) and a raid on a military warehouse (leading to the death of one person).[46] In this case, the majority of the House of Lords considered that attention should be given to the proximity of the means used in light of the political goal pursued. To determine this direct link, the Court established that two main elements should be considered. The first one was the means used to achieve the crime and, more specifically, whether the crime targeted a military or government target or, on the contrary, a civilian one. The second one pertained to whether the crime was likely to lead to indiscriminate killings or injure members of the public foreign to the political struggle.[47] Although this case did not take place within an extradition proceeding but concerned an application for political asylum of an individual suspected of having committed a serious non-political crime within the meaning of article 1F of the 1951 Geneva Convention, it provided essential cues as to the determination of the political nature of a crime within the British context that would equally apply to extradition cases. By casting light on the proximity of the crimes committed and the purpose that they pursued, it introduced a clear element of proportionality, further enriching the British understanding of the incidence theory. [48]

Overall, the British approach has remained relatively loyal to the original incidence test but nevertheless adapted to changing needs.[49] This was, for instance, visible in the *Kolczynski* case, in which, in a very different geopolitical context than the one of the original definition of the political offence exception, the nature of the regime requesting the extradition entered into consideration in the determination of the political nature of the crime. The introduction of the 'at odds' criterion by the *Schtraks* and *Cheng* cases equally modernised the British incidence test as they helped more clearly define what types of political crimes were covered by the exception, that is crimes that specifically oppose the plaintiff to the requesting state. Later cases concerning IRA members not only cemented this 'at odds' criterion but also introduced elements of intentionality to the courts' interpretation of the incidence theory normally only focusing on contextual elements to determine the political nature of an offence. To this increasingly elaborate approach, the *T v. Secretary of State for the Home Department* case added concerns on proportionality by requiring that due consideration be given to the nature of the target of the crime (civilian or not), as well as to whether the crime was likely to generate indiscriminate killings. As a result of the mentioned cases, even if the British approach to the incidence test has remained overall centred on the criteria developed in the early days, it has become a multi-layered test including several additional factors to determine the political nature of a crime.

46 T v. Secretary of State for the Home Department (1996) 2 All ER 865.
47 T v. Secretary of State for the Home Department (1996) 2 All ER 865.
48 G. Gilbert, *Responding to International Crime* (Martinus Nijhoff Publishers, Leiden, Boston 2006) 208.
49 C. Van den Wijngaert (n 1) 115–116; G. Gilbert (n 48) 208.

The U.S. approach to the political incidence theory

In the United States, the case law stuck to a stricter interpretation of the incidence theory as developed in the early *Castioni* and *Meunier* cases. The emphasis has thus generally been put on the fact that the crime for which extradition was requested be committed during a political uprising and that it be incidental to or form part of it.[50] This reasoning was first applied by analogy in 1894 in the *Ezeta* case, where the court refused the extradition to El Salvador of a military general and four of his subordinates who were accused of having committed crimes of murder and robbery in their unsuccessful attempt to quash a revolution.[51] In the examination of this case, the district court paid particular attention to whether the crime took place against the backdrop of a rebellion against the existing government and whether the crimes were committed in the furtherance of this political movement before it concluded that they were indeed connected to the political conflict and were thus political.[52]

The same logic of strict adherence to the incidence theory underpinned the decision of the Supreme Court in the *Ornelas* ruling. The case took place in 1896 and concerned an extradition request issued by the Mexican government for three men accused of crimes of murder, arson, robbery, and kidnapping committed during an attack on a village. Noting that no Mexican government forces were present at the time of the attack and that the men had run away with the stolen goods, the Supreme Court rejected the argument that these crimes were political and authorised the extradition.[53] Interestingly, however, while the Supreme Court authorised the extradition using a rationale very close to the original interpretation of the incidence theory as laid out in *Castioni*, Epps notes that the district court had initially rejected it on grounds of the offences being political. She argues in this respect that the decision of the Supreme Court to reverse the ruling was linked to a letter sent by Secretary of State Gresham to the minister of Mexico in which he shared his view that the crimes were not purely political. Epps therefore offers another reading of the case according to which political considerations impacted the final decision of the Supreme Court.[54]

A similar concern transpired in the *Mylonas* case. The latter involved an anti-communist political figure who was a member of the community council of a Greek town and became the president of the community council of the town. In 1954, the communists won the elections, and Mylonas was the only

50 D. M. Lieberman, 'Sorting the Revolutionary from the Terrorist: The Delicate Application of the "Political Offense" Exception in U.S. Extradition Cases' [2006] *Stan. Law Rev.* 181, 188–189.

51 In re Ezeta. In re Bolanos, In re Colocho. In re Cienguegos. In re Bustamante, 62 F. 972 (N.D. Cal 1894) 997–999.

52 J. Jansson (n 13) 61.

53 Ornelas v. Ruiz 161 U.S. 502 (1896) 510–512.

54 V. Epps (n 35) 69–70.

member of his party to be re-elected. He subsequently immigrated to the United States and was shortly after requested for extradition on charges of embezzlement. The U.S. district court refused the extradition on grounds of his offence being political because the latter was incidental to, and formed part of, political disturbances.[55] In this case, although the district court stuck to a strict application of the incidence test to refuse the surrender, Van Den Wijngaert raised the question of whether the outcome of the ruling would have been different if Mylonas was not anti-communist,[56] a view shared by Epps, who underlined that while the extradition request had a clear political motive, there was no reason to believe that the embezzlement of which Mylonas was accused participated to an effort to overthrow the communist regime as Mylonas was himself the mayor of the community at the time of the crime. Epps therefore argued that a rather liberal interpretation of the political offence exception was adopted in this case to prevent the extradition of an anti-communist figure.[57] The *Ornelas* and *Mylonas* cases thus show that despite a more conservative application of the incidence theory by U.S. courts, concerns on political alignment of the requested country with U.S. foreign policy found its place into the courts' decisions.

This was equally visible in the *Gonzalez* case that pertained to an extradition request issued by the Dominican Republic for Clovodeo Ortiz Gonzalez for crimes of murder and torture of political prisoners that Gonzales committed in a military or quasi-military capacity under the Trujillo regime. Of note, while the crimes were committed under the Trujillo regime, which was at odds with U.S. foreign policy, the extradition requests were issued after the regime change in the Dominican Republic.[58] In assessing the political nature of the crime, the Court ruled that these crimes did not take place against the backdrop of a disturbed political situation that could lead to their qualification as political and that there was no political motive behind the commission of these crimes that could justify a relaxation of the 'political disturbance' requirement. The fact that Gonzalez committed those crimes under military capacity and out of personal commitment to military discipline further confirmed, in the view of the Court, that the crimes were not political.[59] The British argument that the nature of the regime requesting the extradition was of interest to the final decision on whether to use the political offence exception clause clearly fuelled this conclusion, as in a footnote to the case, Judge Tyler specifically referred to the *Kolczynski* case, and pointed out that the history of the political offence exception in Anglo-Saxon countries indicate that this clause could be used more liberally when the extradition request emanates from a totalitarian

55 In re Mylonas, 187 F. Supp. 716 (N.D. Ala. 1960) 721.
56 C. Van den Wijngaert (n 1) 117.
57 V. Epps (n 35) 73–74.
58 V. Epps (n 35) 73–74.
59 In re Gonzalez, 217 F. Supp. 717 (S.D.N.Y. 1963) 721–722.

country seeking the extradition of people who opposed that regime in the name of freedom.[60] Van Den Wijngaert noted in this respect that, on top of the influence of the *Kolczynski* ruling in the United States approach, this case also illustrates one of the major shortcomings of the incidence theory, that is, the absence of regard to the seriousness of the acts committed in the determination of the political nature of the crime.[61]

This rigorous application of the incidence test where consideration of the seriousness of the crime does not find its place in the courts' decision has equally been observed in the infamous *Artukovic* case. Andrija Artukovic was the minister of interior in the pro-Hitler Pavelic government in the 'Independent State of Croatia' (a German puppet state)[62] during World War II.[63] He was notably tasked with setting up and managing concentration camps. When he left for the United States, his extradition was requested by the then Yugoslavian government for war crimes and genocide.[64] To oppose his extradition, Artukovic invoked the political offence exception, arguing that his acts were incidental to the political conflict taking place during World War II.[65] This argument was accepted by both the district court and the court of appeals. The latter stated that considering that the acts of Artukovic took place in the context of a power struggle between different theories of government and that his crimes were strongly linked to a political element, Artukovic's crimes were political.[66] Because of the loophole this case created to protect tyrants, it has been one of the most roundly criticised cases of U.S. extradition history, costing the political offence exception clause its reputation of safeguard against despotic and tyrannic regimes.[67]

The narrow interpretation of the incidence test by U.S. courts later continued in cases involving IRA members who enjoyed protection from extradition under the political offence exception clause up until 1986.[68] In those cases, the courts considered that because there were political disturbances in Northern Ireland at the time and because the crimes for which IRA members were requested were committed as part of, and in furtherance of the political

60 In re Gonzalez, 217 F. Supp. 717 (S.D.N.Y. 1963) 721–722.

61 C. Van den Wijngaert (n 1) 117–118.

62 R. Soucy, 'Varieties of Fascism' (Encyclopaedia Britannica) <https://www.britannica.com/topic/fascism/Varieties-of-fascism> accessed 5 December 2023.

63 Matter of Extradition of Artukovic, 628 F. Supp. 1370 (C.D. Cal. 1986) 1377–1378.

64 Matter of Extradition of Artukovic, 628 F. Supp. 1370 (C.D. Cal. 1986) 1377–1378.

65 C. Van den Wijngaert (n 1) 118.

66 Karadzole v. Artukovic 247 F.2d 198 (9th Cir. 1957). The decision on the case was later vacated by the Supreme Court that remanded the case for a hearing on the extradition complaint. Karadzole v. Artukovic 355 U.S. 393 (1958). The decision on the political nature of the offence was eventually confirmed by the District Court. United States v. Artukovic, 170 F. Supp. 383 (S.D. Cal. 1959) 393.

67 C. H. Pyle, *Extradition, Politics and Human Rights* (Temple University Press, Philadelphia 2001) 138–139.

68 G. Gilbert (n 48) 214–215.

goal pursued by the IRA, the crimes were political.[69] These refusals generated great unease for the U.S. government, torn between the large number of Irish descendants in the United States preventing it from openly condemning the IRA and the U.S. government's privileged relationship with the United Kingdom. The United States' neutrality vas-à-vis the Irish conflict changed following the 1979 IRA attack killing Lord Mountbatten and three others, as well as another attack at army barracks killing 18 soldiers. After these events, the U.S. government started to show support for British policies on the matter. However, while the government's approach changed, the courts did not immediately follow suit and continued protecting IRA members, including in the two *McMullen* and *Mackin* cases that triggered great political concern about the tenability of the U.S. approach to the incidence test in light of the growing need to combat terrorism.[70]

In the *McMullen* case, the Court refused the extradition of Peter McMullen because it considered that the bombing of military barracks was a political offence since the bombing was part of a political uprising and was directed against the British army.[71] An equally strict application of the incidence test was used in the *Mackin* case, where the Court contemplated that the attempted murder of British soldier Stephen Wooton amounted to a political crime for which extradition could not be granted because the Provisional Irish Republican Army (PIRA) was conducting a political uprising at the time and place the offence was committed, because Mackin was an active member of the PIRA, and because the offence was incidental to the furtherance of the political fight of the PIRA.[72] Following these cases, a serious academic and political debate took place in the United States, where concerns over the United States becoming a safe haven for terrorists multiplied.[73]

A few years later, however, the practice of protecting IRA members from extradition with the political offence exception continued being applied by U.S. courts, most notably in the *Doherty* case. The case concerned Joseph Doherty, a member of the PIRA who was accused of killing a British army captain in an exchange of gunfire in Belfast in 1980. In this case, the district court considered that Doherty's offence was political, not only because it was committed in the course of and in furtherance of the Irish fight but also because of other factors to which the Court gave due consideration. These included the nature of the act, its context, the status of the person committing it, the nature of the organisation on behalf of which the act is committed, and

69 G. Gilbert (n 48) 214–215.
70 J. Jansson (n 13) 144–147.
71 In re McMullen, No. 3–78–1099 MG (N.D. Ca. 11 May 1979). McMullen would eventually be extradited several years later following the adoption of a Supplementary Extradition Treaty between the United States and the United Kingdom. J. Jansson (n 13) 154.
72 In re Mackin, 668 F.2d 122 (2d Cir. 1981).
73 J. Jansson (n 13) 147–149.

the specificities of the place where it is committed.[74] In this case, the Court noted that Doherty did not perform indiscriminate killings or target civilians. It also took note of the fact that Doherty committed his crime in the territory where he wished to see political change and that he did not violate principles of international law as enshrined in the Geneva Convention. Finally, the Court considered that PIRA had organisation, discipline, and command, which, in the Court's view, set it apart from other less structured groups like the Black Liberation Army or the Red Brigades.[75] What thus appears from this case is that, although the Court was very mindful of respecting traditional markers of the incidence test, namely by looking at whether Doherty committed his crime in the course of and in the furtherance of a political commotion, the Court considered these criteria to merely be the starting point of its analysis. By considering the additional elements mentioned earlier, the Court thus went beyond a narrow understanding of the incidence test as applied in the early days of the U.S. case law on the matter and introduced an element of proportionality to the American approach to the incidence test.

The focus on proportionality equally found its place in the *Eain* case that concerned Abu Eain, a member of the Palestine Liberation Organization, who had killed two young boys and injured more than 30 other persons by placing a bomb in a crowded Israeli market. The Seventh Circuit Court rejected the argument that this offence was political because it considered that the latter was not incidental to the political conflict. On appeal, the application of the political offence exception to this case was again rejected. Noting the severe criticisms targeting the U.S. extradition law for adhering too strictly to the original understanding of the incidence test, the Seventh Circuit Court of Appeals contemplated that the exception was not meant to protect wanton crimes simply because they took place during a time of political upheaval. The Court thus established that the indiscriminate bombing of civilians – whatever the claimed political objective of the perpetrator – could not amount to a political offence and benefit from the protection attached to the exception.[76] In this sense, the *Doherty* and *Eain* rulings aligned on the need to steer away from the blind application of the original incidence test as first applied by U.S. courts and introduced the idea that, although the existence of an uprising may be the starting point in assessing the political nature of an offence, it cannot be the determining factor.[77] The overall impact of the *Eain* ruling on U.S. extradition practice, however, was limited. Indeed, only courts under the Seventh Circuit's jurisdiction were bound by this precedent, and other jurisdictions did not follow suit on this ruling, which was widely criticised for failing to provide a proper guideline on the exclusion of the political offence exception

74 In re Doherty, 599 F. Supp. 270 (S.D.N.Y. 1984) 275.
75 In re Doherty, 599 F. Supp. 270 (S.D.N.Y. 1984) 275–276.
76 Eain v. Wilkes, 641 F.2d 504 (7th Circ. 1981) 519–521.
77 G. Gilbert (n 48) 217.

in cases involving attacks against civilians as it did not exclude all attacks of the sort from the scope of the political offence exception and because it did not specify either whether attacks against non-military government staff would be equally covered by the exception. The emotionalism it allowed and the room it gave to judges' personal preferences to find their place in the determination of the political nature of an offence were other points on which the ruling came short, according to commentators.[78] In the later *Quinn* ruling, for instance, the Court rejected the approach adopted in this case and conversely contended that it saw no good reason for distinguishing between attacks on military or civilian targets and that the incidence test should be applied in an objective manner, that is in a way that judges abstain from sharing views on which revolutionary tactic would actually be successful in changing the government.[79]

The *Quinn* case thus reverted to an application of the incidence test more in line with the original understanding of the incidence test as applied in the United States. The case concerned William Joseph Quinn, a U.S. citizen, wanted by the United Kingdom so he could face charges of murder of a police officer and conspiracy to cause explosions endangering human life. While the district court initially refused his extradition based on the political offence exception, the Ninth Circuit Court in turn allowed it. In their decision, the judges focused on two main elements, namely that a violent political uprising existed at the time of the commission of the offence (noting in passing that these uprisings are temporally and spatially limited) and that Quinn's crimes were committed to further the political uprising.[80] In this case, the Court noted that there was indeed a political uprising in Northern Ireland but not in England, where Quinn had committed his crimes. In the view of the Court, the meaning of the uprising prong of the incidence test was to be understood as it being conducted by the people living on the land and wishing for a change in government. By perpetrating the attack in England and not Northern Ireland, Quinn, whom the Court emphasised was not even a Northern Irish national, and his co-conspirators were said to have merely exported the conflict to another location and could not be said to have tried to initiate a change in their own country and against their own government.[81] As a result, the Court ruled that he could not be protected from extradition by the political offence exception.[82] Had Quinn committed his crimes in Northern Ireland, the Court found that his actions would have indeed qualified as being incidental to the IRA activities.[83] This focus on the geographical criterion perplexed

78 J. Jansson (n 13) 135.
79 Quinn v. Robinson, 783 F. 2d 776 (9th Cir. 1986) 820.
80 Quinn v. Robinson, 783 F. 2d 776 (9th Cir. 1986) 817.
81 Quinn v. Robinson, 783 F. 2d 776 (9th Cir. 1986) 813–814.
82 Quinn v. Robinson, 783 F. 2d 776 (9th Cir. 1986) 818.
83 Quinn v. Robinson, 783 F. 2d 776 (9th Cir. 1986) 812.

some commentators of the case who feared that this interpretation could constrain the definition of the political offence exception in undesirable ways[84] and that it contravened previous rulings on the matter, including the *McMullen* one, where the political offence exception applied despite the offence being committed in North Yorkshire, England.[85] Others argued, on the contrary, that this interpretation was in line with the original purpose of the political offence exception, which was to afford protection to people subjected to and seeking to overthrow oppressive regimes rather than to foreign fighters.[86] Breaking with the traditional protection of IRA members, the *Quinn* case marked the first extradition of an IRA member from the United States to the United Kingdom.[87]

The strict application of the incidence test in the United States has long been criticised for providing a safe haven to terrorists.[88] Authors like Gilbert have argued that, for a long time, all that essentially mattered in the U.S. application of the incidence test was to demonstrate that a political uprising existed and that the crime under consideration was linked, however remotely, to furthering the political struggle of the movement.[89] Because of this, the test has been criticised for being simultaneously, in the words of John Groarke, over- and under-inclusive. Its over-inclusiveness is owed to the fact that any act committed as part of political turbulence could virtually be (and have been) protected with this approach (as observed in the *Artukovic* case and cases involving IRA members, for instance). Its under-inclusiveness conversely stems from the fact that political crimes that are not committed as part of a recognised uprising will not be considered political.[90] So, while the incidence test offers an arguably more objective approach to assessing the political nature of a crime due to its focus on the existence of a political uprising rather than on the motives of the perpetrator, its overly strict observance has fallen short of giving due consideration to other important factors, such as the seriousness of the offence.[91] Despite criticism on the uncompromising adherence of U.S. courts to the approach developed in the *Castioni* ruling,[92] however, U.S. case law has showed consideration to additional factors over time, such as

84 A. D. Soafer, 'The Political Offense Exception and Terrorism' [1986] *Denv. J. Intl'l. Law & Pol'y.* 125, 130; D. M. Lieberman (n 50) 198.
85 J. Jansson (n 13) 151.
86 K. A. Basso, 'The 1985 U.S.-U.K. Supplementary Extradition Treaty: A Superfluous Effort?' [1989] *B.C. Int'l. & Comp. Law Rev.* 301, 329, cited in J. Jansson (n 13) 151.
87 J. Jansson (n 13) 150.
88 J. Jansson (n 13) 151.
89 G. Gilbert (n 48) 214.
90 J. P. Groarke, 'Revolutionaries Beware: The Erosion of the Political Offense Exception under the 1986 United States-United Kingdom Supplementary Extradition Treaty' [1988] *U. PA. Law Rev.* 1515, 1525.
91 J. Jansson (n 13) 62.
92 C. Van den Wijngaert (n 1) 118–119.

political alignment, for example in the *Ornelas*, *Gonzalez*, or *Mylonas* cases,[93] or proportionality, as visible in the *Doherty* or *Eain* case.[94] Yet these external considerations have only limitedly contributed to refining and modernising the U.S. application of the incidence test, which has overall yielded mixed results in overcoming the difficulty of defining political crimes.[95]

The 'continental' theories

While the Anglo-Saxon approaches to defining political crimes can overall be grouped under the incidence test, authors like Van Den Wijngaert point out that the same cannot be said of continental theories that very much differ in their assessments of the political nature of a crime and are often applied with greater flexibility than the incidence test. Two main models nevertheless stand out: the French injured rights theory and the Swiss proportionality test.[96]

The French injured rights theory

The French approach to defining political crimes has traditionally been characterised as the injured rights theory, which focuses on the nature of the rights injured in the commission of the crime. This theory stems from the French Extradition Law of 10 March 1927 that sought to frame the political offence exception clause in a narrow way to eschew potential abuses stemming from a too-liberal understanding of the notion of political offence.[97] This test found its most prominent application in the *Giovanni Gatti* case that took place in 1947. The case concerned the condemnation *in absentia* of a San Marino national, Giovanni Gatti, for the murder of a member of a communist cell. Gatti contested his extradition by invoking the political nature of his crime. However, in its advisory opinion, the Court of Appeal of Grenoble noted that the motives of the offenders were not a determining factor in the assessment of the political nature of a crime and that only the nature of the rights injured were.[98] More specifically, the Court delineated crimes targeting the state, its normal functioning, its organisation, and its rights as those eligible under the political offence exception.[99]

Around the same period as the *Gatti* case, this understanding of the political offence exception was consolidated in several rulings concerning Belgian requests for wartime collaborators who, despite great judicial uproar on the

93 V. Epps (n 35) 69.
94 G. Gilbert (n 48) 216–217.
95 G. Gilbert (n 48) 217.
96 C. Van den Wijngaert (n 1) 120.
97 M. R. García-Mora, 'The Nature of Political Offenses: A Knotty Problem of Extradition Law' [1962] *Va. Law Rev.* 1226, 1249.
98 C. Van den Wijngaert (n 1) 121.
99 In re Gatti, Annual Digest 70 (1947) 145, cited in M. R. García-Mora (n 97) 1236.

question, were protected by the political offence exception because of the political nature of the rights injured.[100] The choice to protect collaborators with the political offence exception was, however, a very controversial one and led several courts to conversely apply the injured rights test in a way that would allow the surrender of collaborators by focusing on the idea that political crimes are crimes against the state – and therefrom interpreting the notion of 'crime against the state' in a restrictive manner – rather than being merely satisfied with the political nature of the right injured. In the *Colman* case, for instance, in assessing whether providing intelligence to the enemy, carrying arms against Belgium and murder amounted to a political crime, the Paris Court of Appeal reasoned that collaboration with the enemy in an occupied country at a time of war did not amount to a crime against the state that could be protected by the political offence exception.[101] The same reasoning was later applied in the *Spiessens* case in which the Court of Appeal of Nancy authorised the extradition of a Belgian national accused of collaboration with the enemy by arguing that collaboration with an enemy occupying the territory at a time of war did not qualify as a crime against the state.[102]

While the injured rights theory offers a relatively objective measure to determine the political nature of a crime as it mostly eliminates the risk of abuse, for it does not allow the protection of common crimes on the sole ground of the alleged political intention of their authors, its only focus on the nature of the rights affected by the crime makes it a rather incomplete approach that falls short of considering important elements surrounding the case, such as the seriousness of the acts or the context within which the crime is committed. This was, for instance, visible in the examples mentioned earlier of wartime collaborators being protected by the political offence exception clause. If some courts chose to rectify the issue of problematic protections resulting from a too rigid application of this test by toying with the notion of 'crime against the state', as visible in the *Colman* and *Spiessens* cases, the fact remains that this test's reliance on one criterion only makes it unable to capture the complexity of the notion of political crime and account for the reality within which these crimes take place. Van Den Wijngaert argues, in this respect, that, under this test, absolute political crimes such as espionage and treason, which would be committed for personal motives, would benefit from the political offence exception.[103] Conversely, common crimes committed for political reasons would not be offered protection.[104]

The limits of the injured rights theory have led the French courts to borrow from different approaches over the years to determine the political nature of

100 C. Van den Wijngaert (n 1) 122.
101 M. R. García-Mora (n 97) 1250.
102 L. C. Green (n 35) 341.
103 C. Van den Wijngaert (n 1) 122.
104 M. R. García-Mora (n 97) 1251.

crimes. In the *da Palma* case for instance, Van Den Wijngaert notes that the Court of Appeal of Paris focused on the intention of the perpetrator to establish that the robbing of the Portuguese national bank was a political crime. The Court indeed contended that considering the well-known political activities of da Palma and that despite the seriousness of the offence, the latter was linked to the political activities of the defendant, who was clearly acting out of political motives, the crime was political.[105] Similarly, in the *Hennin* case, the Court refused the extradition of Hennin, a separatist from the Bern region wanted by Switzerland for having conducted bombings, on grounds that Hennin had political motives and was pursuing political objectives.[106] More compellingly perhaps, in the *Holder* case, the mere allusion to Angela Davies of U.S. nationals who hijacked an aircraft while also extorting half a million dollars from the airline company sufficed to convince the Court that the crimes were political.[107]

In other cases French courts have leaned towards a mixed approach bordering on the Swiss proportionality test.[108] This was for example visible in the famous *Croissant* case that took place in 1977. Klaus Croissant, who was the lawyer for a number of members of the Baader–Meinhof Group, was suspected of having contributed to setting up and operating an information system between imprisoned terrorists and their partners in liberty and, in doing so, of having facilitated the activities of a criminal organisation. He was also accused of having aided the criminal organisation by means of propaganda, press conferences, and organisation of hunger strikes.[109] Although the Court refused the extradition on the latter ground because these acts did not constitute extraditable offences under French law, it did accept the extradition for the former offence.[110] Croissant opposed his extradition, invoking the political offence exception on grounds of his activities being related to the Baader–Meinhof Group. The Court of Appeal of Paris, however, refused the argument, retorting that the actions of the Baader–Meinhof Group were not political in nature but criminal in that they did not form part of a system fighting against or in favour or something and that, on the contrary, they could only be characterised by the fact that they were committed in complete contempt for the lives of its victims that were foreign to motives

105 Inacio da Palma (Cour d'Appel de Paris, 1967) No. 15387, cited in C. Van den Wijngaert (n 1) 122.

106 Hennin (Cour d'Appel de Paris, 1967) No. 15274, cited in C. Van den Wijngaert (n 1) 123.

107 C. Van Den Wijngaert, 'The Political Offence Exception to Extradition: Defining the Issues and Searching a Feasible Alternative' [1983] Report Presented at the International Seminar on Extradition, International Institute of Higher Studies in Criminal Sciences 741, 745.

108 C. Van Den Wijngaert, 'The Political Offence Exception to Extradition: Defining the Issues and Searching a Feasible Alternative' [1983] Report Presented at the International Seminar on Extradition, International Institute of Higher Studies in Criminal Sciences 746.

109 T. E. Carbonneau, 'Extradition and Transnational Terrorism: A Comment on the Recent Extradition of Klaus Croissant from France to West Germany' [1978] *Int. Lawyer.* 813, 820.

110 T. E. Carbonneau, 'Extradition and Transnational Terrorism: A Comment on the Recent Extradition of Klaus Croissant from France to West Germany' [1978] *Int. Lawyer.* 813, 820.

of the group, noting in passing the political motivations of the group did not suffice to qualify its crimes as political.[111] In this decision, the Court thus balanced several interests (*i.e.* the gravity of the offences and their political motives) before it concluded that the seriousness of the offences giving rise to extradition trumped their potential political character.[112] A similar focus on the gravity of the offence was found in the *Piperno* and *Pace* cases that concerned members of the Italian Red Brigades suspected of being involved in the kidnapping and murder of Aldo Moro, the Italian prime minister of the time. Thomas Carbonneau pinpointed here that unlike in other similar cases involving members of the Red Brigades or the Baader–Meinhof Group, where the Court of Appeal of Paris first sought to determine whether the activities of the group amounted to a political undertaking, in this case, the Court immediately held that the seriousness of the crime outweighed any political motivation and therefore excluded the possibility of qualifying the crime as political.[113]

Although the French approach to defining political crimes is usually characterised as the injured rights theory, French courts have thus wobbled significantly over the years on this issue and eventually came closer to the Swiss proportionality test that, unlike other theories, puts a great emphasis on the seriousness of the acts under examination.

The Swiss proportionality test

The proportionality test, also known as the predominance, preponderance, or political motivation theory, balances the political and the common aspects of a crime to determine the nature of an offence. If the political elements of the crime outweigh its common crime aspects, the offence will be considered political.[114] This approach originated in the Federal Act of 22 January 1892 on extradition to foreign states, whose article 10 provides that extradition cannot be granted for political crimes but that it can, however, be granted if the crime for which the extradition is requested is predominantly a common crime, even if the defendant invokes a political motive or end.[115]

Clearer guidance on how to balance the political and common elements of the crime was provided in the *Wassilieff* case of 1908 that concerned a Russian national accused of the murder of a local police chief. Although Wassilieff claimed his crime was political because he had committed it to further the

111 Croissant (Cour d'Appel de Paris, 1977), cited in C. Van den Wijngaert (n 1) 124.

112 T. E. Carbonneau, 'The Political Offense Exception as Applied in French Cases Dealing with the Extradition of Terrorists' [1983] *Mich. J. Int. Law*. 209, 217–218.

113 T. E. Carbonneau, 'The Political Offense Exception as Applied in French Cases Dealing with the Extradition of Terrorists' [1983] *Mich. J. Int. Law*. 225.

114 G. Gilbert (n 48) 218.

115 Federal Act of 22 January 1892 on Extradition to Foreign States 1892 (Repealed in the Meantime by the Federal Act on International Mutual Assistance in Criminal Matters 1981 (Mutual Assistance Act, IMAC)).

cause of the Russian Revolutionary Socialist Party that sought to overthrow the tsar, the Federal Tribunal refused the argument and granted the extradition on the ground that the murder did not seek to realise a purely political offence and that other means of achieving the political goal existed, which gave the offence a predominantly common crime character.[116] The Tribunal indeed held that three criteria must be respected for an offence to qualify as political: first, the act should be directly linked to a pure political offence; second, it should represent a truly effective means of reaching the political goal pursued; and, third, the political elements of the crime should outweigh their common components.[117]

While the first criterion of the proximity of the crime with its political goal resembles the approach of the Anglo-Saxon incidence test, the Swiss theory is stricter because it requires a very clear relationship between the act and the political goal pursued.[118] Garcia-Mora highlighted in this respect that this requirement is most likely to be fulfilled when the crime is incidental to a more general political struggle.[119] This was especially visible in the *Kaphengst* case that concerned the extradition of a German national accused of bombings in Prussia. In the case, the Federal Tribunal ruled out the possibility of recognising political attributes to a purely terrorist offence before it added that, for an offence to qualify as political, it should be related to a general movement seeking to achieve a political objective.[120] Accordingly, in the *Nappi* case, the court established that, for a direct relation between the offence and the end sought, the offence must constitute a truly effective means to achieve the end, be an integral part of acts leading thereto, or else be an incident in a more general political movement wherein competing parties have recourse to these types of methods.[121] In the later *Della Savia* case of 1969, the Federal Tribunal held that participation in a number of bombings and membership to the criminal organisation of 22 October, an anarchist-nihilist organisation, could not be considered predominantly political, first, because the crimes were not committed as part of a real political struggle, in that the democratic governance in Italy was not threatened to a point where a revolutionary movement across the country could be established; second, because there was no direct link, in time or in space, between the offence and the local political agitation; and, finally, because there was no reasonable proportion between the criminal act and the political end these pursued. The Federal Tribunal condemned in no uncertain terms the use of gratuitous violence by the perpetrator that it declared as being

116 M. R. García-Mora (n 97) 1254.
117 R. S. Phillips, 'The Political Offence Exception and Terrorism: Its Place in the Current Extradition Scheme and Proposals for Its Future' [1997] *Dickinson J. Int. Law.* 337, 346–347.
118 C. Van den Wijngaert (n 1) 127.
119 M. R. García-Mora (n 97) 1253.
120 In re Kaphengst, Ann. Dig. 292 (No. 188, 1930), quoted in M. R. García-Mora (n 97) 1253.
121 In re Nappi I.L.R. 19 (1952) 375.

unacceptable to any civilised conscience.[122] Although the Swiss requirement of proximity between the offence and the goal pursued is stricter than the one applied in the Anglo-Saxon incidence test, Van Den Wijngaert nevertheless pointed out that in cases involving totalitarian regimes, Swiss courts have somewhat relaxed this criterion, as was also observed in British and U.S. decisions. Accordingly, she described how, in the *Kavic*, *Bjelanovic*, and *Arsenijevic* cases, which echo the British *Kolczynski* ruling, the Swiss Federal Tribunal deemed that the hijacking perpetrated by the three Yugoslav defendants was predominantly political even though there was no political struggle in Yugoslavia at the time to which the acts could be linked.[123] In this case, the Federal Tribunal accepted the argument of the defendants according to which the hijacking was the only available means for them to leave the country. The Tribunal indeed considered that the political offence exception must be applied more liberally to cases involving totalitarian regimes, as the traditional means to fight oppressive regimes may not be available or bear any chances of success. It thus accepted that, in such situations, flight abroad may be the only available means for opponents of the regime to resist it and that this passive opposition was not less worthy of protection than active participation in a fight for political power. The Tribunal also took note of the fact that the offences against the other members of the crew were not very serious before it finally concluded that the political offence exception should be applied to this case.[124]

The second and third criteria of the Swiss proportionality test, namely the effectiveness of the means used to achieve their goal and the proportionality of the common elements of the crimes to their political goal are intertwined and mostly assessed together. The Federal Tribunal has indeed consistently repeated that crimes involving acts of atrocity will be considered common crimes for which extradition can be granted.[125] It is therefore expected that the means used to achieve a political aim be not only effective but also be proportionate to reach their goal. When considering crimes against life, the Federal Tribunal has often been of the opinion that recourse to this type of means should be used as a last resort, when no other alternatives are available to achieve the political goal pursued.[126] In its assessment of the *ultima ratio* principle, the Federal Tribunal has for a long time looked at whether other alternatives existed to achieve the desired goal. Van Den Wijngaert noted in this respect that, in the *Ktir* case, for instance, The Federal Tribunal considered that the murder of a member of the Algerian National Liberation Front – a movement seeking to free Algeria from the French colonial administration – who

122 Della Savia v. Ministero pubblico della Confederazione 95. ATF 1 462 (Switz., Fed.Tr. 1969) 469–470.
123 C. Van den Wijngaert (n 1) 128.
124 *In re Kavic, Bjelanovic and Arsenijevic*, 78 *ATF* 1 39 (Switz., Fed.Tr. 1952).
125 M. R. García-Mora (n 97) 1254.
126 C. Van den Wijngaert (n 1) 129.

was suspected of treason, was not a political crime because the assassination of the suspected traitor did not constitute the only way to achieve the political goal pursued that was to safeguard the interests of the National Liberation Front.[127] This approach contrasted with the one the Federal Tribunal later adopted in the *Watin* case, wherein it did not focus on the objective availability of other options but rather on the subjective perception of the perpetrator as to the availability of other options.[128] Watin had been sentenced *in absentia* for participating in an attack of the Secret Army Organisation, a far-right paramilitary organisation opposing Algerian independence, on the person of the General de Gaulle, the French president of the time.[129] In this case, the Federal Tribunal argued that, even though other ways to achieve the desired result existed (*e.g.* elections), what mattered was whether the assassination attempt was perceived by the defendant as the last available resort to achieve his political goal, especially when, as was the case here, the targeted person was thought to embody the system the defendant was attacking and that therefore there was a reasonable ground to believe that the disappearance of de Gaulle may have led to a change in the system he represented.[130]

If the proximity, effective means and proportionality criteria are the main focus of the predominance test, certain authors have argued that the motivation of the perpetrator has also been a determining factor in some cases – even if the motivation of the perpetrator *alone* is not enough to qualify a crime as political under the Swiss predominance test.[131] In the *Ockert* case, for instance, Garcia Mora noted that the Federal Tribunal defined political offences as acts that appear as common crimes and that are on the list of extraditable offences but which, because of the surrounding circumstances and the motive of the perpetrator in particular, become predominantly political.[132] The same reasoning was applied in the in the *Peruzzo* case in which, in considering whether the incitement to or complicity in the murder of a fascist was a relative political offence, the Federal Tribunal held that a common offence becomes predominantly political when the motives inspiring it or its purpose or the attendant circumstances are principally political, emphasising in passing the importance of the motive and object in this respect.[133]

In comparison to the other tests, the predominance test thus takes into account a wide variety of factors in the determination of the political nature of an offence, which is why it is widely accepted as the most well-rounded approach to defining

127 C. Van den Wijngaert (n 1) 129.
128 G. Gilbert (n 48) 219.
129 R. S. Phillips (n 117) 347.
130 In re Watin, 90 ATF 1 298 (Switz., Fed. Tr. 1964) 300–301.
131 D. P. King, 'The political Offence Exception in International Extradition' [1980] *CILSA*. 247, 255; M. R. García-Mora (n 97) 1252.
132 M. R. García-Mora (n 97) 1252.
133 M. R. García-Mora (n 97) 1252.

the political nature of an offence.[134] Because of its reliance on subjective criteria to determine the political nature of an offence, however, the proportionality theory has been criticised for its arbitrariness. Its application indeed proves to be difficult because it does not provide objective standards against which to measure the common and political elements of crimes.[135] Van Den Wijngaert emphasised in this respect that the criterion of effectiveness is particularly prone to fall prey to subjectivism as, more often than not, there is no way to determine if and to what extent an act has helped the attainment of a political goal.[136] Overall, however, the predominance test has been hailed as the most developed approach to the determination of the political nature of a crime.[137] Unlike the other tests outlined in this chapter, consideration as to the seriousness of the acts is baked into the proportionality theory. The criterion of proportionality and the *ultima ratio* principle that underpins it leave indeed little room for the protection of very serious offences.[138] Van Den Wijngaert noted on this point that while the criterion of the effectiveness of a means to achieve its goal is always disputable, the seriousness of an offence is not as debatable. Accordingly, the Federal Tribunal has more often than not deemed that serious crimes do not constitute predominantly political offences.[139] Similarly, acts of terrorism have almost automatically been excluded from the protection of the political offence exception with this theory because of the combined requirements of proximity and proportionality.[140] Due to its explicit focus on the seriousness of the act, Van Den Wijngaert therefore advanced that this test achieves what the incidence theory or the injured rights theory do not, which is strike a good balance between the political components of a crime and the gravity of its consequences. She indeed underlined that while the other tests focus on the evaluation of the political character of an offence based on the intentions, context, or consequences of an act, the proportionality theory focuses on whether an offence is *predominantly* political, which means that not all political crimes will be protected under the Swiss approach.[141]

Popularity of the proportionality test

For all these reasons, the predominance test is largely considered the most adequate test and has been endorsed by the courts of many countries, including, but not limited to, Dutch, German, Belgian, Argentinian, Brazilian, Chilean, and Italian courts.[142] Equally, although most extradition treaties remain silent on

134 G. Gilbert (n 48) 218; M. R. García-Mora (n 97) 1256.
135 C. Van den Wijngaert (n 1) 131.
136 C. Van den Wijngaert (n 1) 131–132.
137 G. Gilbert (n 48) 220.
138 C. Van den Wijngaert (n 1) 132.
139 C. Van den Wijngaert (n 1) 132.
140 G. Gilbert (n 48) 220.
141 C. Van den Wijngaert (n 1) 132.
142 M. R. García-Mora (n 97) 1255–1256.

how to determine the political nature of an offence, certain bilateral extradition treaties have made reference to the proportionality test.[143] At the international level, the Swiss test has also been accepted as the standard against which to assess the political nature of an offence in various arenas. At the UN level, for instance, although no clear guidance is provided on how to assess the political offence exception within the framework of the Model Treaty on Extradition, very clear recommendations on how to determine the political nature of an offence in the application of 1F (b) of the 1951 United Nations Convention Relating to the Status of Refugees pertaining to the grounds for exclusion from refugee exist and unmistakably refer to the Swiss predominance test. They indeed state that in deciding whether an offence is political or not, the nature and purpose of the act should be considered first. More specifically, special consideration should be granted to whether the crime was committed with genuine political motives or for personal reasons or gain. There should also be a direct and close causal link between the crime and its purported political purpose. In addition, the political aspect of the crime should predominate over its common-law character. This would, for instance, not be the case if the acts in question are grossly out of proportion to the objective they seek to achieve. Accordingly, crimes involving acts of an atrocious nature are unlikely to be considered political.[144]

The predominance test has equally been adopted by Interpol for the assessment by its member countries of the political nature of the cases introduced in Interpol requests.[145] Article 3 of Interpol's Constitution in the context of the processing of information via Interpol's channels precludes the organisation from undertaking any intervention or activities of a political, military, religious, or racial character. This measure aims to ensure the independence and neutrality of the organisation, align with the international extradition law practice, and protect individuals from persecution.[146] To guide its member countries on their assessment of the political nature of an offence, the General Assembly adopted a resolution in 1951 that agreed on the application of the predominance test under international extradition law even if, in the requesting country, the facts of the offence amount to an offence of ordinary law. The 1951 resolution, however, only refers to, but does not describe, the predominance test.[147] In a later resolution of 1984, the General Assembly made a

143 M. R. García-Mora (n 97) 1255–1256.

144 UNHCR, Handbook on Procedures and Criteria for Determining Refugee Status Under the 1951 Convention and the 1967 Protocol Relating to the Status of Refugees. HCR/1P/4/ENG/REV.4 (UNHCR, Geneva 1979, reissued in 2019) 36.

145 Interpol, Interpol Repository of Practice for the Application of Article 3 of Interpol's Constitution in the Context of the Processing of Information via Interpol's Channels (Interpol, 2013) 5.

146 Interpol, Interpol Repository of Practice for the Application of Article 3 of Interpol's Constitution in the Context of the Processing of Information via Interpol's Channels (Interpol, 2013) 6.

147 Interpol, Request for International Inquiries (Resolution No AGN/20/RES/11) 1951.

clearer reference to the criteria of the predominance test by underlining how the direct connection of the offence to the cause pursued or political life of the offender's country was of particular importance in this assessment and that, in the absence of such a direct link, even if the motive of the offender is political, the crime could not be considered falling within the scope of article 3 precluding the organisation's involvement due to the political nature of the case.[148] The resolution further outlines how the fact that the offence takes place within a conflict area is of paramount importance in that respect and that the victims should be connected with the aims or goals of the offender as well as with the political situation or conflict area.[149] Over the years, Interpol has refined its guidelines on how to conduct a predominance test and included additional information to be considered, such as the identity of the source of information, the position expressed by a member or authorised international entities other than the source of information, or the implications on the neutrality of the organisation.[150] Doing so, it went beyond the traditional application of the predominance test, without however, changing it substantially.

Conclusion

The political offence exception to extradition is a deep-rooted practice of international extradition law that emerged around the time of the French Revolution that carved the idea that people fighting tyranny should be protected from extradition. The clause quickly gained popularity and became a standard practice of extradition law worldwide. Today, the political offence exception is found in various forms in most bilateral and multilateral extradition treaties. Despite the wide acceptance of the clause, however, the notion of political offence still generates intense debates and several theories trying to capture its substantive elements coexist. The most common theories are the Anglo-Saxon incidence test, the French injured rights theory test, and the Swiss proportionality test. The incidence test essentially looks at whether the offence was 'incidental to' and formed 'part of' a political commotion to determine the nature of an offence. In the United Kingdom, the application of the incidence test largely evolved over the years to adapt to changing needs and eventually became a multi-layered test taking several elements into account, such as the nature of the regime requesting the extradition and the fact that the offence should target the requesting state, and has occasionally focused on intentionality as well as proportionality. By contrast, in the United States, the case law stuck to a stricter application of the

148 Interpol, Application of article 3 of the Constitution (Resolution No AGN53/RES/7) 1984, 2.

149 Interpol, Application of article 3 of the Constitution (Resolution No AGN53/RES/7) 1984, 3.

150 Interpol, 'Frequently Asked Questions' (Interpol) <https://www.interpol.int/Who-we-are/Commission-for-the-Control-of-INTERPOL-s-Files-CCF/Frequently-Asked-Questions> accessed 8 February 2024.

incidence test, although concerns of political alignment as well as of proportionality equally transpired in the assessment of U.S. courts. The approach adopted in France widely differed and rather focused on the nature of the right injured to determine the political nature of an offence. In this sense, the French test restrains political crimes to crimes targeting the state, its normal functioning, its organisation and its rights. It is thus very limiting in its strict application, which has led French courts to borrow from various other approaches over the years, which eventually brought them closer to the Swiss proportionality test. The Swiss test is in fact largely accepted as the most developed test of all to determine the political nature of an offence, as it considers various criteria, such as the direct link between the offence and a pure political offence, the effectiveness of the means used to reach the goal pursued, the proportionality of the means used, and the intentionality of the author of the crime.

While the incidence, injured rights, and proportionality tests all aim to ascertain the political nature of an offence by examining its characteristics, the past few decades have witnessed a shift driven by the increasing imperative to combat terrorism. This shift has led to the implementation of various counterterrorism measures – at international, regional, and national levels – that significantly limit the application of the political offence exception. These measures have effectively defined the political offence 'negatively' by excluding certain crimes from the protection offered by the political offence exception. In doing so, they have clarified what political offences cannot be, without, however, providing a positive definition of what they actually are. The following chapters focus on those tools adopted as part of counterterrorism efforts. They will more specifically explore how the protection of political offenders from extradition was substantially reduced in the CoE framework that incorporated the offences listed in the United Nations' conventions on terrorism in its own counterterrorism conventions, and how this tendency to depoliticise crimes for the purpose of combatting terrorism continued and intensified in the EU framework where the political offence exception clause was eventually abolished among EU member states.

Bibliography

Legislation, official publications

United Nations

Model Treaty on Extradition (Adopted by General Assembly Resolution 45/116) 1990.

UNHCR, Handbook on Procedures and Criteria for Determining Refugee Status Under the 1951 Convention and the 1967 Protocol Relating to the Status of Refugees. HCR/1P/4/ENG/REV.4 (UNHCR, Geneva 1979, reissued in 2019).

Interpol

Interpol, Application of article 3 of the Constitution (Resolution No AGN53/RES/7) 1984.

Interpol, Interpol Repository of Practice for the application of article 3 of Interpol's Constitution in the context of the processing of information via Interpol's channels (2nd, Interpol, 2013).
Interpol, Request for International Inquiries (Resolution No AGN/20/RES/11) 1951.

Regional treaties

Acuerdo Sobre Extradición entre el Mercosur, la República de Bolivia y la República de Chile (CMC 15/98) 1998.
The Arab States and the Arab League Extradition Agreement, 1952.
ECOWAS Convention on Extradition (A/PI/8/94) 1994.
European Convention on Extradition (ETS 24) 1957.
Inter-American Convention on Extradition, 1981.
The London Scheme for Extradition within the Commonwealth, Incorporating the Amendments agreed at Kingstown in November 2002.
Riyadh Arab Agreement for Judicial Cooperation, 1983.

Switzerland

Federal Act of 22 January 1892 on Extradition to Foreign States 1892 (Repealed in the Meantime by the Federal Act on International Mutual Assistance in Criminal Matters 1981 (Mutual Assistance Act, IMAC)).

Case law

France

Croissant (Cour d'Appel de Paris, 1977).
Hennin (Cour d'Appel de Paris, 1967) no. 15274.
In re Gatti, Annual Digest 70 (1947).
Inacio da Palma (Cour d'Appel de Paris, 1967) No. 15387.

Switzerland

Della Savia v. Ministero pubblico della Confederazione 95. ATF 1 462 (Switz., Fed. Tr. 1969).
In re Kaphengst, Ann; Dig. 292 (No. 188, 1930).
In re Kavic, Bjelanovic and Arsenijevic, 78 ATF 1 39 (Switz., Fed.Tr. 1952).
In re Nappi I.L.R. 19 (1952).
In re Watin, 90 ATF 1 298 (Switz., Fed. Tr. 1964).

United Kingdom

In re Castioni (1891) 1 QB 149.
In re Meunier (1894) 2 QB 415.
Regina v. Governor of Brixton Prison, Ex Parte Kolczynski and others (1955) 2 QB 540.
Schtraks v. Government of Israel and Others (1964) AC 556, (1962) 3 All ER 529, (1962) 3 WLR 1013.
T v. Secretary of State for the Home Department (1996) 2 All ER 865.
Tzu-Tsai Cheng v. Governor of Pentonville Prison (1973) 2 All ER 204.

United States

Eain v. Wilkes, 641 F.2d 504 (7th Circ. 1981).
In re Doherty, 599 F. Supp. 270 (S.D.N.Y. 1984).
In re Ezeta. In re Bolanos, In re Colocho. In re Cienguegos. In re Bustamante, 62 F. 972 (N.D. Cal 1894).
In re Gonzalez, 217 F. Supp. 717 (S.D.N.Y. 1963).
In re Mackin, 668 F.2d 122 (2d Cir. 1981).
In re McMullen, No.3–78–1099 MG (N.D. Ca. 11 May 1979).
In re Mylonas, 187 F. Supp. 716 (N.D. Ala. 1960).
Karadzole v. Artukovic 247 F.2d 198 (9th Cir. 1957).
Karadzole v. Artukovic 355 U.S. 393 (1958).
Matter of Extradition of Artukovic, 628 F. Supp. 1370 (C.D. Cal. 1986).
Ornelas v. Ruiz 161 U.S. 502 (1896).
Quinn v. Robinson, 783 F. 2d 776 (9th Cir. 1986).
United States v. Artukovic, 170 F. Supp. 383 (S.D. Cal. 1959).

Books

Bassiouni C., *International Extradition: United States Law and Practice* (6th edn, Oxford University Press, Oxford 2014).
Gilbert G., *Responding to International Crime* (Martinus Nijhoff Publishers, Leiden, Boston 2006).
Jansson J., *Terrorism, Criminal Law and Politics: The Decline of the Political Offence Exception to Extradition* (Routledge, Abingdon, New York 2020).
Papadatos P., *Le Délit Politique: Contribution à l'Étude des Crimes contre l'État* (Librairie E. Droz, Geneva 1955).
Pyle C. H., *Extradition, Politics and Human Rights* (Temple University Press, Philadelphia 2001).
Shearer I. A., *Extradition in International Law* (Manchester University Press, Manchester 1971).
Van den Wijngaert C., *The Political Offence Exception to Extradition: The Delicate Problem of Balancing the Rights of the Individual and the International Public Order* (Kluwer, The Netherlands 1980).

Journal articles

Basso K. A., 'The 1985 U.S.-U.K. Supplementary Extradition Treaty: A Superfluous Effort?' [1989] *B.C. Int'l. & Comp. Law Rev.* 301.
Carbonneau T. E., 'Extradition and Transnational Terrorism: A Comment on the Recent Extradition of Klaus Croissant from France to West Germany' [1978] *Int. Lawyer.* 813.
Carbonneau T. E., 'The Political Offense Exception as Applied in French Cases Dealing with the Extradition of Terrorists' [1983] *Mich. J. Int. Law.* 209.
Epps V., 'The Validity of the Political Offender Exception in Extradition Treaties in Anglo-American Jurisprudence' [1979] *Harv. Int'l. Law J.* 61.
García-Mora M. R., 'The Nature of Political Offenses: A Knotty Problem of Extradition Law' [1962] *Va. Law Rev.* 1226.
Green L. C., 'Political Offences, War Crimes and Extradition' [1962] *ICLQ.* 329.
Groarke J. P., 'Revolutionaries Beware: The Erosion of the Political Offense Exception under the 1986 United States-United Kingdom Supplementary Extradition Treaty' [1988] *U. PA. Law Rev.* 1515.

King D. P., 'The Political Offence Exception in International Extradition' [1980] *CILSA*. 247.

Lévy-Bruhl H., 'Les Délits Politiques. Recherche d'une Définition' [1964] *Rev. Fr. Sociol.* 131.

Lieberman D. M., 'Sorting the Revolutionary from the Terrorist: The Delicate Application of the "Political Offense" Exception in U.S. Extradition Cases' [2006] *Stan. Law Rev.* 181.

O'Higgins P., 'Extradition. Offence of a Political Character. Terrorism' [1973] *CLJ*. 181.

Phillips R. S., 'The Political Offence Exception and Terrorism: Its Place in the Current Extradition Scheme and Proposals for Its Future' [1997] *Dickinson J. Int. Law*. 337.

Soafer A. D., 'The Political Offense Exception and Terrorism' [1986] *Denv. J. Intl'l. Law & Pol'y*. 125.

Academic reports

Van Den Wijngaert C., 'The Political Offence Exception to Extradition: Defining the Issues and Searching a Feasible Alternative' [1983] Report Presented at the International Seminar on Extradition, International Institute of Higher Studies in criminal Sciences 741.

Online resources

Interpol, 'Frequently Asked Questions' (Interpol) <https://www.interpol.int/Who-we-are/Commission-for-the-Control-of-INTERPOL-s-Files-CCF/Frequently-Asked-Questions> accessed 8 February 2024.

Soucy R., 'Varieties of Fascism' (Encyclopaedia Britannica) <https://www.britannica.com/topic/fascism/Varieties-of-fascism> accessed 5 December 2023.

3 Evolution of the political offence exception in CoE Conventions

The 1957 Convention on Extradition offers a strong protection of political offenders

Historical context: common heritage of CoE member states enabling cooperation

In the aftermath of World War II, many pro-European movements advocated for the establishment of an organisation that would promote peace, freedom, and democracy. The goal was to foster cooperation among European countries to prevent the rise of totalitarian regimes and avoid future conflicts. As a result, and to ensure stability, economic growth, and social cohesion on the continent,[1] the Council of Europe was established in 1949, making it the oldest political organisation in Europe.[2] The declared purpose of the Council of Europe was "to achieve a greater unity between its members for the purpose of safeguarding and realising the ideals and principles which are their common heritage".[3] Countries wishing to join the Council of Europe thus had to meet certain prerequisites, the most crucial being respect for the rule of law, fundamental freedoms, and a genuine commitment to the Council's objectives.[4] These conditions made the Council a key forum for negotiating tools of cooperation in criminal matters to protect its core values,[5] despite the initial reluctance due to criminal law being a cornerstone of state sovereignty. At the time, the legal systems of other nations were viewed as foreign, and states were generally disinclined to enhance their effectiveness by extraditing

1 International Democracy Watch, 'Council of Europe' (International Democracy Watch) <http://www.internationaldemocracywatch.org/index.php/council-of-europe> accessed 19 August 2019.

2 CVCE, 'The origins of the Council of Europe' (CVCE 2016) <https://www.cvce.eu/en/education/unit-content/-/unit/026961fe-0d57-4314-a10a-a4ac066a1801/13839cdf-3e7e-4985-995f-2b6d9b534633> accessed 22 August 2018.

3 Statute of the Council of Europe (ETS 1) 1949 (Art. 1).

4 Statute of the Council of Europe (ETS 1) 1949 (Art. 3).

5 W. Wagner, 'Building an Internal Security Community: The Democratic Peace and the Politics of Extradition in Western Europe' [2003] *J. Peace Res.* 695, 702–703.

DOI: 10.4324/9781003425847-3

individuals who had fled their jurisdictions.[6] However, the shared values and common heritage among member states fostered an environment conducive to the negotiation of effective extradition regimes. This shared foundation created a presumption of goodwill,[7] making this European project of achieving a "closer unity between all like-minded countries of Europe"[8] possible.

In 1953, the Committee of Ministers of the Council of Europe instructed the secretary-general to convene a committee of governmental experts to examine the possibility of establishing a number of principles in extradition that would be acceptable to all members of the Council.[9] The accumulation of these principles, one of which was the political offence exemption, formed the first multilateral convention on extradition concluded in Europe. Until then, extradition and mutual cooperation agreements in criminal matters in general were concluded bilaterally. The Council of Europe thus offered the first European multilateral platform for the negotiation and adoption of tools of cooperation in criminal matters among European countries.[10] Later, it would represent a laboratory of cooperation for the nascent European Coal and Steel Community, which was then only collaborating on industrial coal and steel production.

The 1957 European Convention on Extradition[11] is the first tool of cooperation in criminal matters that was adopted to get closer to the Council of Europe's objective of unity. It provides for the extradition of persons wanted for criminal proceedings or the carrying of a sentence. It contains 32 articles covering general issues such as non-extradition for political offences, military offences, the special case of fiscal offences, the non-extradition of nationals, the possibility to refuse extradition if there is a risk of capital punishment, and more. This convention, which took precedence over bilateral agreements previously concluded, is the founding tool from which all ensuing conventions and protocols on extradition at the European level later derived. It is thus a cornerstone of this book because it is the starting point that provides the frame of reference to understand how political crimes evolved from there on in European criminal law, as all subsequent conventions and protocols amended and built on the notion of political crimes as worded in this convention.

6 W. Wagner, 'Building an Internal Security Community: The Democratic Peace and the Politics of Extradition in Western Europe' [2003] *J. Peace Res.* 703.
7 W. Wagner, 'Building an Internal Security Community: The Democratic Peace and the Politics of Extradition in Western Europe' [2003] *J. Peace Res.* 703.
8 Statute of the Council of Europe (n 3) (Preamble).
9 Committee of Ministers of the Council of Europe, European Convention on Extradition (Resolution (53)4) 19 March 1953.
10 A. C. Kiss, 'La Convention Européenne d'Extradition' [1958] *AFDI.* 493, 493.
11 European Convention on Extradition (ETS 24) 1957.

Strong protection of political offenders (art. 3)

Article 3 of the Convention, concerning political crimes, provides the following:

1. Extradition shall not be granted if the offence in respect of which it is requested is regarded by the requested Party as a political offence or as an offence connected with a political offence.
2. The same rule shall apply if the requested Party has substantial grounds for believing that a request for extradition for an ordinary criminal offence has been made for the purpose of prosecuting or punishing a person on account of his race, religion, nationality or political opinion, or that that person's position may be prejudiced for any of these reasons.
3. The taking or attempted taking of the life of a Head of State or a member of his family shall not be deemed to be a political offence for the purposes of this Convention.
4. This article shall not affect any obligations which the Member states may have undertaken or may undertake under any other international convention of a multilateral character.[12]

The convention thus precludes extradition in case the offence for which extradition is requested is a political offence. What stands out is that the political offence is not defined. More than that, the term is actually used as a basis to define another category of offence, the ones 'connected with a political offence', which are also exempt from extradition. By not defining the political offence, the convention thus confers a very broad protection to political offenders, as political crimes and their associated protection are not limited in any way. This means that, according to the wording of this convention, virtually any crime could be considered political, provided they are connected to a political situation.

The second paragraph of the article further provides for the protection of what is commonly called a discrimination clause. The latter means that extradition cannot be granted if there are grounds for believing that the requested person is persecuted "on account of his race, religion, nationality or political opinion, or that that person's position may be prejudiced for any of these reasons". This clause is humanitarian in nature because it seeks to protect potential victims of state repression from extradition. Together with the first paragraph, the text of the article therefore provides both for the protection of persons who would have actively participated in a political endeavour resulting in a crime and of persons who would have been passive victims of political persecution. As a result, the protection from extradition provided by this convention covers both active and passive agents of political situations. This proscription is also valid in case of transit.[13]

12 European Convention on Extradition (ETS 24) 1957 (Art. 3).
13 European Convention on Extradition (ETS 24) 1957 (Art. 21).

The only crime excluded from the protection of the political offence exemption is the taking or attempted taking of the life of a head of state or a member of their family. This first restriction is a Belgian legacy to the European extradition framework. It followed events that unfolded in 1854, when two French nationals residing in Belgium attempted to take the life of Napoleon III during a visit to Belgium. This unsuccessful attempt led to the drafting of a bill excluding regicides from the scope of the political offence exemption. This clause, commonly called the *clause d'attentat* or *clause belge*, was integrated into the Belgian legal order in 1856 and later incorporated in many bilateral and multilateral extradition agreements.[14] As the sole and only restriction to the political offence exemption in the convention, it conveys a clear message regarding the legitimate targets of political crimes: the head of state (and their family) is off-limits.

Generous reservation regime used as a way to increase the protection of political offenders (art. 26)

In addition to the quite substantial possibilities that it puts in place to protect political offenders, the Convention offers the possibility to contracting parties to introduce reservation regarding any provision of the Convention, which has served as a venue to further increase the protection of political offenders for contracting parties to the Convention.[15] Indeed, among the 46 member states of the Council of Europe that ratified the Convention (later joined by Israel, South Korea, South Africa, and now Russia), only three have introduced restrictions to the political offence exemption. This indicates that the restriction regime has not been widely adopted to limit this protection.[16] On the contrary, ten member states used it to reserve the right not to extradite a person if the person is claimed on the basis of the taking of attempted taking of the life of a head of state or member of their family, thus further enlarging the already substantial protection offered by the Convention. Authors like Kiss observed that this generous reservation regime, rather unusual in treaties dealing with such matters, was the result of tense debates on the format of the Convention.[17] In order to convince reluctant member states and get as many of them as possible on board, the Council of Europe provided the chance to its

14 E. Crabit, *Recherches sur la Notion d'Espace Judiciaire Européen* (Presses Universitaires de Bordeaux, Bordeaux 1988) 76.

15 European Convention on Extradition (n 11) (Art. 26§1).

16 Council of Europe, 'Reservations and Declarations for Treaty No. 24 – European Convention on Extradition' (Council of Europe) <https://www.CoE.int/en/web/conventions/full-list/-/conventions/treaty/024/declarations?p_auth=6DZu2522&_CoEconventions_WAR_CoEconventionsportlet_enVigueur=false&_CoEconventions_WAR_CoEconventionsportlet_searchBy=state&_CoEconventions_WAR_CoEconventionsportlet_codePays=RUS&_CoEconventions_WAR_CoEconventionsportlet_codeNature=2> accessed 29 August 2018.

17 A. C. Kiss (n 10) 493.

member states to easily introduce important reservations, an opporunity that many seized. This reservation regime was, however, later criticised because it was said to undermine the multilateral nature of the Convention. Some indeed argue that because of the variable geometries these reservations generate, the multilateral conventions having them can result in engendering more disputes than if bilateral treaties were applied.[18] Belgium, for example, reported signing the Convention only much later because it considered that all the reservations to the Convention turned the latter to a sort of compilation of bilateral agreements rather than truly providing a multilateral tool.[19] Nevertheless, this Convention offered a multilateral platform connecting countries which did not, and maybe would have not, have extradition agreements between them otherwise.[20]

The 1975 Additional Protocol to the European Convention on Extradition: excluding most violent crime from the scope of the political offence exception

Context of the adoption of the Protocol

On the tenth anniversary of the entry into force of the European Convention on Extradition, the Council of Europe convened a meeting of experts responsible for the application of the Convention at national level to discuss its efficacity. The opinion of the majority of experts was that the 1957 Convention no longer corresponded to the needs of the time in terms of inter-state cooperation in criminal matters. Revising it, however, was considered premature. The 1975 Protocol was thus drafted in order to address some of the issues raised at the meeting.[21] The discussions led to conclusions on numerous topics, but the Protocol, comprising nine articles in total, ultimately addressed two of them: political crimes (art. 1) and of the *ne bis in idem* principle (art. 2).[22] Both in fact raise two essential points regarding political crimes. The first one relates to the threshold of violence that can be reached in the commission of political crimes; the second one, to the legitimate targets of such crimes.

18 F. Honig, 'Extradition by Multilateral Conventions' [1956] *ICLQ.* 549, 551.

19 G. Gilbert, *Responding to International Crime* (Martinus Nijhoff Publishers, Leiden, Boston 2006) 33.

20 P. O'Higgins, 'The European Convention on Extradition' [1960] *ICLQ.* 491, 497–498.

21 Council of Europe, Explanatory Report to the Additional Protocol to the European Convention on Extradition (1975) 1.

22 Council of Europe, Explanatory Report to the Additional Protocol to the European Convention on Extradition (1975) 3. The *Ne bis in Idem* principle is a fundamental principle in criminal law according to which one cannot be prosecuted for the same offence twice. As such, it seeks to contain the *ius puniendi* of the states. M. Wasmeier, 'The Principle of Ne Bis In Idem' [2006] *RIDP.* 121.

The Protocol excludes the most violent crimes from the scope of the political offence exception (art. 1)

The question of the level of violence tolerated in the commission of a political crime appears in the first article of the Protocol that enumerates a number of crimes that are not to be considered political anymore. The first one is the crime of genocide. The Convention criminalises not only the commission of genocide but also the conspiracy, the direct and public incitement, the attempt, and the complicity in the commission of genocide.[23] The implications of this are that, although resorting to violence and causing unintended casualties in pursuit of a political goal may be seen as an unavoidable and necessary side effect for achieving a legitimate aim, the Protocol sets clear boundaries. It suggests, first, that the killings cannot be a primary objective of the political endeavour and, second, that this level of violence exceeds any political justification. The same goes for grave breaches of the Geneva Conventions to which the Protocol refers and excludes from the scope of the political offence exception. These breaches include the "willful killing, torture or inhuman treatment, including biological experiments, wilfully causing great suffering or serious injury to body or health . . . , not justified by military necessity and carried out unlawfully and wantonly"; the "extensive destruction and appropriation or property" (also not justified by military necessity); "compelling a prisoner of war to serve in the forces of the hostile Power or wilfully depriving a prisoner of war of the rights of fair and regular trial"; and, finally, "the unlawful deportation or transfer or unlawful confinement of a protected person, compelling a protected person to serve in the forces of a hostile Power, or wilfully depriving a protected person of the rights of fair and regular trial" in addition to "the taking of hostages". The Protocol further excludes "any comparable violations of the laws of war" from the scope of the political offence exemption.[24]

The most violent crimes, even taking place in a context of generalised violence (*i.e.* the one of armed conflicts), are thus hereby excluded from the protection of political crimes. The idea is that some crimes are so monstrous that it would be inconcevable that their perpetrator enjoys immunity from extradition and prosecution.[25] If the political offence exemption was applied to these crimes, the state in which the offender is located might not have the jurisdiction to prosecute the offenders.[26] This rationale, however, does not apply to state actors, as visible from the fact that the Protocol clarifies for some of these crimes that they are not protected by the political offence exception when committed 'unlawful or not justified by military necessity'.

23 Convention on the Prevention and Punishment of the Crime of Genocide (No. 1021) 1948 (Art. 3).

24 Additional Protocol to the European Convention on Extradition (ETS 86) 1975 (Art. 1 c).

25 Council of Europe, Explanatory Report to the Additional Protocol to the European Convention on Extradition (n 21) 3.

26 Council of Europe, Explanatory Report to the Additional Protocol to the European Convention on Extradition (n 21) 6–7.

The Protocol redefines legitimate targets of political crimes (art. 1 and 2)

In addition to the issue of the level of violence tolerated in the commission of political crimes, the Protocol raises the question of the legitimate targets of these crimes. This already appears in the first article, which not only suggests that civilian populations not involved in the conflict are off-limits but also, and more interestingly, that certain offences against military and diplomatic staff – even in times of war – are considered to cross a line. It is indeed noteworthy that the Convention puts some of the most violent crimes possible on an equal footing with the ones where state staff are used against the state they serve (forcing diplomatic staff to work against their country or the military to fight for hostile powers).

The second article of the Protocol, modifying the *ne bis in idem* principle, further comforts the idea that state interests deserve special protection. The Protocol indeed extends the application of the *ne bis in idem* principle to cases where a final judgement was rendered in a contracting party to the Convention, as long as it satisfies certain conditions.[27] As such, this article does not formally and directly affect the definition of political crimes, but it very much does so in practice. Indeed, until this Protocol, the *ne bis in idem* principle was applied only with respect to judgments made in the requested state. The Protocol extends the judicial security provided by this principle by adding new instances where extradition should not be granted (art. 2§2), short of cases in which the

a) offence in respect of which judgment has been rendered was committed against a person, an institution or any thing having public status in the requesting State,
b) if the person on whom judgment was passed had himself a public status in the requesting State,
c) or if the offence in respect of which judgment was passed was committed completely or partly in the territory of the requesting State or in a place treated as its territory.[28]

The intent of this provision is explicit: it allows a state to prosecute individuals when it has a "special interest"[29] to do so.[30] This is particularly significant for

27 Council of Europe, Explanatory Report to the Additional Protocol to the European Convention on Extradition (n 21) 6–7.
28 Additional Protocol to the European Convention on Extradition (n 24) (Art. 2§3). This change had actually already been initiated in the Conventions on the international validity of criminal judgments and on the transfer of proceedings in criminal matters that contained a very similar provision, but the fact that it was also applied to extradition is noteworthy. European Convention on the International Validity of Criminal Judgments (ETS 70) 1970 (Art. 53§2); European Convention on the Transfer of Proceedings in Criminal Matters (ETS 73) 1972 (Art. 35§2).
29 Council of Europe, Explanatory Report to the Additional Protocol to the European Convention on Extradition (n 21) 6–7.
30 Additional Protocol to the European Convention on Extradition (n 24) (Art. 2§3c).

political crimes, which are likely to target the state. While this change pertains specifically to the *ne bis in idem* principle and does not directly alter the definition of political crimes, it nonetheless represents a significant political manoeuver. By excluding judicial security for these offences, the Protocol effectively casts a shadow of illegitimacy over actions directed against the state.

Overall, however, the 1957 Convention on Extradition and its 1975 Additional Protocol offer very strong protection to political offenders. The 1957 Convention on Extradition indeed provides an unbridled protection of political offenders, short of cases in which the offender targets a head of state or member of their family. As for the 1975 Protocol, although it does introduce the idea that the 'special interests' of the state deserve special protection, it only formally proscribes extremely violent crimes – such as genocide and crimes against humanity – from the scope of protection of political crimes. The 1975 Protocol thus does not affect the protection associated with political crimes in a considerable or objectionable way, but, together with the 1957 Convention on Extradition, it introduces the idea that heads of state and state interests in general deserve greater protection. When, in later years, the Council of Europe started dealing with terrorism, protecting state interests became a dominant concern, which greatly impacted the protection of political offenders.

The 1977 Convention on the Suppression of Terrorism: depoliticising crimes for the purpose of combatting terrorism

Strategic venue-shopping and diverging interests of CoE member states in combating terrorism

The 1977 Convention is the first significant tool of cooperation on terrorism at the European level.[31] Its adoption followed the increase of attacks on European soil starting from the early 1950s, from groups like the Italian Red Brigades, the German Red Army Faction, the Belgian Communist Combatant Cells, the French Action Directe group, the Provisional Irish Republican Army, the Basque Euskadi Ta Askatasuna (ETA), or the Corsican National Liberation Front.[32] Most significantly, the Munich attacks committed by the Black September organisation prompted serious reflections among policy-makers on how to overcome existing obstacles to cooperation in combatting terrorism.[33] The need for cooperation became clear when it appeared that the states

31 C. Murphy, 'The Legal Response to Terrorism of the European Union and Council of Europe' in B. Saul (ed), *Research Handbook on International Law and Terrorism* (Edward Elgar Publishing, 2014) 685.

32 B. Galloux-Fournier, *Histoire de l'Europe au XXe siècle (de 1974 à nos jours)* (Complexe, France 1995) 160–163.

33 B. Blumenau, 'Taming the Beast: West Germany, the Political Offence Exception, and the Council of Europe Convention on the Suppression of Terrorism' [2015] *Terror Polit. Violenc.* 310, 314.

affected by these attacks generally had the necessary legislation to respond to domestic attacks but lacked tools of international cooperation to retaliate to transborder crimes.[34] In response to these attacks (especially the one in Munich), the Parliamentary Assembly of the Council of Europe repeatedly urged its members to start cooperating on the fight against terrorism.[35] These recurrent calls eventually led to the adoption of a secretly negotiated European Convention on the Suppression of Terrorism.[36]

Compared to the texts dealing with extradition outlined earlier that only mildly affected the definition and protection of political crime, this Convention – and the fight against terrorism in general – changed this protection in an unprecedented way. The main purpose of this Convention is to depoliticise crimes to facilitate their extradition (art. 1 and 2). This approach arose from the frequent invocation of the political offence exemption in extradition cases involving alleged terrorists. The exemption was often used due to confusion and, perhaps more critically, disagreements over the distinction between terrorists and freedom fighters.[37] Defining terrorism has been a long-lasting problem that very few counterterrorism tools have overcome. In fact, the United Nations – where most international tools to combat terrorism had been adopted up to that point – had been very cautious in that respect. It only criminalised targeted crimes (such as the unlawful seizure of aircraft, hostage-taking, etc.) while deliberately avoiding the unclear term *terrorism* in its conventions (adopted as part of its counterterrorism efforts), precisely because of the ambiguity of the notion. The Council of Europe crossed that barrier with this Convention by directly referring to the term *terrorism*.[38] Despite its proclaimed goal of combatting terrorism, the Convention does not define it.

The choice of the Council of Europe as an arena to combat terrorism, however, was neither obvious nor unanimous. Many European countries were of the opinion that the United Nations should remain the forum of choice for these matters and perceived the Council of Europe as a secondary platform that should deal with legal issues only, and not political ones, such as terrorism.[39] It is only when the United Nations reached a stalemate on the adoption of its Convention on the taking of hostages that the Council of Europe became a more attractive venue to undertake work on terrorism.[40]

34 N. Gal-Or, *International Cooperation to Suppress Terrorism* (Routledge, New York 1985) 194–195.

35 C. Walter, 'Combatting Terrorism and Organized Crime' in S. Schmahl & M. Breuer (eds), *The Council of Europe: Its Law and Policies* (Oxford University Press, 2017) 673.

36 N. Gal-Or (n 34) 275.

37 O. Lagodny, 'The European Convention on the Suppression of Terrorism: A Substantial Step to Combat Terrorism?' [1989] *U. Colo. Law Rev.* 583.

38 G. Guillaume, 'Terrorism and International Law' [2004] *ICLQ.* 537, 539.

39 B. Blumenau (n 33) 314–315.

40 B. Blumenau (n 33) 315.

There was, however, competition in that respect, as the European Communities were also trying to carve themselves a role as important actors in the field of counterterrorism, albeit with a more operational focus. Noemi Gal-Or noted on this point that, while the dynamic between the United Nations and the Council of Europe was largely dominated by complementarity, the relation of the Council of Europe to the European Economic Community was rather that of competition and rivalry.[41] Initially, the member states of the European Communities – that were also part of the Council of Europe – were more favourable to discussing these issues in a more restricted and confidential setting. They argued that while the Council of Europe was a good platform to discuss general ideas, the European Communities were more suitable for immediate and effective responses.[42] This approach changed around 1975 when Germany pointed out that it would be useful to have a regional framework that allowed going beyond practical cooperation between security forces and to have a general convention on the suppression of terrorism.

Germany was keen on having this Convention adopted because it was seeking to send a message of unity and determination to combat terrorism to the world, and to the United Nations in particular. This effort was intended to overcome the deadlock on the adoption of the hostage Convention and finally have an international tool to prevent situations like the one of the Munich attacks.[43] Alongside Germany, Italy and the United Kingdom were also facing terrorist attacks at the time, showed a strong interest in limiting the scope of the political offence exemption.[44] French and Irish authorities, however, held a different view. France, land of refuge – including for controversial political figures such as Basque and Palestinian militants Klaus Croissant (lawyer and alleged militant of the Red Army Faction)[45] and Abu Daoud (instigator of the Munich attacks)[46] – was reluctant to encroach on the protection of the political offence exemption. It consequently vetoed one of the earlier versions of the 1977 Convention. Only after it made substantial changes to the text following an active German campaign to wrap up the negotiations was the text finally adopted. This adoption, however, came at the cost of an Irish abstention. Because of its history with the United Kingdom,[47] Ireland believed that impinging on the political offence exemption would go against international customary law.[48] The Convention is therefore often described as a tool of compromise because of the conflicting interests of the CoE

41 N. Gal-Or (n 34) 217.
42 N. Gal-Or (n 34) 221.
43 B. Blumenau (n 33) 318.
44 B. Blumenau (n 33) 324.
45 L. Israël, 'Défendre le Défenseur de l'Ennemi Public: l'Affaire Croissant' [2012] *MS.* 67.
46 B. Blumenau (n 33) 321.
47 N. Gal-Or (n 34) 251–253.
48 B. Blumenau (n 33) 316–320.

member states stemming not only from their different levels of exposure to varying forms of terrorism but also from their very diverging legal responses to it.[49] The main goal of this 16-article-long Convention is to depoliticise certain crimes to make them extraditable while reminding CoE member states that this does not impose an obligation on them to extradite a person who may be persecuted on the grounds of race, religion, nationality, or political opinion.

Obligation to depoliticise certain offences (art. 1)

The most pressing issues identified at the time of the negotiation of the 1977 Convention were extradition and the political offence exemption.[50] By depoliticising political crimes for the purpose of combatting terrorism, this Convention confirmed for the first of a long series of instances the ambiguous relation of political crimes to terrorism. The authors of the Convention did not, however, seek to clarify the grey area between the two.[51] In 1973, the Parliamentary Assembly of the Council of Europe called on its members to adopt a common definition of the notion of political offence so as to prevent the possibility of justifying a terrorist crime endangering the lives of innocent people by invoking its political nature.[52] However, this call went unheeded and remained unadressed.[53]

The argument brought forward for the depoliticisation of crimes was that certain crimes are so abhorrent in their methods or consequences in relation to their motives that it was no longer reasonable to classify them as 'political offences' exempt from extradition.[54] Interestingly, as is true for all the conventions discussed in this chapter and the next, defining the crimes listed in this Convention as non-political meant that the political nature of an offence was acknowledged only at the moment of its depolitisation.[55] The idea was that in the 19th and 20th centuries, it might have been acceptable for liberal democracies to protect offenders who committed those acts against conservative and reactionary regimes.[56] By 1977, however, it was argued that the democratic nature and strong commitment to human rights of the Council of Europe

49 N. Gal-Or (n 34) 189–192.

50 B. Blumenau (n 33) 315.

51 M. B. Baker, 'The Western European Legal Response to Terrorism' [1987] *Brook. J. Int'l. Law.* 1, 5.

52 Parliamentary Assembly, International Terrorism (Recommendation 703) 1973.

53 Years later, in 1999, the Parliamentary Assembly would still (unsuccessfully) try advocating for a common definition of political offences. Parliamentary Assembly, European Democracies Facing up to Terrorism (Recommendation 1426) 1999, 2.

54 Council of Europe, Explanatory Report to the Convention on the Suppression of Terrorism (1977) 1.

55 F. Tulkens, 'Analyse Critique de la Convention Européenne pour la Répression du Terrorisme' [1979] *Deviance Soc.* 229, 232.

56 B. Blumenau (n 33) 312.

member states had fostered a climate of mutual trust among these countries. This environment no longer warranted the protection of individuals who committed terrorist crimes within another Council of Europe member state.[57] The relevance of maintaining protection from countries that were not only not considered illiberal anymore but that were considered democratic and likeminded allies was called into question.

This depoliticisation of political crimes took place in two steps in this Convention. The first one was the the obligation to depoliticise certain crimes as laid out in article 1 of the Convention. This first article of the Convention lists six offences that can no longer be considered "political offences, offences connected with a political offence, or offences inspired by political motives" by CoE member states. The offences in question refer to the unlawful seizure of (a civil) aicraft,[58] unlawful acts against the safety of civil aviation,[59] and attacks against internationally protected persons,[60] which all refer to offences listed in specialised UN Conventions tackling specific aspects of terrorism.[61] The article further prohibits the protection of "an offence involving kidnapping, the taking of a hostage or serious unlawful detention"; the use of explosives or automatic firearm, endangering the lives of people indiscriminately;[62] and, finally, the attempt to commit any of the offences listed earlier, as well as the participation to the attempt/offence.[63]

Perhaps more distinctly than in any other instrument, each of the provisions of this Convention is linked to specific events that took place in the years leading up to the adoption of the Convention. For instance, the rise in airplane hijackings during that period[64] led to the first two paragraphs of the

57 Council of Europe, Explanatory Report to the Convention on the Suppression of Terrorism (n 54) 2. Because of this, this convention was only open to member states of the Council of Europe and not to third parties (such as Israel, South Korea, and South Africa, which are contracting parties to other CoE conventions). Council of Europe, Explanatory Report to the Convention on the Suppression of Terrorism (n 54) 4.

58 The Convention refers to the unlawful seizure of aircraft as defined in the Convention for the Suppression of unlawful seizure of aircraft. Convention for the Suppression of Unlawful Seizure of Aircraft (860 UNTS) 1970 (Art. 1).

59 As defined in the Convention for the Suppression of Unlawful Acts against the Safety of Civil Aviation. Articles 1 and 2, Convention for the Suppression of Unlawful Acts Against the Safety of Civil Aviation (974 UNTS) 1971 (Art. 1–2).

60 More specifically, "a serious offence involving an attack against the life, physical integrity or liberty of internationally protected persons, including diplomatic agents". European Convention on the Suppression of Terrorism (ETS 90) 1977 (Art. 1c).

61 C. Walter (n 35) 678.

62 The article refers to 'an offence involving the use of a bomb, grenade, rocket, automatic firearm or letter or parcel bomb if this use endangers persons'. European Convention on the Suppression of Terrorism (n 60) (Art. 1e).

63 More specifically, "an attempt to commit any of the foregoing offences or participation as an accomplice of a person who commits or attempts to commit such an offence". European Convention on the Suppression of Terrorism (n 60) (Art. 1f).

64 R. Mankiewicz, 'La Problématique de la Piraterie Aérienne' [1977] *Etud. Int.* 100, 100–102.

article.[65] Similarly, the third provision was influenced by the increasing attacks against diplomats in the 1960s, particularly in South America and Europe, with West Germany being notably affected.[66] The fourth provision addresses hostage-taking and kidnappings, which were prevalent in the violent political activism of that era.[67] The final two paragraphs cover more traditional violent terrorist attacks. In response to all these events, the Convention laid an obligation upon its contracting parties not to consider any of these offences as political in extradition proceedings. However, the Convention did not create an obligation to extradite, as it is not an extradition treaty; any potential extradition still requires a separate legal framework or arrangement designed for that purpose.[68]

This first article raises several significant aspects regarding counterterrorism and state power. Notably, by condemning, in the words of its explanatory report, these "odious" attacks against "like-minded" and "democratic" states that are "respectful of human rights," the Convention constructed an imaginary community of such states needing protection from these attacks. Despite the fact that the groups perpetrating these acts pursued different objectives and employed diverse methods, they were portrayed as a uniform threat against the homogeneous community of democratic states (which, as demonstrated by their differing concerns during negotiations, were quite varied). This rhetoric not only enabled CoE member states to position themselves as a community of good values that needed protection, it also legitimised a strong retaliation.

Conversely, the requirement that all attacks listed in the Convention must be committed "unlawfully" (a stipulation found in all CoE tools) implies that if the same actions are carried out by the state, they are considered acceptable. Authors like Hunt pointed out that in this regard, some viewed this as not only an important legal setback at the international level regarding the notion of state terrorism but also a self-serving approach to the idea of wrongdoing.[69] That said, the Convention nevertheless implicitly allows the use of discriminate violence in some instances. Although the provision of the Convention referring to offences that make "use of a bomb, grenade, rocket, automatic firearm or letter or parcel bomb if this use endangers persons" condemns the

65 The Parliamentary Assembly had already, in 1972, called on the member states of the Council of Europe to take action against terrorism and, more specifically, sign and ratify the two conventions against aviation offences in reaction to the terrorist activities being conducted in those years, "of which the Munich tragedy [was considered] a particularly horrifying example". Parliamentary Assembly, International Terrorism (Recommendation 684) 1972.

66 B. Blumenau, *The United Nations and Terrorism. Germany, Multilateralism, and Antiterrorism Efforts in the 1970s* (Palgrave Macmillan, Basingstoke 2014) 104–105.

67 B. Blumenau, *The United Nations and Terrorism. Germany, Multilateralism, and Antiterrorism Efforts in the 1970s* (Palgrave Macmillan, Basingstoke 2014) 122.

68 Council of Europe, Explanatory Report to the Convention on the Suppression of Terrorism (n 54) 5.

69 A. Hunt, 'The Council of Europe Convention on the Prevention of Terrorism' [2006] *EPL*. 603, 615.

use of means that could lead to indiscriminate killings, it simultaneously suggests that targeted killings might be considered a legitimate means to achieve a political goal.[70]

In addition to the issue of the legitimate use of violence, this first article also raises the issue of attacks against state symbols. It establishes that attacks on internationally protected persons are of a particularly odious character. The explanatory report of the Convention indicates in this respect that this method of excluding some crimes because of their odious nature had actually already been applied in the past to crimes such as genocide, war crimes, and the attempted taking of the life of a head of state or a member of their family and that this Convention only followed suit.[71] It is therefore noteworthy that the taking or attempted taking of the life of a head of state and attacks on internationally protected persons were categorised alongside crimes like genocide

70 Claude Debrulle, honorary general director of the former directorate general on legislation at the Belgian Ministry of Justice, mentioned in this respect that the negotiations on this provision of the article led to heated discussions on the kind of weapons that could be allowed for the commission of a political crime. The premise for the discussions was that it was conceivable that a person be killed in the framework of a political endeavour, provided that the murder of that person could indeed lead to believe that it could generate a big political change. The problem was thus not the killing *per se*, but the number and type of casualties. Innocent and multiple victims were not admissible casualties. This is why weapons that engender indiscriminate killings (explosives or automatic firearms), potentially reaching innocent victims, were excluded by the Convention. If automatic firearms were unanimously agreed to be ruled out from the protection of the political offence exemption, the issue of semi-automatic firearms, by comparison, was more difficult to settle. It was, in the end, rejected. Interview with Claude Debrulle, Honorary General Director of the former Directorate General on Legislation at the Belgian Ministry of Justice (Walloon Brabant, 15 April 2014). The non-inclusion of non-automatic firearms was thus deliberate, which tacitly left room for manoeuvre for the use of political violence. In the famous case of Fehriye Erdal involving Belgium and Turkey, this specific issue on the use of semi-automatic firearms found a practical application. Fehriye Erdal, a DHKP-C activist, was accused of having participated, in 1996, in the assassination of a Turkish businessman with a semi-automatic firearm. The DHKP-C is a Marxist-Leninist revolutionary party in Turkey that is on the EU list of terrorist organisations. Council Decision 2019/25 Amending and Updating the List of Persons, Groups and Entities Subject to Articles 2, 3 and 4 of Common Position 2001/931/CFSP on the Application of Specific Measures to Combat Terrorism, and Repealing Decision (CFSP) 2018/1084 [9 January 2019] OJ L L6. When Turkey requested her extradition, Belgium considered that she had committed a political crime and that the restrictions foreseen by the 1977 Convention did not apply in this case because her accomplices had used a semi-automatic weapon. She ended up being prosecuted and convicted in Belgium for this as well as other offences but was not extradited to Turkey on the grounds that she committed a political crime. Interview with Paul Bekaert, Lawyer of Fehriye Erdal (West Flanders, 29 November 2018). It thus looks like, in 1977, a certain level of violence was still accepted in the pursuit of a political aim. This tolerance would be later criticised in 1991 by the Parliamentary Assembly that deplored the fact that the Convention did not include non-automatic firearms at the time. Parliamentary Assembly, Strengthening the European Convention on the Suppression of Terrorism (Recommendation 1170) 1991.

71 Council of Europe, Explanatory Report to the Convention on the Suppression of Terrorism (n 54) 3.

and crimes against humanity as particularly egregious, even if committed only against targeted persons who are especially susceptible, due to their role, to be the targets of political crimes.

Invitation to depoliticise violent offences (art. 2)

The depoliticisation of crimes for purposes of combating terrorism continues in article 2 of the Convention. This article invites (but does not oblige) member states not to consider "as a political offence an offence, or as an offence connected with a political offence or as an offence inspired by political motives a serious offence involving an act of violence . . . against the life, physical integrity or liberty of a person", [72] offences "involving an act against property . . . if the act created a collective danger for persons"[73] (for instance, following an explosion of a major facility, such as a nuclear installation or a dam),[74] or the "attempt to commit any of the foregoing offences or participation as an accomplice of a person who commits or attemtps to commit such an offence".[75] Contrary to the previous article that allows for targeted violence to be used, this one excludes the possibility of employing violence that could endanger people. It is, in this sense, broader in what it seeks to exclude from the scope of the political offence exemption than the first article. However, its efficacity in reducing the scope of the political offence exemption is limited by the fact that it does not actually create an obligation not to consider these offences as political but only offers a possibility to do so.

Enhancing safeguards with the discrimination clause (art. 5)

With these two new restrictions on the protection of political offenders, it was considered necessary to include safeguards against potential misuses of the Convention. Three major safeguards were included in that respect. One of them is the discrimination clause allowing it to comply not only with the Convention for the Protection of Human Rights and Fundamental Freedoms[76] but also with the principle of *non-refoulement* enshrined in the Geneva Convention.[77] The discrimination clause that was, until then, incorporated in article 3 of the Convention on Extradition concerning political crimes became

72 European Convention on the Suppression of Terrorism (n 60) (Art. 2a).
73 European Convention on the Suppression of Terrorism (n 60) (Art. 2b).
74 Council of Europe, Explanatory Report to the Convention on the Suppression of Terrorism (n 54) 6.
75 European Convention on the Suppression of Terrorism (n 60) (Art. 2b)
76 Council of Europe, Explanatory Report to the Convention on the Suppression of Terrorism (n 54) 7.
77 A. Weyembergh and E. Bribosia, 'Extradition et Asile: Vers un Espace Judiciaire Européen?' [1997] *RBDI*. 69, 82.

a fully fledged article in this Convention.[78] Authors like Tulkens pointed out in this respect that, to the extent that the Convention seeks to automatise the extradition of actions that usually generate such situations of potential persecution, the actual level of protection that the discrimnation clause really offers is rather low, not to mention that its application is compromised by the diplomatic tensions to which the use of the clause may give rise. She therefore argues that this clause actually only filters extradition requests that would be manifestly issued for political motives by the state.[79]

Enhancing safeguards with the denunciation clause (art. 14)

In addition to the development of the discrimination clause into a self-standing article, the Convention includes an unusual article among the final clauses of the CoE conventions enabling the member states to denounce the Convention in exceptional circumstances, in particular in case the democratic regime in another Council of Europe contracting party is overthrown. While a denunciation clause was already added to the European Convention on Extradition, it was not especially linked to a situation where the democratic regime of the denounced state in question would be overthrown. The choice to specifically clarify this here thus showed that CoE contracting parties were mindful of the potential backlash of the Convention on fundamental rights in case CoE member states did not align with the CoE values.[80]

Enhancing safeguards with reservation possibility (art. 13)

The Convention also provides the opportunity for its contracting parties to declare that they

> reserve the right to refuse extradition in respect of any offence mentioned in Article 1 which [they] consider to be a political offence, an offence connected with a political offence or an offence inspired by political motives, provided that [they] undertake to take into due consideration, when evaluating the character of the offence, any particularly serious aspects of the offence, including: (a) that it created a collective danger to the life, physical integrity or liberty of persons; or (b) that it affected persons foreign to the motives behind it; or (c) that cruel or vicious means have been used in the commission of the offence.[81]

78 European Convention on the Suppression of Terrorism (n 60) (Art. 5).
79 F. Tulkens (n 55) 235.
80 Council of Europe, Explanatory Report to the Convention on the Suppression of Terrorism (n 54) 11; European Convention on Extradition (n 11) (Art. 31).
81 European Convention on the Suppression of Terrorism (n 60) (Art. 13).

This article is interesting not only because it actually enables the states to completely frustrate the whole purpose of the Convention but also because it offers an unanticipated venue for the definition of political crimes in the CoE framework. While, officially, the Council of Europe could not provide a definition of political crimes, this article outlines rather precise criteria for assessing the political nature of an offence. Noteworthy is the fact that more than a third of the contracting parties to the Convention used the possibility provided by this article to reserve the right not to consider the offences listed in article 1 as political (thereby offsetting the whole purpose of the Convention),[82] indicating – if not their willingness to preserve the political offence exemption – their chilliness to renounce it overall at the time. This wide use of the possibility of introducing a reservation would later be perceived as a major weakness of the Convention.[83] However, as for the 1957 Convention on Extradition, observers like Cardona pointed out that the inclusion of this possibility was necessary to accommodate the different political and legal traditions of member states, which would have otherwise prevented the accession of several of them to the Convention. In this sense, the Convention is said to represent the highest achievable degree of consensus at the time of its elaboration.[84]

Ensuring prosecution with the obligation to prosecute in case of refusal to extradite (art. 7)

In case of a refusal to extradite, however, the requested state is under the obligation to prosecute the person itself.[85] The subordination of prosecution to extradition is, in this regard, another major blow of the Convention to the protection of political offenders. Indeed, traditional extradition tools – which this Convention is not – usually abide by the *aut dedere aut judicare* principle, giving the contracting parties the choice to either extradite or prosecute, with no hierarchy between the two.[86] This Convention, however, prioritises extradition over prosecution in the requested state, thereby further undermining the position of political offenders by not only ensuring their prosecution but also giving priority to the judge of the territory where the offence was committed.[87]

82 Council of Europe, 'Reservations and Declarations for Treaty No. 090 – European Convention the Suppression of Terrorism' (Council of Europe) <https://www.CoE.int/en/web/conventions/full-list?module=declarations-by-treaty&numSte=090&codeNature=0> accessed 8 February 2022.

83 M. B. Baker (n 51) 6–7.

84 M. Cardona, 'The European Response to Terrorism' [1992] *Terror Polit. Violenc.* 245, 251–252.

85 European Convention on the Suppression of Terrorism (n 60) (Art. 7).

86 A. Weyembergh and E. Bribosia (n 77) 79.

87 A. Weyembergh and E. Bribosia (n 77) 79.

Challenges and criticism of the Convention

Despite the safeguards put in place to counterbalance the potentially detrimental effects of the Convention on human rights and national traditions, the latter came with its fair share of criticism, attesting to the scepticism of commentators on the proclaimed goal of the Convention to protect human rights and democracy. Three main concerns were raised.

The first one referred to the fact that the Convention gutted the political offence exemption of its protection by going well beyond its claimed goal of depoliticising particularly odious crimes endangering the lives of innocent people.[88] This was partly due to the vagueness of the terms used in the first two articles of the Convention, creating uncertainty and ambiguity around the crimes to suppress.[89]

The imprecise wording of the Convention further contributed, according to human rights defenders, to a feeling of uncertainty regarding what constitutes a political crime or a terrorist crime and who will be afforded protection and who will not, which was considered particularly problematic in the field of criminal law based on the principle of legality.[90] Fears about the toll this Convention would have on fundamental rights were such that, at the time the Convention was being adopted, a member of the European Parliament questioned whether the CJEU, despite not being its primary role, should oversee the protection of human rights – particularly the right to political asylum – in the application of the Convention among EU member states.[91] It was indeed argued that the approach taken by the Convention, which is to deny the political nature of the offence in all situations, oversimplified the problem and did not allow sufficient legal differentiation.[92]

The third criticism concerned the aim of the Convention, which, far from being the protection of innocent people from political violence, was said to give the means to *repress*[93] internal political dissent[94] and delegitimise any form of political violence used against CoE member states.[95] As such, the Convention was perceived as jeopardising the progress and achievements made in Western European democracies regarding the protection of both human rights and an ideological culture and heritage. This included concerns about

88 J. J. A. Salmon, 'La Convention Européenne pour la Répression du Terrorisme - un Vrai Pas en Arrière' [1977] *JT.* 497, 500.

89 N. Gal-Or (n 34) 276.

90 F. Tulkens (n 55) 232.

91 European Parliament, 'Written question 1147/79 by Mrs Vayssade to the Commission of the European Communities (15 November 1979)' [17 March 1980] OJ C 66, 79–80.

92 R. Linke, 'International Cooperation in the Fight Against Terrorism', Conference on Defence on Democracy, AS/Col/Poll/Terr(32)3, 4, cited in N. Gal-Or (n 34) 285.

93 Françoise Tulkens notes that the regulatory approach adopted in the Convention is one of repression. This, she says, appears more clearly in the French title of the Convention that uses the term 'repression' instead of 'suppression'. F. Tulkens (n 55) 229.

94 F. Tulkens (n 55) 230.

95 J. J. A. Salmon (n 88) 500–501; F. Tulkens (n 55) 230.

its impact on the accepted right to use political violence for self-defence or liberation from oppressive regimes, a stance that was openly supported at the time.[96] Gal-Or, for instance, reminded that during World War II, Western democracies used political violence to combat fascist and oppressive regimes. She questioned the idea that while these methods were used for democratic regimes to emerge victorious from the war, these same countries now deny the use of those methods against themselves. Warning that there is no guarantee that European democracies will not descend into fascism or create a different form of oppression in the future, she contended that the excessive reaction of current governments to perceived threats calls for a soul-searching into the type of society we have built.[97]

Even if it met initial objections, this Convention eventually became the stepping stone of the fight against terrorism in the CoE framework. Despite the safeguards it put in place to mitigate its potential backlashes on human rights (through an enhanced discrimination clause, an intentional denunciation clause, and large reservation possibilities), the Convention opened the path of depoliticising crimes for purposes of extradition. Later conventions on counterterrorism would build on this approach to considerably expand the types of crime to be depoliticised, eventually leaving very little room for the protection of political offenders.

The 2003 Protocol amending the 1977 Convention on the Suppression of Terrorism

Historical context: lowered tolerance towards violence

Despite the 1990s being marked by significant events such as the Good Friday Agreement, the disbandment of the Red Army Faction, an extended ceasefire announced by the ETA, and the Oslo Accords (which notably reduced Palestinian terrorism in Europe), leading to a significant decrease in attacks,[98] tolerance for political violence still diminished, and the fight against terrorism continued to advance. In those years, Interpol, the police organisation that had vowed to never get involved in political cases (namely terrorism),[99] started engaging in cases of terrorism.[100] The atmosphere at the Council of Europe was also one of urgency. CoE member states were repeatedly invited to ratify

96 N. Gal-Or (n 34) 281–282.

97 N. Gal-Or (n 34) 283.

98 F. Gaub, 'Trends in Terrorism' (European Union Institute for Security Studies April 2017) <https://www.iss.europa.eu/sites/default/files/EUISSFiles/Alert_4_Terrorism_in Europe_0.pdf> accessed 21 March 2019.

99 M. Barnett and L. Coleman, 'Designing Police: Interpol and the Study of Change in International Organizations' [2005] *ISQ* 593, 605–607.

100 J. Jansson, *Terrorism, Criminal Law and Politics. The Decline of the Political Offence Exception to Extradition* (Routledge, Abingdon, New York 2020) 168–172.

existing tools of cooperation in criminal matters and on terrorism adopted so far,[101] as well as to withdraw the reservations they had introduced on any of these conventions.[102] The Parliamentary Assembly even suggested to remove the possibility to introduce reservations altogether.[103] As regards the use of violence to further a political cause, the position of the Parliamentary Assembly toughened. In recommendations issued in 1979, it condemned the use of violent means when other pacific solutions existed.[104] The next year, it issued another recommendation in which it stated that it could not support political organisations advocating for or using violence to solve political, economic or social problems; this time disconnecting the rejection of the use of violence from the existence of pacific means to achieve political change.[105] Finally, in 1991, it called on CoE member states to outlaw and depoliticise all crimes involving violence, to allow extradition for those crimes, and to consider as non-political all the crimes listed in article 2 of the Convention on the Suppression of Terrorism.[106]

In 1999, the Assembly drafted its own definition of terrorism.[107] The definition not only included violence but also the threat of its use as part of the terrorist offence. It was as broad as to define separatist ambitions, extremist ideologies, fanatism and other "irrational and subjective factors"[108] as terrorist motivations. The Assembly generally considered that the aim of terrorist acts was to undermine democratic values, parliamentary institutions, and the territorial integrity of sovereign states,[109] as well as to destabilise legitimately constituted governments.[110] In the view of the Assembly, terrorism threatened the

101 Parliamentary Assembly, Defence of Democracy Against Terrorism in Europe (Recommendation 982) 1984, 2; Parliamentary Assembly, European Response to International Terrorism (Recommendation 1024) 1986, 1.

102 Committee of Ministers of the Council of Europe, Resolution (78)43 on Reservations Made to Certain Provisions of the European Convention on Extradition (Resolution (78)43) 1978; Parliamentary Assembly, Conference on 'Defence of Democracy against Terrorism in Europe - Tasks and Problems' (Strasbourg, 12–14 November 1980) (Recommendation 916) 1981, 1; Parliamentary Assembly, Extradition of Criminals (Recommendation 950) 1982, 2; Parliamentary Assembly, European Response to International Terrorism (Resolution 863) 1986, 2; Parliamentary Assembly, Democracies Facing Terrorism (Resolution 1258) 2001, 2.

103 Parliamentary Assembly, Recommendation 1426 (n 53) 2.

104 Parliamentary Assembly, Terrorism in Europe (Recommendation 852) 1979, 1.

105 Parliamentary Assembly, Recommendation 916 (n 102) 2

106 Parliamentary Assembly, Recommendation 1170 (n 70) 1.

107 The Parliamentary Assembly suggested this definition, but it did not get adopted at the Council of Europe level.

108 Parliamentary Assembly, Recommendation 1426 (n 53) 1.

109 Parliamentary Assembly, Recommendation 1426 (n 53) 1.

110 Committee of Ministers of the Council of Europe, Guidelines on Human Rights and the Fight Against Terrorism Adopted by the Committee of Ministers at its 804th Meeting (11 July 2002) 3.

moral and social fibre of democratic societies and must be condemned because it attacked the most fundamental right of all, the right to life.[111]

Following the 9/11 attacks, the CoE adopted an unprecedented number of declarations and tools. The day after the attacks, the Committee of Ministers of the Council of Europe issued a declaration that not only expressed the wish to update the Convention on the Suppression of Terrorism and urged the contracting parties to remove their reservations, but that also suggested opening the Convention to non-CoE members.[112] The Parliamentary Assembly supported this idea and took it a step further by stating that terrorism and support for it should be declared crimes against humanity in all existing conventions. It also recommended removing the provision in the 1977 Convention on the Suppression of Terrorism that allowed member states to make reservations. It finally suggested for the first time extending the use of the European arrest warrant – a groundbreaking extradition tool being negotiated at the time within the EU (discussed in the next chapter) – to CoE members for the purpose of combating terrorism.[113] At the time, terrorism was still not defined at the CoE level (it still is not),[114] which did not prevent the CoE from forging ahead with the adoption of increasingly robust measures to combat it.

In light of these calls, a specialist group of experts, the Multidisciplinary Group on International Action against Terrorism (GMT) was set up.[115] The latter was tasked with reviewing and assessing existing tools to combat terrorism and determining if they needed updating.[116] The first instrument they decided to revise was the 1977 Convention on the Suppression of Terrorism, which they amended with a Protocol.[117] Although it never entered into force, this Protocol of 19 articles sought to bring about five main changes to the 1977 Convention. The first was to further enlarge the list of offences that should be depoliticised to cover all offences listed in the relevant UN Conventions and

111 Committee of Ministers of the Council of Europe, Guidelines on Human Rights and the Fight Against Terrorism Adopted by the Committee of Ministers at its 804th Meeting (11 July 2002) 3.

112 Committee of Ministers of the Council of Europe, Declaration of the Committee of Ministers on the Fight Against International Terrorism (12 September 2001) 1–2.

113 Parliamentary Assembly, Democracies Facing Terrorism (Recommendation 1534) 2001, 1–2. This last suggestion was reiterated the next year and again three years later. Parliamentary Assembly, Combatting Terrorism and Respect for Human Rights (Recommendation 1271) 2002, 2; Parliamentary Assembly, Challenge of Terrorism in Council of Europe Member States (Recommendation 1677) 2004, 2.

114 Despite repeated calls – started in the 1980s – to find a definition. The suggestion was made to adopt the EU definition of terrorism, but this idea did not materialise. Parliamentary Assembly, Recommendation 916 (n 102) 2; Parliamentary Assembly, Combatting Terrorism and Respect for Human Rights (Recommendation 1550) 2002, 1.

115 The latter would later be replaced by the comité d'experts sur le terrorisme (CODEXTER), an intergovernmental forum of experts in various disciplines, that would take over the activities of the GMT. C. Walter (n 35) 676.

116 A. Hunt (n 69) 605.

117 A. Hunt (n 69) 605–606.

Protocols on terrorism. The second was to introduce a simplified amendment procedure to facilitate the addition of new offences to that list. The third change pertained to opening the 1977 Convention to Observers to the CoE. A fourth update concerned the amendment of the discrimination clause to allow member states to refuse extradition in case there was a risk of application of a death sentence, torture, or life imprisonment without parole. Finally, the Protocol sought to set up a follow-up mechanism (Conference of States Parties against Terrorism [COSTER]) to ensure the proper application of certain provisions of the Protocol, such as new rules concerning reservations.

List of terrorist offences to cover all relevant UN Convention on terrorism (art. 1)

The Protocol first sought to extend substantively the list of offences not to be considered political by referring to all existing specialised UN treaties on counterterrorism in its first article. It more specifically listed eight categories of offences to be considered terroristic:

- offences listed in the 1973 Convention on the Prevention and Punishment of Crimes Against Internationally Protected Persons, Including Diplomatic Agents (art. 1c),
- offences listed in the 1979 International Convention Against the Taking of Hostages (art. 1d),
- offences listed in the 1980 Convention on the Physical Protection of Nuclear Material (art. 1e),
- offences listed in the 1988 Protocol for the Suppression of Unlawful Acts of Violence at Airports Serving International Civil Aviation (art. 1f),
- offences listed in the 1988 Convention for the Suppression of Unlawful Acts Against the Safety of Maritime Navigation (art. 1g),
- offences listed in the 1988 Protocol for the Suppression of Unlawful Acts Against the Safety of Fixed Platforms Located on the Continental Shelf (art. 1h),
- offences listed in the 1997 International Convention for the Suppression of Terrorist Bombings (art. 1i), and
- offences listed in the 1999 International Convention for the Suppression of the Financing of Terrorism (art. 1j).

Doing so, the Protocol greatly reduced the possibilities for non-state actors to undertake legitimate acts of violence for a political purpose.[118] The first article further clarifies that the attempt to commit any of these offences, the participation as an accomplice or the organisation of it are all to be excluded from the political offence exemption.[119] Of note, when combined with the

118 C. Walter (n 35) 679.
119 Protocol Amending the European Convention on the Suppression of Terrorism (ETS 190) 2003 (Art. 1).

UN Conventions cited in the Convention on the Suppression of Terrorism of 1977, this Protocol covers all UN instruments adopted to fight terrorism at the time, except for two (the 1963 Convention on Offences and Certain Other Acts Committed On Board Aircraft and the 1991 Convention on the Marking of Plastic Explosives for the Purpose of Detection).

By referring to a list of UN Conventions rather than individual offences, the 2003 Protocol equally continued the work of previous instruments protecting the state from being a legitimate target of political crimes. Indeed, the Protocol introduced, for the first time in the CoE framework, the idea that trying to "compel a Government or an international organisation to do or to abstain from doing any act" should be addressed as part of counterterrorism efforts. Although this provision was not included in the Protocol itself but is rather found in a number of the UN Conventions to which the Protocol refers,[120] it nevertheless introduced a great shift in the approach of the Council of Europe regarding political offenders. One might indeed argue that political offenders more often than not try to "compel a Government or an international organization to do or to abstain from doing" something. And even though the cases cited in this Protocol are always in relation to a specific offence such as hostage taking or funding terrorism, which means that the intention is not criminalised *per se*, this development is still noteworthy, as it indicates that compelling the state to do or not to do something should also be dealt with counterterrorism tools.

Making the optional depoliticisation of the 1977 Convention mandatory (art. 2 and 3)

Article 2 of the Protocol further excludes from the protection of political offences the participation in any of the offences listed in the second article of the Convention on the Suppression of Terrorism, whose depoliticisation was only optional until then. In addition, whereas in the Convention the "attempt to commit any of the . . . offences [cited in the Convention] or participation as an accomplice of a person who commits or attempts to commit such an offence" was criminalised, the Protocol sought to go further by adding the organisation "of, or directing others to commit or attempt to commit" any of the offences listed in the article.[121]

These first two articles seeking a greater depoliticisation of offences are interesting in many ways, especially as regards the tolerated use of (non-state) violence.

120 International Convention Against the Taking of Hostages (No. 21931) 1979; Convention for the Suppression of Unlawful Acts Against the Safety of Maritime Navigation (No. 29004) 1988; Protocol for the Suppression of Unlawful Acts Against the Safety of Fixed Platforms Located on the Continental Shelf, 1988; International Convention for the Suppression of Terrorist Bombings (No. 37517) 2001; International Convention for the Suppression of the Financing of Terrorism (No. 38349) 1999.

121 Protocol Amending the European Convention on the Suppression of Terrorism (n 119) (Art. 2).

Indeed, the Protocol further lowered the threshold of accepted violence against people, regardless of whether the latter led to loss of lives and/or injuries. By including hostage-taking in anti-terrorism efforts, as well as the threat

> to kill, to injure or to continue to detain another person . . . in order to compel a third party, namely, a State, an international intergovernmental organization, a natural or juridical person, or a group of persons, to do or abstain from doing any act,

the Protocol established that harm does not need to be done for an act to already be considered terrorism (if the aim is to compel a third party to do/not do something). The 1977 Convention already criminalised acts supporting the preparation and commission of the offence, as well as attempts thereof, but in that case, the criminalisation concerned upstream actions that were supposed to lead to violent outcomes. What strikes here compared to the 1977 Convention is the fact that an action does not need to deploy any level of violence (since a threat of attempt suffices) for it to be considered terroristic.

A similar intent lies behind the replacement of the third sub-paragraph of the 1977 Convention, depoliticising offences "involving an attack against the life, physical integrity or liberty of internationally protected persons, including diplomatic agents"[122] by the whole of the UN Convention on the Prevention and Punishment of Crimes Against Internationally Protected Persons, Including Diplomatic Agents. This change might seem insignificant, but it is not. In the Convention on the Suppression of Terrorism, the decision not to reference the UN Convention was deliberate. The rationale given for this choice was that only the most odious crimes – such as attacks against internationally protected persons – should be depoliticised, whereas attacks against infrastructure were not included in this approach.[123] By referencing to the UN Convention, this Protocol condemned once more not only attacks against internationally protected persons but also attacks against premises, accommodations, and transport linked to protected persons[124] deliberately circumvented in the previous Convention because the level of gravity of those crimes was not considered high enough to be tackled with counterterrorism tools.

Introducing an open-ended understanding of terrorism (and ignoring the work conducted at the EU level; art. 9 and 13)

Even if this Protocol sought to step up the fight against terrorism, it did not provide additional guidance on the definition of terrorism. This was in fact

122 European Convention on the Suppression of Terrorism (n 60) (Art. 1c).

123 Council of Europe, Explanatory Report to the Convention on the Suppression of Terrorism (n 54) 3.

124 Convention on the Prevention and Punishment of Crimes Against Internationally Protected Persons, Including Diplomatic Agents (No. 15410) 1973 (Art. 2). International Convention Against the Taking of Hostages (n 120) (Art. 1).

a matter of intense discussion among the experts negotiating the Protocol because, at the time of its negotiation, the European Union had adopted its own definition of terrorism in the European Council Common Position of 7 December 2001 on the application of specific measures to combat terrorism (2001/931/CFSP). The group of experts involved in the drafting of the Protocol considered adopting that definition but eventually decided against it. They argued that the EU definition was designed for the purpose of the Common Position (no mention was made of the proposal for a Council Framework Decision on combatting terrorism that also offered a definition of terrorism, which could have been another option if the fact that the former definition was adopted for the purpose of the Common Position was considered problematic). Additionally, they were reluctant to change the aim of the Protocol, which was to depoliticise crimes for the purpose of extradition.[125]

As the combined texts of the 1977 Convention of its 2003 Additional Protocol refer to almost all specialised anti-terror UN instruments to define the acts criminalised to fight terrorism, the Council of Europe *de facto* adopted the UN 'definition' of terrorism. If it is true that the United Nations does not have a common definition of terrorism, it does have a series of conventions adopted as part of its counterterrorism efforts, listing a number of acts to be criminalised to that purpose. Crucially, the Protocol introduced a simplified amendment procedure to allow any future anti-terror UN Convention to be added to the list of terrorist offences ex post, enabling an open-ended definition.[126] Limits are, however, introduced to the amendment procedure, as the article expressly states that the UN Conventions have to be specifically dealing with international terrorism and that they must have entered into force.[127] Regarding political crimes, this decision to use an open-ended definition of terrorism results in diminished protection for such crimes and, more importantly, leaves open the possibility for further reduction in protection over time. It also means that no definition of political crimes is possible in the framework of the Council of Europe as long as the one of terrorism remains open-ended.[128]

125 Council of Europe, Explanatory Report to the Protocol Amending the European Convention on the Suppression of Terrorism (2003) 7.

126 Protocol Amending the European Convention on the Suppression of Terrorism (n 119) (Art. 13).

127 Protocol Amending the European Convention on the Suppression of Terrorism (n 119) (Art. 9).

128 The CoE would later openly state that political crimes could not be defined 'positively', as the notion was bound to evolve over time, leaving it to be defined 'negatively', alongside the changes in the 'definition' of terrorism. European Committee on Crimes Problems (CDPC) - Committee of Experts on the Operation European Conventions in the Penal Field, Summary report of the 47th meeting, Strasbourg 15–17 September 2003, PC-OC (2004) 03 rev (2004) 5.

Enhancing safeguards for people at risk of torture, death penalty or life imprisonment without parole (art. 4)

As in the 1977 Convention on the Suppression of Terrorism, the reduction of the protection of political offenders was accompanied by a strengthened discrimination clause. The 2003 Protocol indeed sought to protect passive agents of injustices, victims of discrimination, and people who would be at risk of being exposed to torture, the death penalty, or life imprisonment without parole.[129] The Protocol thus introduced new barriers to cooperation in case of potential human rights violations[130] and in cases of inhuman and degrading treatment.[131] Here again, as in the 1977 Convention, a reason must be provided for the refusal to cooperate on basis of this clause.[132] This stronger protection of victims thus contrasts with and serves as a balancing act to the stronger criminalisation of active political agents using violence in the rest of the Protocol.[133]

Ensuring prosecution by restricting possibilities for reservations (art. 12)

Contrary to the 1977 Convention that offered a generous reservation regime to the contracting parties to the Convention, this Protocol sought to establish a much stricter approach to reservations as a way to comply with the United Nations Security Council Resolution 1373 (2001) of 28 September 2001 urging all States to ensure that claims of political motivation are not accepted as valid reasons for denying extradition requests for alleged terrorists.[134]

To that end, article 12 of the Protocol started by clarifying that any reservation made prior to the opening for signature of the Protocol would not be applicable to the Convention as amended by the latter,[135] unless the contracting

129 Protocol Amending the European Convention on the Suppression of Terrorism (n 119) (Art. 3).
130 European Convention for the Protection of Human Rights and Fundamental Freedoms as amended by Protocols No. 11 and No. 14 (ETS 5) 1950 (Art. 3).
131 European Court of Human Rights, Factsheet: Life Imprisonment (2023) 1.
132 Council of Europe, Explanatory Report to the European Convention on the Suppression of Terrorism (2003) 10.
133 In a report published the year after the adoption of the Protocol, a member of the committee of experts on the operation European Conventions in the Penal Field indirectly confirmed that the discrimination clause was used as a way to compensate for the reduction of the political offence exemption by stating that although the protection associated to political offences had been reduced, additional grounds for refusals were introduced to cover cases in which the person would be at risk of a death sentence, life imprisonment without parole, or torture. European Committee on Crimes Problems (CDPC) – Committee of Experts on the Operation European Conventions in the Penal Field (n 128) 4–5.
134 Council of Europe, Explanatory Report to the European Convention on the Suppression of Terrorism (n 132) 16.
135 Protocol Amending the European Convention on the Suppression of Terrorism (n 119) (Art. 12§1).

parties reintroduced them at the time of signature, ratification, acceptance, or approval of the Protocol.[136] This represented a clear effort to address the extensive list of reservations that had long been a concern for the Council of Europe by forcing the member states to reconsider and re-submit them if necessary. The Protocol also insisted that the use of reservations to the Convention for the protection of political offences be made on a case-by-case basis and applied through a duly reasoned decision.[137] The clause further sought to limit the scope of reservations, both in content and duration, by requiring the contracting parties to specify for which offences their reservations apply[138] and creating a time limit of three years to the ones introduced (making the contracting parties re-evaluate their reservations every three years). In case the contracting parties failed to renew the reservations on time, the Protocol foresaw their extension for another 6 months, but if they failed again to notify the secretary general of the Council that they wished to renew them, the reservations lapsed.[139] The Protocol also added that any state that wished to renew a reservation was expected to provide a justification for its continuance.[140] In addition, the Protocol created a new body, the COSTER, that acted as a follow-up mechanism, especially for one peculiar task, the examination of the reservations.[141] If, despite all this, the contracting parties chose to maintain and apply them, the Protocol foresaw that the requested state would have to submit the case to its competent authorities for prosecution unless otherwise agreed between the parties involved,[142] in line with the 1977 Convention.

Ensuring prosecution by offering the possibility to use the 1977 Convention as a basis for extradition (art. 3)

The Protocol thus really sought to maximise cooperation to the point that – contrary to what was explicitly stated in the explanatory report to the original Convention[143] – it allowed the contracting parties to the Convention and Protocol to use the Convention as a legal basis for extradition for the

136 Council of Europe, Explanatory Report to the European Convention on the Suppression of Terrorism (n 132) 16.
137 Protocol Amending the European Convention on the Suppression of Terrorism (n 119) (Art. 12§3).
138 Protocol Amending the European Convention on the Suppression of Terrorism (n 119) (Art. 12§4).
139 Protocol Amending the European Convention on the Suppression of Terrorism (n 119) (Art. 12§5–6).
140 Protocol Amending the European Convention on the Suppression of Terrorism (n 119) (Art. 12§6).
141 C. Walter (n 35) 679.
142 Protocol Amending the European Convention on the Suppression of Terrorism (n 119) (Art. 12§7).
143 Council of Europe, Explanatory Report to the European Convention on the Suppression of Terrorism (n 54) 5.

offences mentioned in the Convention as amended by the Protocol.[144] This willingness to cooperate was so strong that it was also considered appropriate to open the Convention to the Observer States to the Council of Europe as well. This was, however, explicitly excluded from the Convention itself, as it was agreed that such cooperation should be limited to "like-minded states" operating in a "climate of mutual confidence".[145]

This perceived need to increase cooperation with more countries and address a broader range of issues reflected the climate of political urgency following the 9/11 attacks.[146] The explanatory report to the Protocol used words such as "monstrous" and "barbaric" to describe these attacks that it contended necessitated urgent and collective action.[147] Duplicating the words of the explanatory report of the 1977 Convention, the report further noted that the acts the Protocol referred to may indeed be considered political offences but that in the absence of a common definition of the notion of political crime, the protection of political offenders from extradition created a lacuna in existing international agreements on the extradition of people accused or convicted of terrorism.[148] As a result, the report explained that this Protocol sought to fill that gap by eliminating or restricting the possibility to invoke the political nature of an offence to refuse an extradition.[149]

The 2005 Convention on the Prevention of Terrorism

Context

All the changes that could not materialise because the 2003 Protocol did not enter into force would later find their place in the 2005 Convention on the Prevention of Terrorism.[150] In the early 2000s, the Parliamentary Assembly issued another series of calls for the adoption of a comprehensive Convention on terrorism, as the existing one was considered unfit to combat modern-day terrorism.[151]

144 Protocol Amending the European Convention on the Suppression of Terrorism (n 119) (Art. 3).
145 Council of Europe, Explanatory Report to the European Convention on the Suppression of Terrorism (n 132) 3.
146 Protocol Amending the European Convention on the Suppression of Terrorism (n 119) (Preamble); Council of Europe, Explanatory Report to the European Convention on the Suppression of Terrorism (n 132) 1.
147 Council of Europe, Explanatory Report to the European Convention on the Suppression of Terrorism (n 132) 2.
148 Council of Europe, Explanatory Report to the European Convention on the Suppression of Terrorism (n 132) 4.
149 Council of Europe, Explanatory Report to the European Convention on the Suppression of Terrorism (n 132) 4.
150 European Convention on the Prevention of Terrorism (ETS 196) 2005.
151 Parliamentary Assembly, Draft Protocol Amending the European Convention on the Suppression of Terrorism (Opinion 242) 2003, 1; Parliamentary Assembly, Terrorism: A Threat to Democracies (Recommendation 1644) 2004, 2; Parliamentary Assembly, Recommendation 1677 (n 113) 2.

This led to the adoption of the Convention on the Prevention of Terrorism. Legislators initially aimed to create a comprehensive convention with a broad definition of terrorism. However, the final version was much narrower in scope than originally intended. This limitation arose because, as the Council of Europe began working on the new Convention, the EU hindered these ambitions by stating it would not support the initiative. The EU indeed declared that similar work was already underway at the UN level and that duplication of efforts should be avoided.[152] Some argue that this episode was very representative of the competition that took place in the post-9/11 period between the European Union and the Council of Europe to establish dominance as the leading regional security actor,[153] particularly in the fight against terrorism. According to commentators, the European Union's actions represented a deliberate attempt to sabotage the Council of Europe's ambitions in this area.[154] Because of the limited support from the European Union, the Council of Europe scaled back its ambitions and opted for a Convention with a narrower scope. The Council of Europe was indeed reluctant to pursue a Convention that would lack the support of a majority of its members, many of whom were also EU member states.[155] The post-2001 period thus marked a time when the European Union emerged as the leading force in the field of counterterrorism policies, leaving the Council of Europe with more of a supporting role, with the notable exception of the European Court of Human Rights that plays a prominent role in overseeing the application and abuses of European counterterrorism policies than the Court of Justice of the European Union.[156] The 32-article-long Convention on the Prevention of Terrorism sought to strengthen the CoE member states' fight against terrorism in two main ways. The first was the criminalisation of certain acts that may lead to the commission of terrorist offences (public provocation, recruitment, and training). The second one was by strengthening cooperation on prevention at both the national level (with national prevention policies) and the international level (with enhanced extradition and mutual legal assistance arrangements).

Defining the terrorist intent in a broad manner (preamble)

The 2005 Convention did not offer a formal definition of terrorism as originally intended. However, it did do something important: drawing on the EU definition of terrorism adopted in a Framework Decision three years earlier, it

152 A. Hunt (n 69) 606.
153 E. Guild, 'The Uses and Abuses of Counter-Terrorism Policies in Europe: The Case of the "Terrorist Lists"' [2008] *JCMS*. 173, 178.
154 M. Kolb, *The European Union and the Council of Europe* (Palgrave Macmillan, London 2013) 87.
155 A. Hunt (n 69) 608.
156 C. Murphy (n 31) 687–693.

formally outlined, and for the first time in a CoE tool, possible terrorist intents in its preamble. The Convention delineated these intents as follows:

> to seriously intimidate a population or unduly compel a government or an international organization to perform or abstain from performing any act or seriously destabilize or destroy the fundamental political, constitutional, economic or social structures of a country or an international organization.[157]

This preambular provision raises a few questions.

First, as previously argued, political crimes often aim to "compel a Government or an international organisation to do or to abstain from doing" something. Classifying this intent as a terrorist one effectively restricts legitimate goals that political offenders may seek to pursue.

In addition, the terrorist intent identified in the preamble is very broad. Indeed, categorising the purpose of "seriously destabiliz[ing] or destroy[ing] the fundamental political, constitutional, economic or social structures of a country or an international organization" as a terrorist one leaves little to no room for the protection of political offenders. One burning question in this respect is that of current political parties that openly share some of the purposes condemned by the Convention. Contrary to the EU tool from which this definition was borrowed, the intents listed here are not to be taken in conjunction with certain acts to form a terrorist offence; they are self-standing terrorist intents. The delineation of these intents as terroristic, however, raises the question of communist or separatist parties that seek to reform the economic or constitutional structure of a state. According to the wording of the preamble, the goal pursued by these parties would technically be terrorist ones. Regarding these types of political objectives, the European Court of Human Rights ruled on different occasions that promoting a change in the legal framework or the legal and constitutional structure of the state is a legitimate political aim, as long as two conditions are respected. The first one is that the means used to achieve that goal must be legal and democratic, and the second is that the proposed change itself be aligned with democratic principles.[158] The Court thus seems to accept the promotion of subversive political goals, such as separatism, provided that they are achieved peacefully and democratically. The methods of communication around these goals must have a limited impact and avoid celebrating violence or inciting hatred, revenge, retaliation, or armed resistance.[159] The Court also stated that crucial to the democratic process is the existence

157 European Convention on the Prevention of Terrorism (n 150) (Preamble).

158 Yazar, Karataş, Aksoy and the People's Labour Party (HEP) v. Turkey, Applications nos. 22723/93, 22724/93 and 22725/9 (ECtHR 09/04/2002); European Court of Human Rights, Factsheet: Political Parties and Associations (2016) 2–3.

159 A. Salinas de Frias, *Counter-Terrorism and Human Rights in the Case Law of the European Court of Human Rights* (Council of Europe Publishing, Strasbourg 2012) 138–139.

of diverse political projects and the possibility to freely debate them even if they call into question the current organisation of the state, as long as they do not present a threat to democracy itself.[160] The case law of the Court on the legitimate aims of political parties thus suggests that the broad understanding of the terrorist intent in the Convention is not to be blindly applied but rather on a case-by-case basis, with particular attention to the use of or incitement to violence and respect of democratic values.

The 2005 Convention defines terrorist offences with a list of UN Conventions (art. 1): implementing changes brought by the 2003 Protocol that did not enter into force

In addition to defining possible terrorist intents, the Convention sought to criminalise preparatory acts that can lead to the commission of a terrorist crime (public provocation to commit terrorist offences, recruitment for terrorism, and training for terrorism). It also aimed to enhance international cooperation for better prosecution of these crimes.[161] To do this, the text of the Protocol effectively implemented what the Protocol Amending the European Convention on the Suppression of Terrorism could not accomplish, as it had not entered into force. Indeed, the first article of the Convention defines terrorist offences by referring to the same list of UN tools to combat terrorism to which the Protocol referred.[162] As in the Protocol amending the 1977 Convention, this new Convention on the Prevention of Terrorism includes the simplified amendment procedure first introduced in the Protocol.[163] This new Convention equally offers the possibility to use the Convention as a basis for extradition,[164] opens the Convention to observer states,[165] and enlarges the discrimination clause by referring to inhumane and degrading treatment.[166] It is also worth noting that the Convention allows states to introduce reservations only for the articles mentioned earlier, following the same reservation

160 See Socialist Party and Others v. Turkey, 20/1997/804/1007 (ECtHR25/05/1998); Freedom and Democracy Part (ÖZDEP) v. Turkey, No. 699, 08/12/1999]. This is as long as they do 'not encourage violence, armed resistance or insurrection'. See HADEP and Demir v. Turkey, Application No. 964 (ECtHR 14/10/2010); Party for a Democratic Society (DTP) and Others v. Turkey, Applications nos. 3870/10, 3870/10, 3878/10, 15616/10, 21919/10, 39118/10 and 37272/10 (ECtHR 12/01/2016).

161 C. Walter (n 35) 679.

162 European Convention on the Prevention of Terrorism (n 150) (Art. 1). The list in this Convention is only longer by one additional UN Convention, the one 'for the Suppression of Acts of Nuclear Terrorism' adopted in 2005, after the adoption of the Protocol. It was actually the same at the moment of the adoption, but the list was later amended. Council of Europe, Explanatory Report to the European Convention on the Prevention of Terrorism (2005) 7.

163 European Convention on the Prevention of Terrorism (n 150) (Art. 28).

164 European Convention on the Prevention of Terrorism (n 150) (Art. 19).

165 European Convention on the Prevention of Terrorism (n 150) (Art. 49).

166 European Convention on the Prevention of Terrorism (n 150) (Art. 21).

regime established in the Protocol Amending the Convention on the Suppression of Terrorism. This regime includes a three-year time limit for reservations and requires states to justify the introduction and renewal of these reservations. Reservations are not permitted for the remaining parts of the Convention. As in previous treaties, if a contracting party decides not to extradite a person, it is expected to immediately submit the case to competent authorities for prosecution.[167] In case of a refusal to extradite on the grounds that the offence for which extradition is requested is political, an additional mechanism, the Consultation of the Parties, is put in place to smooth and ease the procedure to ensure better prosecution.[168] This possibility to introduce reservations was only used by four member states (all EU member states).[169] The latter contrasts strongly with the 1977 Convention on the Suppression of Terrorism, in which member states seemed significantly more inclined to ensure wide protection of political offenders and profusely used the possibility to introduce reservations to the Convention. Using the political offence exemption for the public provocation, recruitment and training for terrorism, as well as other ancillary offences listed in the Convention is also excluded.[170]

The 2005 Convention thus not only ensured the implementation of the provisions from the Additional Protocol to the Convention on the Suppression of Terrorism but also further enlarged the possibilities to criminalise dissident actions. Although the Convention does not label pre-emptive offences as terrorism but criminalises them instead, it provides robust mechanisms to suppress dissent pre-emptively. The negotiators were aware of this risk, particularly concerning the impact on freedom of expression.[171] It was, however, considered appropriate to curtail freedom of expression in certain situations.[172] The justification provided for this was that terrorist offences listed in CoE conventions can have no political justification, by whoever and for whatever reason committed.[173] Because of that, it was considered this Convention did not pose a threat to citizens' political rights, particularly due to the climate of mutual confidence among like-minded democratic states that respect human rights (referring to CoE member states *and* observer states) that surrounded its adoption.[174]

167 European Convention on the Prevention of Terrorism (n 150) (Art. 18).
168 European Convention on the Prevention of Terrorism (n 150) (Art. 20).
169 Council of Europe, 'Reservations and Declarations for Treaty No. 196 – European Convention for the Prevention of Terrorism' (Council of Europe) <https://www.coe.int/en/web/conventions/full-list?module=declarations-by-treaty&numSte=196&codeNature=0> accessed 24 August 2022.
170 European Convention on the Prevention of Terrorism (n 150) (Art. 20).
171 Council of Europe, Explanatory Report to the European Convention on the Prevention of Terrorism (n 162) 5, 11.
172 Council of Europe, Explanatory Report to the European Convention on the Prevention of Terrorism (n 162) 12.
173 European Convention on the Prevention of Terrorism (n 150) (Preamble).
174 Council of Europe, Explanatory Report to the European Convention on the Prevention of Terrorism (n 162) 4.

The 2017 Additional Protocol to the 2005 Convention on the Prevention of Terrorism

The optimism on the compliance of CoE contracting parties with CoE human rights standards faded with the adoption in 2017 of the Additional Protocol to the 2005 Convention.[175] The intense focus on combating terrorism following the Paris attacks indeed led to increasing concerns over the human rights impact of the fight against terrorism. The 14-article Protocol was adopted as part of this trend to securitisation and sought to go even further in the criminalisation of pre-emptive actions potentially leading to the commission of a terrorist offence (including taking part in an association or group for the purpose of terrorism, receiving terrorist training, travelling abroad for the purposes of terrorism, and financing or organising travel for this purpose). This generated outrcy from not only human rights watchdog organisations but also the CoE Parliamentary Assembly itself. The latter, traditionally a strong advocate of increasing state powers to fight terrorism, questioned the necessity to expand the existing framework on combating terrorism. It also shared the concerns raised by major non-governmental actors such as Amnesty International, the International Commission of Jurists, or the Open Society Justice Initiative on the potential negative consequence of the Protocol on a number of human rights. Criticism was also voiced about the lack of clarity between its application in times of peace and war and what this meant in terms of the applicability of international humanitarian law. Further reservations concerned the criminalisation of preparatory acts that do not necessarily require a direct intent to commit an act of terrorism and that are quite remote from the potential commission of a terrorist crime.[176] In its resolution on "Human Rights and the fight against terrorism", the Parliamentary Assembly reminded that while the member states need to have the necessary tools to combat terrorism, a balance must be respected so that counterterrorism measures do not create disproportionate restrictions or undermine democratic control and thereby create a threat to fundamental freedoms and the rule of law in the name of ensuring security.[177] This trend was decried as being all the more problematic that measures adopted initially temporarily to fight a specific problem tend to stay and become permanent even after the situation has changed.[178]

As a result of this trend to securitisation, CoE tools on counterterrorism eventually covered more and more in terms of areas (enlarging the range of action) as well as temporality (becoming increasingly preventive),

175 Additional Protocol to the European Convention on the Prevention of Terrorism (ETS 217) 2017.

176 Parliamentary Assembly, Draft Additional Protocol to the European Convention on the Prevention of Terrorism (Opinion 289) 2015, 1–2.

177 Parliamentary Assembly, Combatting International Terrorism while Protecting Council of Europe Standards and Values (Resolution 2090) 2016, 2.

178 Parliamentary Assembly, Human Rights and the Fight against Terrorism (Resolution 1840) 2011, 1.

enabling the states to criminalise actions very remote to the actual crime they sought to deter and incriminate people very distant from the movement they sought to dissolve. In later conventions, the mere potentiality of the crime and the dissidence of the perpetrators became the new threshold for criminalisation.

Conclusion

This new threshold of criminalisation of acts as terrorism did not happen overnight. Conventions adopted in the aftermath of successive terrorist attacks led to this result over the course of decades. Several dynamics identified in this chapter participated to largely reduce the protection of political offenders from extradition in the CoE context.

The first was the absence of a definition of both political and terrorist crimes. The Parliamentary Assembly urged Council of Europe member states on multiple occasions to draft a definition of political crimes, but these calls never resulted in action. This lack of a definition of political crimes had major repercussions on political offenders since a clear definition would have created boundaries as to what and how much can be depoliticised. Conversely, the absence of a definition for terrorism allowed for an increasingly broad interpretation of what it could encompass. The ever-growing understanding of what terrorist crimes covered was possible due not only to the lack of definition of political crimes but also to the strategy adopted by the Council of Europe to define terrorism by a list of UN Conventions and Protocols dealing with terrorism rather than by a substantive definition of it (although the Council of Europe did refer to the EU definition of the terrorist *intent*, it did not adopt its definition of terrorism). The simplified amendment procedure further made it possible to modify the list of Conventions defining terrorism indefinitely, thereby keeping the definition of terrorism open-ended. The expanding definition of terrorism eventually also came with an ever-growing radius of criminalisation of acts linked to it, eventually reaching more people, more actions and in a wider range of temporality (allowing preventive criminalisation).

Another dynamic at play was the reduction of possibilities to introduce reservations to the treaties discussed in this chapter. Following the adoption of a generous reservation regime in the 1957 Convention on Extradition and the 1977 Convention on the Suppression of Terrorism, the Council of Europe sought to eliminate these reservations in subsequent conventions on terrorism. The shift from a liberal reservation regime to a stricter one, characterised by time limits and increased accountability mechanisms, began with non-binding resolutions and recommendations from various CoE bodies. Notably, the Parliamentary Assembly repeatedly urged member states to withdraw their reservations and eventually proposed to eliminate the possibility to introduce reservations altogether. This drive to limit reservations was later reflected in the treaties themselves, initially in the Protocol Amending the European

Convention on the Suppression of Terrorism, which, although never enacted, set a precedent for subsequent conventions and protocols aimed at combating terrorism. From that point on, possibilities to introduce reservations were strictly limited. The scope of articles available for reservations was restricted, in contrast to the earlier approach that allowed reservations on any aspect of the treaty. Additionally, reservations were subject to a time limit, expiring after three years if not renewed by the contracting parties. The states were thus invited to periodically reconsider and reevaluate them in view of their suppression. The 1977 Convention introduced a clause requiring CoE member states to refer the case to their national competent authorities for prosecution, in the event of refusing extradition. Prior to 1977, the *aut dedere aut judicare* principle – requiring states either to extradite or prosecute – did not apply, which allowed for potential immunity for political offenders. The obligation to extradite or prosecute was later incorporated into the article detailing the reservation procedure, reminding that the refusal to extradite political offenders could not equate to impunity.

The narrowing scope of political crimes in CoE treaties, as reflected in these initial dynamics, was balanced by the increasing importance of the discrimination clause. Initially a supplementary provision in the article on political offence exemptions in the European Convention on Extradition, the discrimination clause evolved into a standalone article in the 1977 Convention and subsequent texts. It was further strengthened with provisions expanding its application to cases where individuals faced risks of torture, the death penalty, or life imprisonment without parole. This expanded role of the discrimination clause in turn made it easier to justify the further depoliticisation of political crimes.

These changes, even if advertised as enhancing democratic principles, eventually served the interests of member states in that they redefined accepted levels, forms and targets of political violence in a way that greatly shielded them. Initially, there were no restrictions on the targets of political crimes, except for the attentat clause protecting heads of state and their families – a principle long established in extradition law prior to the Council of Europe's adoption of the 1957 Convention on Extradition. Over time, however, the scope of protected targets expanded significantly, both in terms of the extent of damage and the types of targets. Indeed, early CoE treaties mainly sought to protect human lives and more specifically groups of innocent people foreign to the motives of the political fight. However, the scope of protection was gradually broadened to encompass a complete prohibition on human casualties. In certain instances, even the mere threat of physical harm was sufficient to disqualify actions from being included under the political offence exception. While early treaties specifically excluded indiscriminate and mass killings, specific individuals, such as heads of state, diplomatic staff and, in certain circumstances, military staff already enjoyed individual protection, indicating that attacks on state symbols were considered severe enough to fall outside the political offence exception. Finally, by categorising the intention to "destabilise or destroy the fundamental political, constitutional, economic or social structures of a country or an international organization" as terroristic,[179] the Convention on the Prevention of Terrorism extended this protection to not only the state structure but also to a certain type of governance.

This reduction of legitimate types of targets came hand in hand with a decreased tolerance for the use of violence against any of the targets of political crimes. In the early days of mutual cooperation in criminal matters, political violence was, to some extent, a common ground between political and terrorist crimes whose categorisation as one or the other was left to the individual appreciation of the state. The general idea was that if there were reasonable grounds to believe that the use of violence could achieve the intended change, it might be accepted. Over time, however, any type of political violence became assimilated into terrorism, restricting the range of action of political activists to strictly non-violent means.

The texts examined in this chapter reveal a gradual yet notable shift from minimal exclusions in the protection of political crimes to an increasing depoliticisation of crimes within the framework of counterterrorism efforts. This shift was justified by the perceived need to safeguard human rights, democracy, and other shared values among the similarly aligned member states of the Council of Europe. Today, the protection of political crimes still formally exists in the CoE framework but is significantly constrained by the counterterrorism framework that bridled the legitimate means, targets, and objectives of political offenders, seriously limiting their ability to benefit from the political offence exception to extradition.

Bibliography

Legislation, cases, official publications

United Nations

Convention for the Suppression of Unlawful Acts Against the Safety of Civil Aviation (974 UNTS) 1971.
Convention for the Suppression of Unlawful Acts Against the Safety of Maritime Navigation (No. 29004) 1988.
Convention for the Suppression of Unlawful Seizure of Aircraft (860 UNTS) 1970.
Convention on the Prevention and Punishment of the Crime of Genocide (No. 1021) 1948.
Convention on the Prevention and Punishment of Crimes Against Internationally Protected Persons, Including Diplomatic Agents (No. 15410) 1973.
International Convention Against the Taking of Hostages (No. 21931) 1979.
International Convention for the Suppression of the Financing of Terrorism (No. 38349) 1999.
International Convention for the Suppression of Terrorist Bombings (No. 37517) 2001.
Protocol for the Suppression of Unlawful Acts Against the Safety of Fixed Platforms Located on the Continental Shelf, 1988.

179 European Convention on the Prevention of Terrorism (n 150) (Preamble).

Council of Europe

Additional Protocol to the European Convention on Extradition (ETS 86) 1975.
Additional Protocol to the European Convention on the Prevention of Terrorism (ETS 217) 2017.
Committee of Ministers of the Council of Europe, Declaration of the Committee of Ministers on the Fight Against International Terrorism (12 September 2001).
Committee of Ministers of the Council of Europe, European Convention on Extradition (Resolution (53)4) 19 March 1953.
Committee of Ministers of the Council of Europe, Guidelines on Human Rights and the Fight Against Terrorism Adopted by the Committee of Ministers at its 804th Meeting (11 July 2002).
Committee of Ministers of the Council of Europe, Resolution (78)43 on Reservations Made to Certain Provisions of the European Convention on Extradition (Resolution (78)43) 1978.
Council of Europe, Explanatory Report to the Additional Protocol to the European Convention on Extradition (1975).
Council of Europe, Explanatory Report to the Convention on the Suppression of Terrorism (1977).
Council of Europe, Explanatory Report to the European Convention on the Prevention of Terrorism (2005).
Council of Europe, Explanatory Report to the European Convention on the Suppression of Terrorism (2003).
Council of Europe, Explanatory Report to the Protocol Amending the European Convention on the Suppression of Terrorism (2003).
European Committee on Crimes Problems (CDPC) - Committee of Experts on the Operation European Conventions in the Penal Field, Summary report of the 47th meeting, Strasbourg 15–17 September 2003, PC-OC (2004) 03 rev (2004).
European Convention for the Protection of Human Rights and Fundamental Freedoms as amended by Protocols No. 11 and No. 14 (ETS 5) 1950.
European Convention on Extradition (ETS 24) 1957.
European Convention on the International Validity of Criminal Judgments (ETS 70) 1970.
European Convention on the Prevention of Terrorism (ETS 196) 2005.
European Convention on the Suppression of Terrorism (ETS 90) 1977.
European Convention on the Transfer of Proceedings in Criminal Matters (ETS 73) 1972.
European Court of Human Rights, Factsheet: Life Imprisonment (2023).
European Court of Human Rights, Factsheet: Political Parties and Associations (2016).
HADEP and Demir v. Turkey, Application no. 964 (ECtHR 14/10/2010).
Parliamentary Assembly, Challenge of Terrorism in Council of Europe Member States (Recommendation 1677) 2004.
Parliamentary Assembly, Combatting International Terrorism while Protecting Council of Europe Standards and Values (Resolution 2090) 2016.
Parliamentary Assembly, Combatting Terrorism and Respect for Human Rights (Recommendation 1271) 2002.
Parliamentary Assembly, Combatting Terrorism and Respect for Human Rights (Recommendation 1550) 2002.
Parliamentary Assembly, Conference on 'Defence of Democracy against Terrorism in Europe - Tasks and Problems' (Strasbourg, 12–14 November 1980) (Recommendation 916) 1981.
Parliamentary Assembly, Defence of Democracy Against Terrorism in Europe (Recommendation 982) 1984.
Parliamentary Assembly, Democracies Facing Terrorism (Recommendation 1534) 2001.

Parliamentary Assembly, Democracies Facing Terrorism (Resolution 1258) 2001.
Parliamentary Assembly, Draft Additional Protocol to the European Convention on the Prevention of Terrorism (Opinion 289) 2015.
Parliamentary Assembly, Draft Protocol Amending the European Convention on the Suppression of Terrorism (Opinion 242) 2003.
Parliamentary Assembly, European Democracies Facing up to Terrorism (Recommendation 1426) 1999.
Parliamentary Assembly, European Response to International Terrorism (Recommendation 1024) 1986.
Parliamentary Assembly, European Response to International Terrorism (Resolution 863) 1986.
Parliamentary Assembly, Extradition of Criminals (Recommendation 950) 1982.
Parliamentary Assembly, Human Rights and the Fight against Terrorism (Resolution 1840) 2011.
Parliamentary Assembly, International Terrorism (Recommendation 684) 1972.
Parliamentary Assembly, International Terrorism (Recommendation 703) 1973.
Parliamentary Assembly, Strengthening the European Convention on the Suppression of Terrorism (Recommendation 1170) 1991.
Parliamentary Assembly, Terrorism in Europe (Recommendation 852) 1979.
Parliamentary Assembly, Terrorism: A Threat to Democracies (Recommendation 1644) 2004.
Party for a Democratic Society (DTP) and Others v. Turkey, Applications nos. 3870/10, 3870/10, 3878/10, 15616/10, 21919/10, 39118/10 and 37272/10 (ECtHR 12/01/2016).
Protocol Amending the European Convention on the Suppression of Terrorism (ETS 190) 2003.
Socialist Party and Others v. Turkey, 20/1997/804/1007 (ECtHR 25/05/1998).
Statute of the Council of Europe (ETS 1) 1949.
Yazar, Karataş, Aksoy and the People's Labour Party (HEP) v. Turkey, Applications nos. 22723/93, 22724/93 and 22725/9 (ECtHR 09/04/2002).

European Union

Council Decision 2019/25 Amending and Updating the List of Persons, Groups and Entities Subject to Articles 2, 3 and 4 of Common Position 2001/931/CFSP on the Application of Specific Measures to Combat Terrorism, and Repealing Decision (CFSP) 2018/1084 [9 January 2019] OJ L L6.
European Parliament, 'Written question 1147/79 by Mrs Vayssade to the Commission of the European Communities (15 November 1979)' [17 March 1980] OJ C 66.

Books

Blumenau B., *The United Nations and Terrorism. Germany, Multilateralism, and Anti-terrorism Efforts in the 1970s* (Palgrave Macmillan, Basingstoke 2014).
Crabit E., *Recherches sur la Notion d'Espace Judiciaire Européen* (Presses Universitaires de Bordeaux, Bordeaux 1988).
Galloux-Fournier B., *Histoire de l'Europe au XXe siècle (de 1974 à nos jours)* (Complexe, France 1995).
Gal-Or N., *International Cooperation to Suppress Terrorism* (Routledge, New York 1985).
Gilbert G., *Responding to International Crime* (Martinus Nijhoff Publishers, Leiden, Boston 2006).
Jansson J., *Terrorism, Criminal Law and Politics. The Decline of the Political Offence Exception to Extradition* (Routledge, Abingdon, New York 2020).

Kolb M., *The European Union and the Council of Europe* (Palgrave Macmillan, London 2013).

Salinas de Frias A., *Counter-Terrorism and Human Rights in the Case Law of the European Court of Human Rights* (Council of Europe Publishing, Strasbourg 2012).

Journal articles

Baker M. B., 'The Western European Legal Response to Terrorism' [1987] *Brook. J. Int'l Law.* 1.

Barnett M. and Coleman L., 'Designing Police: Interpol and the Study of Change in International Organizations' [2005] *ISQ.* 593.

Blumenau B., 'Taming the Beast: West Germany, the Political Offence Exception, and the Council of Europe Convention on the Suppression of Terrorism' [2015] *Terror Polit. Violenc.* 310.

Cardona M., 'The European Response to Terrorism' [1992] *Terror Polit. Violenc.* 245.

Guild E., 'The Uses and Abuses of Counter-Terrorism Policies in Europe: The Case of the "Terrorist Lists"' [2008] *JCMS.* 173.

Guillaume G., 'Terrorism and International Law' [2004] *ICLQ.* 537.

Honig F., 'Extradition by Multilateral Conventions' [1956] *ICLQ.* 549.

Hunt A., 'The Council of Europe Convention on the Prevention of Terrorism' [2006] *EPL.* 603.

Israël L., 'Défendre le Défenseur de l'Ennemi Public: l'Affaire Croissant' [2012] *MS.* 67.

Kiss A. C., 'La Convention Européenne d'Extradition' [1958] *AFDI.* 493.

Lagodny O., 'The European Convention on the Suppression of Terrorism: A Substantial Step to Combat Terrorism?' [1989] *U. Colo. Law Rev.* 583.

Mankiewicz R., 'La Problématique de la Piraterie Aérienne' [1977] *Etud. Int.* 100.

O'Higgins P., 'The European Convention on Extradition' [1960] *ICLQ.* 491.

Salmon J. J. A., 'La Convention Européenne pour la Répression du Terrorisme - un Vrai Pas en Arrière' [1977] *JT.* 497.

Tulkens T., 'Analyse Critique de la Convention Européenne pour la Répression du Terrorisme' [1979] *Deviance Soc.* 229.

Wagner W., 'Building an Internal Security Community: The Democratic Peace and the Politics of Extradition in Western Europe' [2003] *J. Peace Res.* 695.

Wasmeier M., 'The Principle of Ne Bis In Idem' [2006] *RIDP.* 121.

Weyembergh A. and Bribosia E., 'Extradition et Asile: Vers un Espace Judiciaire Européen?' [1997] *RBDI.* 69.

Book chapters

Murphy C., 'The Legal Response to Terrorism of the European Union and Council of Europe' in B. Saul (ed), *Research Handbook on International Law and Terrorism* (Edward Elgar Publishing, 2014).

Walter C., 'Combatting Terrorism and Organized Crime' in S. Schmahl & M. Breuer (eds), *The Council of Europe: Its Law and Policies* (Oxford University Press, 2017).

Online resources

Council of Europe, 'Reservations and Declarations for Treaty No. 24 – European Convention on Extradition' (Council of Europe) <https://www.CoE.int/en/web/conventions/full-list/-/conventions/treaty/024/declarations?p_auth=6DZu2522&_CoEconventions_WAR_CoEconventionsportlet_enVigueur=false&_CoEconventions_WAR_CoEconventionsportlet_searchBy=state&_

CoEconventions_WAR_CoEconventionsportlet_codePays=RUS&_CoEconventions_WAR_CoEconventionsportlet_codeNature=2> accessed 29 August 2018.

Council of Europe, 'Reservations and Declarations for Treaty No. 090 – European Convention the Suppression of Terrorism' (Council of Europe) <https://www.CoE.int/en/web/conventions/full-list?module=declarations-by-treaty&numSte=090&codeNature=0> accessed 8 February 2022.

Council of Europe, 'Reservations and Declarations for Treaty No. 196 – European Convention for the Prevention of Terrorism' (Council of Europe) <https://www.coe.int/en/web/conventions/full-list?module=declarations-by-treaty&numSte=196&codeNature=0> accessed 24 August 2022.

CVCE, 'The Origins of the Council of Europe' (CVCE 2016) <https://www.cvce.eu/en/education/unit-content/-/unit/026961fe-0d57-4314-a40a-a4ac066a1801/13839cdf-3e7e-4985-995f-2b6d9b534633> accessed 22 August 2018.

Gaub F., 'Trends in Terrorism' (European Union Institute for Security Studies April 2017) <https://www.iss.europa.eu/sites/default/files/EUISSFiles/Alert_4_Terrorism_in_Europe_0.pdf> accessed 21 March 2019.

International Democracy Watch, 'Council of Europe' (International Democracy Watch) <http://www.internationaldemocracywatch.org/index.php/council-of-europe> accessed 19 August 2019.

Interviews

Interview with Claude Debrulle, Honorary General Director of the former Directorate General on Legislation at the Belgian Ministry of Justice (Walloon Brabant, 15 April 2014).

Interview with Paul Bekaert, Lawyer of Fehriye Erdal (West Flanders, 29 November 2018).

4 Evolution of the political offence exception in the EU legal framework

Institutional developments allowing stronger cooperation on extradition

Following in the footsteps of the Council of Europe, the European Union eventually developed its own criminal justice system, resulting in a distinct protection regime for political offenders. This evolution did not happen in isolation; instead, it was largely based on the foundational tools and frameworks established by the Council of Europe. Initially, judicial cooperation in criminal matters was managed exclusively within the Council of Europe, which held a long-standing monopoly in this area across Europe. However, this dominance began to shift as the European Communities gradually started to assert their influence and take on a more active role in these matters. This did not really happen before the entry into force of the Maastricht Treaty in 1993.[1] Earlier attempts to initiate judicial cooperation in criminal matters were made by trial and error and mostly resulted in errors. The 1980s were, in this sense, years of great hope but little success in this field for the European Economic Community. Every failed attempt to cooperate on these issues at the Community level led to a fallback onto existing CoE tools. When the European Community eventually managed to adopt its first tools of judicial cooperation in criminal matters, they supplemented the CoE ones rather than replacing them.[2] Gradually, however, the EU began to adopt instruments that would replace those of the Council of Europe, ultimately leading to the creation of an independent criminal justice system.

The development of judicial cooperation in criminal matters within the EU began in the 1970s, a period marked by significant unrest and political turmoil across Europe, as discussed in the previous chapter. Multiple armed groups

1 EU member states did start cooperating on this before 1993, but outside of the Community framework. A. Mégie, 'Généalogie du Champ de la Coopération Judiciaire Européenne' [2006] *C&C (Online)*. 1, 2.

2 These endeavours are not outlined here. For a broad overview of these initiatives, see G. Vermeulen, 'EU Conventions Enhancing and Updating Traditional Mechanisms for Judicial Cooperation in Criminal Matter' [2006] *Int'l. Rev. Penal Law*. 59, 59–95.

DOI: 10.4324/9781003425847-4

from across the continent performed regular – and transborder – attacks in various cities. This not only incentivised the Council of Europe to start discussing and adopting tools to combat terrorism, but it also encouraged the emergence of below-the-radar intergovernmental fora aimed at police cooperation and intelligence sharing.[3] The possibilities in terms of police and judicial cooperation were largely dominated by police cooperation, as all the initiatives to undertake judicial cooperation successively failed at the time.[4] The repeated failures in establishing effective judicial cooperation calmed the enthusiasm of policy-makers to try to initiate any further form of cooperation. The fact that the Council of Europe already offered a platform to do all these things in fact hindered cooperation at the EU level, as some member states reported being keen on confining these issues to the CoE framework.[5]

It took over a decade for EU member states to start cooperating on judicial matters again. It is indeed with the adoption of the 1985 Schengen agreement seeking to abolish internal border checks that the issue of cooperation in judicial matters resurfaced. The gradual removal of these borders necessitated parallel measures to prevent the European Communities from becoming a haven for criminals.[6] In practical terms, this led to enhanced police and judicial cooperation within the framework of the European Economic Community. Even though the Schengen Agreement would become part of the *acquis Communautaire* only a few years later with the entry into force the Amsterdam Treaty (1999), the Maastricht Treaty (1993) nevertheless provided a legal basis for the adoption of these countervailing measures within the Community framework.[7] The intergovernmental method of decision-making continued to apply to these matters. Overall, the treaty was hailed for not only centralising scattered and unscrutinised endeavours in terms of police cooperation under the umbrella of the third pillar but also because it offered a framework for the development of judicial cooperation to accompany as well as monitor the until-then rather secret activities in the field of police cooperation.[8]

Shortly after the adoption of the Maastricht Treaty, the European Union introduced its first-ever extradition tool: the 1995 Convention on simplified extradition procedures between member states. The Convention, supplementing existing CoE tools, did not revolutionise extradition, but it did provide a simplified extradition scheme, smoothing the whole process by lightening the administrative burden on member states insofar as the person to be extradited

3 D. Bigo, 'La Mondialisation de l'(In)sécurité? Réflexions sur le Champ des Professionnels de la Gestion des Inquiétudes et Analytique de la Transnationalisation des Processus d'(In)sécurisation' [2005] *C&C (Online)*. 1, 16

4 G. Vermeulen (n 2) 60.

5 A. Mégie (n. 1) 8.

6 A. Mégie (n. 1).

7 G. Vermeulen and T. Vander Beken, 'New Conventions on Extradition in the European Union: Analysis and Evaluation' [1997] *Penn. St. Int'l. Law Rev.* 265, 273.

8 A. Mégie (n 1) 2–3.

consented to their extradition and that the requested member state also agreed to the simplified procedure.[9] The Convention also provided the individual sought with the option of waiving their right to the protection afforded by the specialty principle. This principle stipulates that a requesting state cannot detain, convict, or sentence the extradited person for any offences other than those for which extradition was requested.[10] It also established that if member states so declared, consent to extradition could automatically amount to a renunciation of the specialty principle.[11]

Political developments: the *Garcia–Moreno* case

A year after the adoption of the 1995 Convention, the EU adopted another convention on extradition. The adoption of two successive tools on extradition was owed to the fact that, at the moment of the negotiation of the 1995 Convention, EU member states – which wanted to adopt a more general convention on extradition – could not agree on all points of discussion. They therefore decided to forge ahead on points of consensus with the 1995 Convention. They left points of dissensus to be ironed out in a later instrument, the 1996 Convention. One of the points of contention concerned the political offence exception,[12] which was at the heart of Spanish concerns for a long time. Spanish authorities had indeed been engaged in negotiations with France on the need to step up cooperation on extradition and to depoliticise crimes from the early 1980s due their fight with the ETA.[13] This goal would finally be achieved following a particular event that took place back in 1993 and whose effects still resonate today.

In 1993, Spanish authorities issued two international arrest warrants against two Basque separatists, Luis Moreno Ramajo and Raquel Garcia Arranz, accused of participating in an unlawful association and an illegal armed band.[14] The Belgian minister of justice initially wanted to grant the extradition despite the opposing advisory opinion of the Court of Appeal of Brussels that argued, first, that there was a risk of violation of human rights[15] and, second, that the

9 Convention Drawn up on the Basis of Article K.3 of the Treaty on European Union, on Simplified Extradition Procedure Between the Member States of the European Union [1995] OJ C 78 (Art. 2).

10 I. A. Shearer, *Extradition in International Law* (Manchester University Press, Manchester 1971) 146.

11 Convention Drawn up on the Basis of Article K.3 of the Treaty on European Union, on Simplified Extradition Procedure Between the Member States of the European Union (n 9) (Art. 9).

12 G. Vermeulen (n 2) 67.

13 E.-P. Guittet, '"Ne Pas Leur Faire Confiance Serait Leur Faire Offense". Antiterrorisme, Solidarité Démocratique et Identité Politique' [2006] *C&C (Online)*. 1, 8.

14 A. Weyembergh and E. Bribosia, 'Extradition et Asile : Vers un Espace Judiciaire Européen ?' [1997] *RBDI*. 69, 73.

15 Interview with Paul Bekaert, Lawyer of Luis Moreno Ramajo and Raquel Garcia Arranz (Tielt, 29 November 2018).

crimes for which the warrants were issued were political, and that therefore extradition should not be granted.[16] Despite the negative advice of the Brussels Court of Appeal, the extradition was thus initially on good tracks to be approved. And indeed, Claude Debrulle, the then general director of the former Directorate General on Legislation at the Belgian Ministry of Justice,[17] as well as his colleague Paul Rietjens, former advisor in the personal office of the Belgian minister of foreign affairs,[18] reported that Belgian authorities had little to no doubt about the couple's complicity in the case.[19] The problem, according to Debrulle, came from the fact that "at the time, we were emerging from Francoism, it was common knowledge that the Guarda Civil continued to torture in Spanish prisons and the political independence of the judiciary in Spain was still under debate".[20]

As a result, when the couple lodged an asylum application in Belgium, it was deemed admissible for consideration. Spanish authorities viewed this acceptance to consider the request as an utterly unfriendly move from Belgian authorities, despite the fact that in Belgium, unlike in many other countries, asylum requests were not reviewed or decided at the governmental level at the time. These decisions were made by the General Commissariat for Refugees and Stateless Persons.[21] Spanish authorities accused Belgium of playing the game of terrorists and of undermining the European fight against terrorism.[22] What was worse for Spanish authorities was that the admissibility of the asylum request also meant that the extradition was put on hold until a decision on asylum was reached, which did not occur before 1994. In the end, the General Commissariat for Refugees and Stateless Persons decided not to grant asylum to Moreno and Garcia. It considered that, although there were cases of abusive behaviours towards Basque secessionists in Spain, these acts remained isolated. In addition, the Commissariat argued that the extraordinary publicity surrounding the case would be an additional safeguard for the couple,[23] who unsuccessfully appealed this decision. The negative decision on the asylum request resulted in the suspension of the extradition being lifted, and the extradition request was eventually accepted in January 1996.

16 A. Weyembergh and E. Bribosia (n 14) 74.
17 Interview with Claude Debrulle, Honorary General Director of the Former Directorate General on Legislation at the Belgian Ministry of Justice (Walloon Brabant, 15 April 2014).
18 Interview with Paul Rietjens, Former Advisor in the Personal Office of the Belgian Minister of Foreign Affairs (Online, 12 December 2021).
19 Interview with Paul Rietjens, Former Advisor in the Personal Office of the Belgian Minister of Foreign Affairs (Online, 12 December 2021).
20 Interview with Claude Debrulle (n 17).
21 Interview with Paul Rietjens (n 18).
22 Interview with Paul Rietjens (n 18).
23 A. Weyembergh and E. Bribosia (n 14) 75.

Moreno and Garcia consequently introduced a procedure for extreme urgency before the Belgian Council of State, which was successful. The president of the Chamber of the Council of State stopped the extradition on grounds that the acts for which extradition was requested did not correspond to any of the offences listed in the 1977 Convention on the Suppression of Terrorism restricting the application of the political offence exemption. Furthermore, the Spanish government had failed to provide a good reason why the acts for which the extradition was requested should not be considered political.[24]

Because of that event, Spanish authorities started a resolute campaign against the protection of political offenders in the European Union. They not only sought to abolish the political offence exception to extradition between EU member states, but they also questioned the need to maintain the right to political asylum for EU nationals in the European Union. Their argument was that the political offence exemption and the non-refoulement principle applied among EU member states both constituted obstacles to European judicial cooperation in criminal matters and to combatting terror.[25] The latter was actually of crucial importance for Spanish authorities, who contemplated the success of the extradition in the *Garcia–Moreno* case as a potential springboard for the implementation of their anti-terrorism agenda at the EU level. Counterterrorism was ranked so high in their priorities that Spanish authorities had repeatedly called for cooperation in these matters long before their accession to the European Communities.[26] Emmanuel-Pierre Guittet argues in this respect that while scholars typically turn to France, Germany, or the United Kingdom to understand the evolution of the EU counterterrorism framework, the strong focus of the latter on extradition was in fact a Spanish doing. Spanish authorities had sent several extradition requests over the years to France to get Basque terrorists back, but French authorities had consistently opposed the political offence exception argument to reject those requests, which prompted Spanish authorities to turn to the EU framework to overcome the French deadlock.[27]

Fortunately for Spanish authorities, they already had a foundation for enhanced counterterrorism collaboration. The early cooperation among police forces, terrorism working groups, and the earlier, albeit unsuccessful, efforts to initiate judicial cooperation in criminal matters – driven by terrorist attacks occurring at the time – demonstrated a clear commitment to adopting tools for combating terrorism. Building on that, the European Parliament adopted several resolutions where it underlined the outdated nature of concepts like

24 A. Weyembergh and E. Bribosia (n 14) 75–76.

25 A. Weyembergh and E. Bribosia (n 14) 76.

26 E.-P. Guittet, 'Political Identity and Democratic Solidarity After 9/11: The Spanish Case' [2004] *Altern. Global Local Polit.* 441, 451.

27 E.-P. Guittet, 'L'Imposition de l'Agenda Politique Espagnol à l'Europe de l'Antiterrorisme' in D. Bigo, L. Bonelli & T. Deltombe (eds), *Au Nnom du 11 Septembre . . . Les Démocraties à l'Épreuve de l'Antiterrorisme* (La Découverte, 2008) 228.

the political offence exception in the EU context. It declared, for instance, that "in the case of terrorist crimes alone, the concept of political motive or political offence in the context of laws governing extradition should have no place within the external frontiers of the Community".[28] In a later resolution, it added that "terrorism, regardless of its motives, is a threat to peace, democracy and human rights and is a grave problem in several member states of the European Union" and that "in European countries, which are based on the rule of law, no ideology can any longer justify terrorist activities, which should be pursued and punished as criminal offences".[29] The commitment to fight terror was thus undoubtedly present, and the *Garcia–Moreno* case was a powerful trigger on the Spanish side to reactivate the work conducted on a Convention on extradition between the EU member states. On top of this, 1995 was marked by a significant number of terrorist attacks worldwide, including one during which ETA members tried to assassinate the future Spanish prime minister, at the time opposition leader, José Maria Aznar.[30] Spanish authorities had been advocating for the necessity to create a European judicial space to effectively combat terrorism during the whole Garcia Moreno debacle.[31] The circumstances were thus favourable for Spanish authorities to advance their counterterrorism strategy at the European level. In this respect, Spain's turn to hold the presidency of the Council of the European Union from July to December 1995 provided an opportune moment to pursue the country's interests.

All aforementioned events prompted the organisation of an informal European Council summit held in Madrid in December 1995 where EU member states adopted the La Gomera Declaration. Fearing that terrorists may benefit from impunity due to the differences in legal treatments among EU member states, the European Council called on its members to improve the coordination and cooperation of their judicial authorities by means of extradition.[32] A few months later, this declaration was followed by a European Parliament resolution addressing the extradition of "presumed ETA militants", specifically Garcia and Moreno.[33] In this resolution, the EP echoed Spain's repeated calls for increased cooperation whose difficulty to materialise was incomprehensible to Spanish authorities in light of their EU membership. In the resolution, the European Parliament, overtly disapproving the Belgian decision to suspend

28 European Parliament, Resolution on the European Judicial Area (Extradition) [1982] OJ C 238, 83.

29 European Parliament, Resolution on Terrorism and Its Effects on Security in Europe [1994] OJ C 91, 236–237.

30 R. Bossong, *The Evolution of EU Counter-Terrorism: European Security Policy After 9/11* (Routledge, London and New York 2013) 29.

31 E.-P. Guittet (n 13) 10.

32 European Council, 'Madrid European Council 15–16 December 1995 Presidency Conclusions' (1995) Annex 3.

33 European Parliament, Resolution on the Extradition of Two Presumed ETA Militants [1996] OJ C 65, 23.

the extradition request during the examination of the asylum application of Moreno and Garcia, argued that this decision on the admissibility of the request for asylum called into question the democratic nature of Spain, which it deemed incompatible with the spirit of the Treaty on the European Union. The resolution further exhorted EU member states to urgently revise the legal framework allowing the protection of persons accused of terrorism in another member state. It also deplored the obstacles that situations like this created on judicial cooperation and the fight against terrorism and called for a common and definitive solution to this problem. To address this issue, the resolution urged the Council to adopt a convention on extradition that would resolve this deadlock by abolishing the political offence exception that it described as an obsolete concept. Mirroring this call, in a meeting between José Maria Aznar and Jacques Chirac in June 1996, Aznar repeated that he found asylum or other obstacles to cooperation among EU member states unacceptable.[34]

The 1996 Convention relating to extradition between the member states of the European Union: attempt to abolish the political offence exception

This context led to the adoption of the 1996 Convention drawn up on the basis of article K.3. of the Treaty of the European Union, relating to extradition between the member states of the European Union.[35] The general purpose of this Convention, composed of 20 articles, was to facilitate the application of already existing CoE and EU tools enabling or updating extradition procedures.[36] The Convention was thus of supplementary nature and did not replace pre-existing CoE tools. To facilitate extradition, the Convention foresaw four main changes to existing extradition arrangements.

The first one was the extension of the list of extraditable offences, namely by defining the situations leading to extradition in a very broad way (covering

> offences which are punishable under the law of the requesting Member State by deprivation of liberty or a detention order for a maximum period of at least 12 months and under the law of the requested Member State by deprivation of liberty or a detention order for a maximum period of at least six months

and precluding refusals "on the grounds that the law of the requested Member State does not provide for the same type of detention order as the law of

34 E.-P. Guittet (n 26) 451.
35 Convention Drawn up on the Basis of Article K.3 of the Treaty on European Union, Relating to Extradition Between the Member States of the European Union [1996] OJ C 313.
36 Convention Drawn up on the Basis of Article K.3 of the Treaty on European Union, Relating to Extradition Between the Member States of the European Union [1996] OJ C 313 (Art. 1).

the requesting Member State").[37] Second, the Convention lifted the double criminality requirement in case of conspiracy and association to commit one or more of the offences listed in articles 1 and 2 of the European Convention on the Suppression of Terrorism or any serious offence in the field of drug trafficking, as well as certain forms of crime against physical integrity and individual freedoms, or creating a collective danger for persons (only if the offence was punishable by a maximum term of deprivation of liberty or a detention order of at least 12 months in the requesting state).[38] The third change the 1996 Convention introduced was to further restrict grounds for refusal by excluding the possibility to refuse extradition for political offences,[39] fiscal offences,[40] on the ground of nationality,[41] or because of the offence for which extradition was requested would be statute barred according to the law of the requested member state[42] (which did not apply in the case of amnesty).[43] Finally, the principle of speciality was further bent to enable prosecution without prior consent of the requested state when the prosecution or trial of the offence did not entail the deprivation of liberty.[44]

Abolishing the political offence exception (art. 5)

As previously mentioned, the Convention abolished the political offence exception by stating that "no offence may be regarded by the requested member state as a political offence, as an offence connected with a political offence or an offence inspired by political motives".[45] Doing so, it reversed the relationship of the 1957 Convention to political crimes.[46] Indeed, while the 1957 Convention specified that no political offence could lead to extradition, this

37 Convention Drawn up on the Basis of Article K.3 of the Treaty on European Union, Relating to Extradition Between the Member States of the European Union [1996] OJ C 313 (Art. 2).
38 Convention Drawn up on the Basis of Article K.3 of the Treaty on European Union, Relating to Extradition Between the Member States of the European Union [1996] OJ C 313 (Art. 3).
39 Convention Drawn up on the Basis of Article K.3 of the Treaty on European Union, Relating to Extradition Between the Member States of the European Union [1996] OJ C 313 (Art. 5).
40 Convention Drawn up on the Basis of Article K.3 of the Treaty on European Union, Relating to Extradition Between the Member States of the European Union [1996] OJ C 313 (Art. 6).
41 Convention Drawn up on the Basis of Article K.3 of the Treaty on European Union, Relating to Extradition Between the Member States of the European Union [1996] OJ C 313 (Art. 7).
42 Convention Drawn up on the Basis of Article K.3 of the Treaty on European Union, Relating to Extradition Between the Member States of the European Union [1996] OJ C 313 (Art. 8).
43 Convention Drawn up on the Basis of Article K.3 of the Treaty on European Union, Relating to Extradition Between the Member States of the European Union [1996] OJ C 313 (Art. 9).
44 Convention Drawn up on the Basis of Article K.3 of the Treaty on European Union, Relating to Extradition Between the Member States of the European Union [1996] OJ C 313 (Art. 10).
45 Convention Drawn up on the Basis of Article K.3 of the Treaty on European Union, Relating to Extradition Between the Member States of the European Union [1996] OJ C 313 (Art. 5§1).
46 A. Weyembergh and E. Bribosia (n 14) 78.

Convention provided that no extradition could be refused on ground of the political offence exemption.[47] The 1996 Convention thus finished the work initiated by the 1977 Convention on the Suppression of Terrorism. It even went beyond the CoE Convention, in which the compulsory depoliticisation of terrorist crimes was limited to the acts listed in its first article. In addition, whilst the latter offered loopholes to the heavy depoliticisation of political crimes it introduced, the 1996 Convention did not. It only provided the possibility for member states to declare that they chose to apply this strict depoliticisation only in relation to articles 1 and 2 of the 1977 Convention on the Suppression of Terrorism – as well as the conspiracy or association to commit the acts thereof,[48] leaving the door slightly open to the political offence exemption for non-violent crimes. In an unofficial statement, the United Nations High Commissioner for Refugees (UNHCR) – which had not been kept informed on the drafting process and only received a copy of the convention through confidential channels once it was completed – expressed concern that this provision might blur the distinction between terrorists and other political offenders.[49] Interestingly, of the 20 signatories to the Convention,[50] 10 ended up using that possibility, with Italy introducing that reservation no later than in 2019, over two decades after its adoption.[51] Greece was also among those member states and had, already at the moment of the adoption of the Convention, annexed a declaration to the Treaty stating its intention to apply the strict depoliticisation only in relation to the first two articles of the 1977 Convention. The Greek Constitution indeed prohibits its authorities from extraditing foreigners whose extradition is requested on the basis of acts conducted in the pursuit of the defence of freedom. However, even Greece maintained that opportunity using the back door to avoid frustrating the objectives of the Convention: it related this protection to a provision of the article safeguarding the discrimination clause from the abolition of the political offence exemption.[52] Despite the fact that this Greek reservation was a right granted by the Convention, its use was frowned upon. Hartmut Nassauer, a German Christian Democrat Party deputy, shared his disbelief that EU

47 Convention Drawn up on the basis of Article K.3 of the Treaty on European Union, Relating to Extradition Between the Member States of the European Union (n 35) (Art. 5).

48 Convention Drawn up on the basis of Article K.3 of the Treaty on European Union, Relating to Extradition Between the Member States of the European Union (n 35) (Art. 5§1).

49 K. Landgren, 'Deflecting International Protection by Treaty: Bilateral and Multilateral Accords on Extradition, Readmission and the Inadmissibility of Asylum Requests' [1999] UNHCR, New Issues in Refugee Research, Working Paper No. 10, 31.

50 There were in fact 21 signatories, but due to Brexit, only 20 are currently EU member states.

51 Journal Officiel du Grand-Duché de Luxembourg, 'Convention Établie sur la Base de l'Article K.3 du Traité sur l'Union Européenne, Relative à l'Extradition Entre les États Membres de l'Union Européenne, Faite à Dublin, le 27 Septembre 1996 - Entrée en Vigueur' (Legilux 2019) <http://legilux.public.lu/eli/etat/leg/div/2019/08/07/a714/jo> accessed 12 February 2021.

52 Convention Drawn up on the basis of Article K.3 of the Treaty on European Union, Relating to Extradition Between the Member States of the European Union (n 35) (Annex).

member states viewed peace in such different ways that these differences could lead to the sheltering of crime.[53] And indeed, legislators did not anticipate that this discrimination clause would ever be applied among EU member states. The explanatory report for the Convention described the clause's benefit as being primarily "academic".[54]

The Spanish dual strategy enabling the abolition of the political offence exception

The adoption of these measures was said to have been made possible by the allegedly strong trust that member states placed in each other's judicial systems, their high regard for human rights, and the secure nature of their democracies. As a result, it was considered only natural to enhance the system of cooperation in criminal matters among EU member states, which included reassessing the necessity of maintaining the political offence exemption in future extradition relations.[55] The background story to this Convention, however, casts doubt about this justification. The environment surrounding the adoption of this Convention was marked more by hostility than trust. Spain had a history of political repression, including the use of death squads, bombings, kidnappings, and extrajudicial killings against Basque activists. This repression extended beyond its borders into France, where Spain conducted a 'dirty war' using GAL death squads[56] to pressure its neighbour into surrendering activists whom France considered to be political offenders. France had long sheltered Basque militants under the political offence exception, causing significant frustration for Spanish authorities. With the Spanish transition to democracy, however, the continued French refusals to extradite Basque militants further soured the Franco-Spanish relations and the issue of the French sanctuary aggravated.[57] Guittet notes in this respect that Spanish authorities were pursuing two simultaneous counterterrorism agendas: an underground one, with the work of GAL death squads, and an official one, with their EU strategy in terms of extradition.[58] With the attacks in France, Spanish authorities also conveyed a (somewhat) veiled threat: if borders were porous for ETA members, they equally were for GAL agents.[59] Their repeated calls for cooperation

53 E.-P. Guittet (n 26) 452.

54 European Union, Convention Relating to Extradition Between the Member States of the European Union – Explanatory Report [1997] OJ C 191, 19.

55 European Union, Convention Relating to Extradition Between the Member States of the European Union – Explanatory Report [1997] OJ C 1, 13, 18 & 20.

56 GAL stands for 'Grupos Antiterroristas de Liberacion'. It was a state-sponsored terrorist group established under the Spanish Socialist Workers' Party (PSOE) to combat Basque terrorism. They were active from 1983 to 1987 and committed 27 murders. E.-P. Guittet (n 13) 5.

57 E.-P. Guittet, *Counter-Terror by Proxy: The Spanish State's Illicit War with ETA* (Manchester University Press, Manchester 2021) 73–91.

58 E.-P. Guittet (n 27) 228–229.

59 E.-P. Guittet (n 13) 5–6.

were, however, frustrated by the French ideal of their country being a land of refuge, and also by their scepticism at Spain's democratic readiness to engage in an extradition policy with them.[60] Of note, these events took place less than a decade before the signature of the 1996 Convention.

In 1995, the year of the Spanish presidency and a year before the adoption of the Protocol on asylum for nationals of Member States of the European Union, the scandal of the GAL death squads and the involvement of numerous Spanish political figures in it sowed great mistrust among Spain and its EU partners. Spanish authorities, however, justified their actions by pointing out the injustice in the European extradition framework, and the political offence exception more specifically, that allowed the protection of terrorists. If anything, according to Spanish authorities, death squads were proof of the necessity to give the means to EU member states to develop a European democratic solidarity for which Spanish authorities had been long advocating by seeking to foster cooperation.[61] It is important to note that during the GAL scandal, numerous accounts of French police involvement emerged, which eventually became undeniable. Guittet argues that this issue represents a skeleton carefully hidden in the closet of EU counterterrorism. Had it been more widely exposed, the justifications for adopting EU counterterrorism measures would have been significantly undermined.[62] The narrative of a trust so great among EU member states that the concept of the political offence exemption had naturally become obsolete is therefore somewhat deceiving. As Karin Landgren underlined, while the EU Convention on Extradition was adopted as an effort to eliminate the possibility for terrorists to be protected by extradition, it instead removed a necessary and healthy margin of discretion to the states in the determination of a crime as terrorist or political.[63]

The impact of this Convention on political crimes was, however, mitigated by two factors. First, the Convention did not actually start being used before 2005 (between the 12 EU member states who had ratified it by then), and it only officially entered into force in November 2019, when its application was extended to 21 member states.[64] In any case, in the meantime, the European arrest warrant, the next EU tool on extradition – not supplementing but replacing all previous conventions, had already entered into force, rendering the 1996 Convention outdated (short of exceptional cases where the European arrest warrant does not apply).[65] Second, the significant changes introduced in the Convention were to be read in conjunction with a joint

60 E.-P. Guittet (n 13) 6–7.
61 E.-P. Guittet (n 27) 230.
62 E.-P. Guittet (n 13) 7–8.
63 K. Landgren (n 49) 39.
64 Council of the European Union, Avis Concernant l'Entrée en Vigueur de la Convention de 1996 Relative à l'Extradition 2019/C 329/02 [2019] OJ C 329/2.
65 European Union, 'Convention on Extradition Between Member States' (European Union 2005) <https://eur-lex.europa.eu/legal-content/EN/TXT/?uri=LEGISSUM:l14015b> accessed 27 June 2019.

declaration annexed to the Convention stating that the latter was without prejudice to the right of asylum, as member states were mindful of the potential repercussions of this Convention on the right to political asylum. Asylum, however, was abolished shortly after.

The 1997 Protocol on Asylum for Nationals of Member States of the European Union, a.k.a. the Aznar Protocol

Abolishing asylum possibilities in the European Union for EU citizens (sole article)

Besides the adoption of the 1996 Convention on extradition, the other consequence of the *Garcia–Moreno* case was the adoption of the Protocol on Asylum for Nationals of Member States of the European Union, colloquially known as the 'Aznar Protocol', named after the man who pushed for its adoption.[66] In the same way as for the 1996 Convention, Spanish authorities framed the right to asylum as a way for terrorists to benefit from impunity and not as a humanitarian safeguard, which opened the way to a discussion on its abolition.[67] This single article Protocol annexed to the Treaty of Amsterdam establishes that

> given the level of protection of fundamental rights and freedoms by the member states of the European Union, member states shall be regarded as constituting safe countries of origin in respect of each other for all legal and practical purposes in relation to asylum matters.[68]

The Protocol thus abolished asylum among EU member states for EU citizens. It nevertheless foresees three exceptional circumstances in which an asylum application can be declared admissible. The first refers to a situation in which a member state of which the applicant is a national suspends parts of its obligations under the European Convention for the Protection of Human Rights and Fundamental Freedoms, as provided by article 15 of the said Convention. The other two circumstances that could lead to a non-application of the Protocol refer to the provision laid down in article 7 of the Treaty on the European Union, whereby a member state would be in serious breach of the values of respect for human dignity, freedom, democracy, equality, the rule of law, and human rights. In the latter case, an asylum application lodged by a national of a country for which the procedure referred to in article 7 has either

66 Consolidated Version of the Treaty on the Functioning of the European Union - PROTOCOLS - Protocol (No. 24) on Asylum for Nationals of Member States of the European Union [2008] OJ C 115 (hereafter 'Protocol on Asylum for Nationals of Member States of the European Union').

67 E.-P. Guittet (n 27) 232.

68 Protocol on Asylum for Nationals of Member States of the European Union (n 66).

been initiated (second exception) or adopted (third exception) can be received as admissible.[69] A last provision nevertheless states that in the event a member state would take the unilateral decision to deem the application admissible, the application should be processed on the presumption that it is manifestly unfounded.[70]

Criticisms of the Protocol

This Protocol was widely criticised.[71] Only the three main criticisms concerning the Protocol are outlined here. The first one concerned the aim of the Protocol to strip EU citizens from asylum possibilities in the European Union. The second one referred to the reasons provided in the preamble of the Protocol to justify its adoption, namely the respect of human rights by EU member states and the possibility of EU nationals to freely move around the European Union. The third one concerned the fact that the Protocol was a response to counterterrorism needs and was not the result of the real obsolescence of the right to asylum for EU citizens in the European Union.

As aforementioned, the first criticism directly concerned the aim of the Protocol to deny EU citizens not only the fundamental right to asylum but also credibility in case they report violations.[72]

In addition to that, the reasons provided in the preamble of the Protocol as to why it was adopted stumped its commentators, which is the second main criticism raised towards this Protocol. The first of the reasons provided for its adoption was that EU member states were all bound to respect human rights, the rule of law, and democratic principles. Karin Landgren noted in this respect that, according to Spanish authorities, seeing that all EU member states observed the rule of law, respected human rights, and were governed by democratic principles, there was no point maintaining the right of asylum among EU member states. Accordingly, Spanish authorities contended that EU nationals lodging an asylum request in another member state were motivated by a nefarious purpose, which was to delay extraditions and sow mistrust among EU member states. Landgren further described how Spanish authorities argued that it made no sense to grant protection to a person who already benefits from a legal status in other EU member states and add asylum to the list of rights enjoyed by EU citizens.[73]

The reality was different. Landgren reminded that despite the supposed adherence of EU member states to international standards of human rights protection, complaints to the European human rights mechanisms continued

69 Protocol on Asylum for Nationals of Member States of the European Union (n 66).
70 Protocol on Asylum for Nationals of Member States of the European Union (n 66).
71 K. Landgren (n 49) 8–22.
72 A. Weyembergh and E. Bribosia (n 14) 89.
73 K. Landgren (n 49) 11.

to be considered admissible by the thousands every year at the time of the adoption of the Protocol. She noted that these complaints were not considered unfounded or susceptible of viable national remedies and that national authorities were eventually often found in breach of their human rights obligations.[74] Equally, Anne Weyemebergh and Emmanuelle Bribosia pointed out that at the time the Protocol was adopted, the European Court of Human Rights was issuing rulings and human rights organisations were drafting reports on the human rights violations taking place in the European Union. They concerned no less than 11 out of 15 of the EU member states at the time. In particular, in 1995, members of the Interior Ministry of Spain were convicted for extra-judicial killings of suspected ETA members.[75] Weyembergh and Bribosia thus warned that even the most developed system of protection of human rights would never be able to reduce the risk of persecution and abuse to zero, which they consider the only acceptable threshold to abolish the right to asylum.[76] Even 14 years after the adoption of the Protocol, in 2011, Elspeth Guild and Madeline Garlick pointed out that EU nationals were still found in need of international protection.[77] So, contrary to what Spanish authorities and the preamble of the Protocol argued, the European Union still created refugees.[78]

The second reason provided for the adoption of the Protocol was that EU citizens have a right to free movement, rendering the possibility of granting EU citizens asylum useless. The idea was thus that, in the unlikely event of persecution by a national's own state, the person had the freedom to move and settle elsewhere. This argument was, again, criticised because it assimilated asylum seekers to regular migrants, depriving asylum seekers of the protection their status entitles them to. Furthermore, the advanced schemes of police and judicial cooperation in the European Union only make the need for protection of EU citizens vis-à-vis their country of origin stronger and not weaker.[79]

The last criticism concerned the fact that this Protocol was adopted as a response to the Spanish wish to improve anti-terrorism cooperation.[80] The abolition of the right to asylum in the tense context of the *Moreno–Garcia* case was already considered questionable. Its removal for anti-terrorism purposes was even more problematic. This policy not only amalgamates people in need of international protection with security threats, but it also sacrifices fundamental rights in the pursuit of security objectives.[81]

74 K. Landgren (n 49) 15.
75 E.-P. Guittet (n 13) 5.
76 A. Weyembergh and E. Bribosia (n 14) 89–90.
77 E. Guild and M. Garlick, 'Refugee Protection, Counter-Terrorism, and Exclusion in the European Union' [2011] *RSQ.* 63, 69–70.
78 E. Guild and K. Zwaan, 'Does Europe Still Create Refugees? Examining the Situation of the Roma' [2014] *QLJ.* 141, 141–163.
79 A. Weyembergh and E. Bribosia (n 14) 90.
80 E.-P. Guittet (n 26) 452.
81 S. Top, 'Prosecuting Political Dissent: Discussing the Relevance of the Political Offence Exception in EU Extradition Law in Light of the Catalan Independence Crisis' [2021] *NJECL.* 107, 114.

Understanding its adoption despite its shortcomings: advancing EU and national interests

The adoption of this Protocol was therefore not driven by the respect for human rights and democratic values by EU member states as was claimed. The struggle of Spanish authorities against the ETA had significantly shaped Spain's counterterrorism landscape, marked by four legislative reforms up to that point (with more to follow)[82] and a growing counterterrorism arsenal. Spain also positioned itself assertively on the European stage. In a meeting held the day before the adoption of the Protocol, Belgian prime minister Jean-Luc Dehaene expressed his reservations about the Protocol, citing its potential breach of states' obligations under international treaties,[83] particularly the Geneva Convention that was also referenced by the Schengen Agreement. José Maria Aznar, who did not appreciate this critique, stressed the importance of adhering to Spanish law, concluded the meeting and left with his delegation.[84] After Aznar left the meeting, Dehaene declared Belgium would adopt a unilateral declaration.[85] If other countries shared Belgium's concerns about human rights protection, they were satisfied with the adoption of a declaration that was annexed to the Protocol, stating that the Protocol did not preclude individual member states taking organisational measures to comply with their obligations under the 1951 Refugee Convention. The purpose of this Declaration was to prevent EU member states from being blatantly at fault with their international obligations.[86] In the end, Belgium was the only member state to abstain during the vote for the adoption of the Protocol and the only one to declare that it would continue to consider all asylum applications it received.[87] All other member states voted in favour of the Protocol.[88]

Despite the initial reluctance of other EU member states to back this Protocol, the Protocol ultimately garnered support for various reasons. Paul Rietjens recalls the fact that when Spain suggested adopting the Protocol, several other EU member states were prey to terrorist attacks on their soil, which made them more receptive to the Spanish arguments. Additionally, Rietjens notes that at the time of the Protocol's negotiation, the concept of European citizenship had just been established with the Maastricht Treaty. Allowing EU citizens to seek asylum in another EU member state while attempting to cultivate a European citizenship and identity was thus defeating the purpose of that new initiative.[89] Karin Landgren further contends that the adoption of the Protocol was linked to political negotiations among EU member states who

82 E.-P. Guittet (n 27) 227–228.
83 Interview with Paul Rietjens (n 18).
84 Interview with Claude Debrulle (n 17).
85 Interview with Paul Rietjens (n 18).
86 K. Landgren (n 49) 11.
87 E. Guild and M. Garlick (n 77) 67.
88 L. Jannin, M. Meneghini, C. Pauti, R. Poupet and F. Moderne, *Le Droit d'Asile en Europe: Étude Comparée* (L'Harmattan, Paris 1999) 201.
89 Interview with Paul Rietjens (n 18).

made concessions on other member states' demands to have theirs satisfied in return.[90] She takes the example of Austria who could not oppose the Spanish demand because they needed the Spanish support to be able to be part of the Schengen area.[91] Equally, the European Union was also concerned at the time with the stability of the euro, which, she argues, weighed on the fact that the political organs of the EU did not raise concerns about the potential human rights breaches the Protocol would generate.[92]

In this context, it is noteworthy that the decision-making process leading to the adoption of the Protocol was political. Indeed, under the Maastricht Treaty, all matters related to justice and home affairs were decided by unanimity voting in the Council.[93] Only the ministers needed convincing, which facilitated the task of Spanish authorities. The UNHCR, however, was very vocal about the numerous dangers posed by the Protocol,[94] which Spanish authorities did not appreciate. According to a Spanish ambassador, the UNHCR's criticism generated a reluctance among EU member states to support the Protocol that might not have otherwise existed.[95] Frustrated by the approach of the UNHCR that Spanish authorities considered too orthodox and insensitive to the EU context and its specificities, they engaged in an aggressive campaign to convince the UNHCR of the suitability of the Protocol in the EU context, which included veiled threats to shut down the UNHCR office in Madrid.[96] Although this campaign did not result in the Protocol being dropped, it appears to have led member states to reflect on and somewhat temper the irrevocability of completely abolishing asylum. Indeed, while the final text of the Protocol allows for three exceptions where member states can still examine an asylum request under exceptional circumstances, the initial draft proposed by Spain did not provide any such provisions.[97]

The 2000s: stepping up the fight against terrorism

Two years after the adoption of the Treaty of Amsterdam to which the Aznar Protocol was attached, the heads of EU member states met in Tampere in a European summit solely dedicated to the establishment of an 'Area of Freedom, Security and Justice'.[98] The flagship outcome of that summit was the

90 K. Landgren (n 49) 14.
91 K. Landgren (n 49) 14.
92 K. Landgren (n 49) 14.
93 CVCE, 'The Third Pillar of the European Union: Justice and Home Affairs' (CVCE) <https://www.cvce.eu/en/education/unit-content/-/unit/02bb76df-d066-4c08-a58a-d4686a3e68ff/9370a173-d882-4484-974a-f4002c3bd17a> accessed 21 April 2021.
94 K. Landgren (n 49) 8–22.
95 K. Landgren (n 49) 22.
96 K. Landgren (n 49) 22.
97 K. Landgren (n 49) 13
98 S. Bot, *Le Mandat d'Arrêt Européen* (Éditions Larcier, Brussels 2009) 89–90.

formal endorsement of the principle of 'mutual recognition of judicial decision' that would revolutionise judicial cooperation in criminal matters.[99] The application of this principle requires that decisions made by one EU member state should be accepted and implemented by other EU member states as if they had been made by their own competent authorities, even if a comparable authority does not exist in that member state, or that this authority could not or would have not made that decision.[100] In practice, this means a higher level of efficiency for judicial cooperation, of automaticity even.[101]

The adoption of the mutual recognition principle in Tampere made another conclusion of the Summit possible: the abolition of formal extradition procedures among EU member states and their replacement by a simple transfer of persons,[102] an initiative tabled by Spanish authorities[103] (under Aznar's leadership).[104] The momentum was favourable for this type of initiative at the time. The imminent accession of 10 new member states created a strong impetus for advancing extradition practices. Negotiating among 15 members was already challenging, reaching agreements with 10 additional members was expected to be even more difficult. Consequently, any ambitious objectives the EU aimed to achieve in the long term needed to be accomplished before the major enlargement of 2004. This context helps explain the transition from the relatively conventional 1996 Convention on extradition to the more radical European arrest warrant (EAW).[105]

Despite the groundwork being laid for the Europeanisation of terrorism policies, negotiations on the EAW stalled for a long time. The pivotal factor that accelerated its adoption was the 9/11 attacks. According to Kaunert and Léonard, the 9/11 attacks constituted a 'precipitating event' in the collective securitisation of terrorism in the European Union. Until then, terrorism was mainly a domestic concern.[106] Indeed, the terrorist threats faced by member states at that time varied greatly in nature, and their responses to these threats

99 A. Willems, *The Principle of Mutual Trust in EU Criminal Law* (Hart Publishing, Oxford, Dublin 2021) 58.

100 European Commission, Communication from the Commission to the Council and the European Parliament – Mutual recognition of Final Decisions in Criminal Matters (COM(2000) 495 final) 2000, 4.

101 V. Mitsilegas, 'The Limits of Mutual Trust in Europe's Area of Freedom, Security and Justice: From Automatic Inter-State Cooperation to the Slow Emergence of the Individual' [2012] *YEL*. 319, 321.

102 European Council, Tampere European Council 15–16 October 1999 Presidency Conclusions (1999) point 35.

103 E. Guild and M. Garlick (n 77) 71.

104 Encyclopedia Britannica, 'Jose Maria Aznar' (Encyclopedia Britannica 2019) <https://www.britannica.com/biography/Jose-Maria-Aznar> accessed 2 July 2019.

105 M. Plachta, 'European Arrest Warrant: Revolution in Extradition' [2003] *Eur. J. Crime Crim. Law & Crim. Just.* 178, 179.

106 C. Kaunert and S. Lénoard, 'The Collective Securitization of Terrorism in the European Union' [2019] *WEP*. 261, 262–266.

were equally diverse.[107] The authors explain in this regard that while France adopted an approach of dialogue and cooperation with terrorists, the United Kingdom, for instance, replied by increased policing and military presence.[108] The differences among EU member states on terrorism extended to their perceptions of which groups should be considered terrorists. For example, France provided refuge to many ETA members, viewing them as freedom fighters for an extended period, while Spain had a markedly different perspective on the matter.[109]

The 9/11 attacks therefore enabled Spanish authorities to truly export their national political agenda on combating terrorism at the European level and subsume their domestic fight against the ETA with the worldwide war on terror. In the direct aftermath of the attacks, Aznar indeed declared that 9/11 had to happen for other countries to understand and join the Spanish fight against terrorism, adding that the Spanish people had been very lonely in this fight until then and had suffered from a lack of solidarity.[110] Aznar was not shy to capitalise on the attacks to demonstrate the necessity of a unified action against terrorism. The first comment he made on the attacks was during an official visit to Estonia during which he noted that the attacks showed the madness of terrorism and the necessity for all free nations to collectively commit to putting an end to it.[111] Equally, in his message of condolence to US authorities and people following the attacks, he stated that everybody should be concerned by terrorism that knows no borders.[112] A week after the attacks, he wrote in the *Financial Times* that the people of Spain have always wanted everybody to understand that all terrorists are the same.[113]

The 9/11 attacks thus showed to the world what Spain had long asserted: terrorism was a common threat that required a common response. Spanish authorities, understanding first-hand the impact of terrorism on a democracy and the crucial role of international solidarity in combatting it, endorsed the American-led war on terror within the European Union.[114] In doing so, Spain became a key ally for the United States in Europe in the fight against terrorism, as the American discourse on terrorism helped legitimise Spain's

107 C. Kaunert and S. Lénoard, 'The Collective Securitization of Terrorism in the European Union' [2019] *WEP*. 263–264.

108 C. Kaunert and S. Lénoard, 'The Collective Securitization of Terrorism in the European Union' [2019] *WEP*. 264.

109 M. Heiberg, 'ETA: Euskadi "ta Askatasuna"' in M. Heiberg, B. O'Leary & J. Tirman (eds), *Terror, Insurgency, and the State: Ending Protracted Conflicts* (University of Pennsylvania Press, 2007) 42, quoted in C. Kaunert and S. Lénoard (n 106) 269.

110 E.-P. Guittet (n 26) 456.

111 E.-P. Guittet (n 26) 456–457.

112 E.-P. Guittet (n 26) 456–457.

113 E.-P. Guittet (n 26) 456–457.

114 E.-P. Guittet (n 27) 443.

desire to address domestic terrorism, which had now been recognised as a common threat.[115] Because the 9/11 attacks had established the war on terror as evidence, the necessity for democratic solidarity had equally become unquestionable.[116]

The 2002 EAW: effectively abolishing the political offence exception

Context and content of the EAW

Following the attacks, the political agreement on the EAW[117] was reached in just over three months at the European Summit of Laeken on 14–15 December 2001. The signature of the agreement was initially supposed to coincide with the Spanish presidency in the first quarter of 2002 in response to Spain's problems with ETA, but the New York attacks precipitated the negotiations.[118] Still, the Protocol's formal adoption took place under the Spanish presidency, with Mariano Rajoy signing the document on 13 June 2002. This event marked the realisation of Spain's long-standing desire to implement this tool.[119] The EAW is the first – and most successful – instrument of the mutual recognition principle in European criminal law.[120]

The framework decision on the EAW, composed of 35 articles, brought about seven main changes to extradition procedures:

1. The first one is the judicialisation of the procedure.[121] The executive power is completely taken out of the equation; the warrants only travel between the hands of judicial authorities;
2. The procedure is of a summary nature. The evidence supporting the warrant is not needed anymore, the warrant suffices;
3. The EAW introduces strict time limits for the surrender of the person: the final decision must be taken within 10 days if the person agrees to their surrender and 60 if they do not.
4. The double criminality principle is abolished for a list of 32 categories of offences, provided that they are punishable by a custodial sentence or detention order of at least three years in the issuing member state;[122]

115 E.-P. Guittet (n 27) 443.
116 E.-P. Guittet (n 26) 457.
117 Council Framework Decision of 13 June 2002 on the European Arrest Warrant and the Surrender Procedures Between Member States 2002/584/JHA [2002] OJ L 190.
118 C. Kaunert and S. Léonard (n 106) 269.
119 E.-P. Guittet (n 13) 2–3.
120 A. Willems (n 99) 57.
121 G. Vermeulen (n 2) 70.
122 J. R. Spencer, 'The European Arrest Warrant' [2004] *Camb. Yearb. Eur. Leg. Stud.* 201, 205–206.

5. The speciality rule has been optionally abolished. This has been done on a reciprocal basis, so it applies only in relation to states that have also chosen to do so. As in the 1996 Convention, the specialty principle is lifted when the prosecution or trial of the offence does not lead to deprivation of liberty;[123]
6. The rights of the person under arrest are still guaranteed but more limited than before. Legal advice and an interpreter must still be available; the person must still have access to a hearing in case they contest their extradition; the discrimination clause remains; similarly, surrender is forbidden if there are risks of torture or inhumane and degrading treatment or punishment; guarantees against trials in absentia or life imprisonment are also foreseen; and every surrender must respect the principles recognised by article 6 of the Treaty on the European Union. However, there is nothing expressly precluding the surrender in case the executing state fears that the rights to a fair trial will not be respected – although the preamble of the framework decision does refer to the EU Charter on Fundamental Rights whose chapter 6 includes the right to a fair trial; [124]
7. Finally, grounds for refusal are strictly limited to three mandatory and seven optional ones. Some of the most classical ones, such as the refusal to extradite for political and fiscal offences, as well as on grounds of nationality are absent from the Framework Decision.[125]

The political offence exception absent from the grounds for refusal

The protection of political crimes was thus effectively abolished with this Framework Decision. Although the 1996 Convention also sought to eliminate it, it still provided loopholes that enabled member states to protect political offenders if they so desired; not to mention that the Convention never actually entered into force among all EU member states. The EAW truly delivered the *coup de grâce* to the protection of political crimes in the European Union by omitting any reference to them. Although often hailed as a revolutionary tool, it was, in reality, a continuation of, and could not have been conceptualised without, the depoliticisation process that had been unfolding in the years leading up to its adoption.[126] The only remainder from the political offence exemption was the discrimination clause included in the preamble,

123 Or "when the person having had an opportunity to leave the territory of the member state to which he or she has been surrendered has not done so within 45 days of his or her final discharge, or has returned to that territory after leaving it". Council Framework Decision of 13 June 2002 on the European Arrest Warrant and the Surrender Procedures Between Member States (n 117) (Art. 27).
124 J. R. Spencer (n 122) 205–206.
125 J. R. Spencer (n 122) 205–206.
126 E.-P. Guittet (n 13) 13.

which has been flagged by certain authors as a strategy betraying the member states' incapacity to agree on the need to impose express obligations.[127]

The discrimination clause (preamble): an unsatisfying alternative for the protection of political offenders

The efficacity of such a clause, both as a safeguard against persecution and as a residual political offence exception clause, is limited for two reasons.

First, if the discrimination clause was, indeed, since 1957, part of the political offence exemption clause, it quickly became a self-standing provision, as outlined in the previous chapter. This holds true in the context of the European Union, where the discrimination clause found its place in the preambles of different conventions on mutual legal assistance while the protection of political offences was being weakened. The discrimination clause can, in theory, protect political offenders but only if they are at risk of being persecuted. This is a major difference between the political offence exemption clause and the discrimination clause. The discrimination clause can protect a political offender *despite* the person having committed an offence but only if they are at risk of political persecution. The political offence exemption protects the offender *because of* the offence they committed. In practice, this might not change much for the person subject to extradition as they can be protected in both cases (and, since the adoption of the Aznar Protocol, the potentially persecuted person cannot claim asylum in the EU anyway – except in Belgium – so the discrimination clause can hardly lead to formal protection). Ideologically speaking, however, their approach is diametrically opposed. One protects victims, the other offenders. The Framework decision on the EAW nevertheless foresees that the surrender mechanism can be suspended "in the event of a serious and persistent breach by one of the member states of the principles"[128] of "liberty, democracy, respect for human rights and fundamental freedoms, and the rule of law".[129] The argument, however, remains valid since the suspension is not meant to protect the offender but the system of the EAW. By protecting EU values on which mutual trust and therefore recognition are based, this provision protects the EAW system from those who would seek to undermine it.

The second reason why the discrimination clause is not a workable alternative to the political offence exception is that using one or the other of the protection mechanisms has substantial effects on the burden of proof for the person sought. With the political offence exemption, the person just needed to assert the political character of the offence they committed. Proving the potential for persecution, by comparison, places a significantly heavier burden

127 H. Nowell-Smith, 'Behind the Scenes in the Negotiations of EU Criminal Justice Legislation' [2012] *NJECL*. 381, 381–393.

128 Council Framework Decision of 13 June 2002 on the European Arrest Warrant and the Surrender Procedures Between Member States (n 117) (Preamble §10).

129 Treaty on European Union (Consolidated Version) - Treaty of Maastricht [1992] OJ C 325/5 (Art. 6(1)).

on both the individual targeted by the warrant and the judicial authorities of the executing state. The person subject to the warrant would need to provide evidence of the risks of persecution in the issuing country. Additionally, the judicial authorities of the executing state would be required to conduct thorough research into the political and rule of law situation in the issuing member state. This process could also lead to diplomatic tensions if the executing state issues a positive assessment regarding the risk of persecution.[130] Indeed, while the principle of neutrality is supposed to protect the states from potential diplomatic backlashes, the *Garcia–Moreno* case showed that it is not always effective in doing so. Nevertheless, without this principle, the issuing state can more easily denounce a judgement from the executing state on its internal affairs and even a foreign interference in domestic affairs.[131] Overall, authors like Weyembergh and Bribosia are thus sceptical of the ability of this discrimination clause in protecting political offenders, as they fear that the interests of the individual would be sacrificed in favour of maintaining good diplomatic relations.[132] Paul Bekaert – the lawyer of Garcia and Moreno, as well as other (separatist) minorities – reported always having recourse to the discrimination clause in extradition proceedings concerning freedom fighters/terrorists/political dissidents but with very limited success.[133] This is unsurprising, given that the EAW also abolished the *prima facie requirement*, which previously obligated the state receiving the extradition request to assess whether the case had merit on the surface. The abolition of this requirement has been widely criticised at the time for enabling politically motivated charges to pass through the net of mutual trust.[134] As far as the discrimination clause is concerned, the abolition of this requirement fundamentally questions its applicability.

The 2002 Framework Decision on Combating Terrorism: politicising terrorism

Defining terrorism (art. 1): criminalising the (political) intent

The date of the formal adoption of the EAW, 13 June 2002, was also the day of the adoption of the Framework Decision on Combating Terrorism.

130 H. van der Wilt, 'The Political Offence Exception in Extradition Law: An Antidote to Prefixed Ideas about Political Integration in Europe' [1997] *MJECL.* 25, 49.

131 H. van der Wilt, 'The Political Offence Exception in Extradition Law: An Antidote to Prefixed Ideas about Political Integration in Europe' [1997] *MJECL.* 25, 49.

132 A. Weyembergh and E. Bribosia (n 14) 84.

133 Interview with Paul Bekaert (n 15).

134 A. Willems, 'The Extradition Saga Continues: Is the Latest Ruling a Win for Puigdemont, Spain, or for Mutual Trust?' (EUROPP blog - LSE 2018) <http://blogs.lse.ac.uk/europpblog/2018/07/18/the-extradition-saga-continues-is-the-latest-ruling-a-win-for-puigdemont-spain-or-for-mutual-trust/> accessed 23 October 2018.

The Framework Decisions on Combating Terrorism[135] and the EAW were both part of a 'package deal' adopted to combat terror in reaction to the 9/11 attacks.[136] One of the main purposes of the 13-article-long Framework Decision on Combating Terrorism is to define terrorism and offences linked thereto. It also requires EU member states to introduce minimum penalties for terrorist offences.

The Framework Decision defines the terrorist offence as a combination of act and intent.[137] The act alone does not constitute a terrorist offence, nor does the intent. It is the combination of both that forms the terrorist offence. Upon examination of the objective part of the definition, which pertains to the acts, it appears that these were already criminal offences long before the adoption of the Framework Decision. In fact, most of these acts were criminalised in the UN Conventions on terrorism, as discussed in the previous chapter:

(a) attacks upon a person's life which may cause death;
(b) attacks upon the physical integrity of a person;
(c) kidnapping or hostage taking;
(d) causing extensive destruction to a Government or public facility, a transport system, an infrastructure facility, including an information system, a fixed platform located on the continental shelf, a public place or private property likely to endanger human life or result in major economic loss;
(e) seizure of aircraft, ships or other means of public or goods transport;
(f) manufacture, possession, acquisition, transport, supply or use of weapons, explosives or of nuclear, biological or chemical weapons, as well as research into, and development of, biological and chemical weapons;
(g) release of dangerous substances, or causing fires, floods or explosions the effect of which is to endanger human life;
(h) interfering with or disrupting the supply of water, power or any other fundamental natural resource the effect of which is to endanger human life;
(i) threatening to commit any of the acts listed in (a) to (h).[138]

What is interesting here is that even though all these acts were already criminalised as part of UN and CoE counterterrorism efforts of which EU member states were part, the EU legislator thought it necessary to specifically define the terrorist intent. The open purpose of the Framework Decision was thus

135 Council Framework Decision of 13 June 2002 on Combating Terrorism 2002/475/JHA [2002] OJ L 164.
136 European Commission, Europe Must Have Common Instruments to Tackle Terrorism (IP/01/1284) 2001.
137 C. Kaunert and S. Léonard (n 106) 269.
138 Council Framework Decision of 13 June 2002 on Combating Terrorism (n 135).

to define, criminalise, and punish more heavily acts committed with a specific intent.[139] The Framework Decision delineates three types of terrorist intent:

1. seriously intimidating a population, or
2. unduly compelling a Government or international organisation to perform or abstain from performing any act, or
3. seriously destabilizing or destroying the fundamental political, constitutional, economic or social structures of a country or an international organization.[140]

The first two are standard provisions that are found in most UN instruments on terrorism, which were subsequently incorporated into CoE tools. The third provision is an EU novelty, also adopted in the CoE Convention on the Prevention of Terrorism, as outlined in the previous chapter. As discussed in Chapter 3, by categorising the intent to "seriously destabilize or destroy the fundamental political, constitutional, economic, or social structures of a country or an international organization" as a terroristic intent, the Framework Decision redefined the political motive behind such crimes as a terrorist motive. This understanding of the terrorist intent was inspired by the anti-terror legislation of the only six EU member states who had specifically codified the terrorist offence in their criminal code (France, Germany, Italy, Portugal, Spain, the United Kingdom).[141] The other EU member states did not have a distinct category for terrorist offences in their legal systems. Embracing the post-9/11 spirit of overcoming national differences in the collective fight against terrorism, the Framework Decision aimed to harmonise the criminal codes of all EU member states with those of the six that had specific terrorist offences.

Whereas the EAW abolished once and for all the protection of political offenders, the Framework Decision on Combating Terrorism thus went a step further and criminalised the political purpose of crimes.[142] Guittet argues that Spanish authorities had a crucial role in designing the latter intent essentially enabling the criminalisation of dissent so that they could frame the Basque opposition as terrorism and use counterterrorism measures to fight them.[143]

139 European Commission, Report from the Commission based on Article 11 of the Council Framework Decision of 13 June 2002 on Combating Terrorism (COM(2004) 409 final) 2004, 5.

140 Council Framework Decision of 13 June 2002 on Combating Terrorism (n 135).

141 European Commission, Explanatory Memorandum of the Proposal for a Council Framework Decision on Combating Terrorism COM/2001/0521 final - CNS 2001/0217 [2001] OJ C 332E, 300–304.

142 J. Jansson, *Terrorism, Criminal Law and Politics. The Decline of the Political Offence Exception to Extradition* (Routledge, Abingdon, New York 2020) 218.

143 E.-P. Guittet (n 26) 458.

With this third intent, the Framework Decision thus reversed the relationship of criminal law to political crimes. While political crimes used to be considered a special category of crimes deserving of protection, the Framework Decision reclassified them as a type of crime that should be subject to further criminalisation. As a result, although the depoliticisation of political crimes culminated with the EAW, they were simultaneously re-politicised with the Framework Decision on Combating Terrorism.

Increasing human rights safeguards

According to the Framework Definition, the "universal values of human dignity, liberty, equality and solidarity, respect for human rights and fundamental freedoms"[144] that unite all member states, and their being "based on the principle of democracy and the principle of the rule of law, principles which are common to the member states" allowed and justified the adoption of this tool.[145] Regardless of the allegedly already high standards of human rights protection in the European Union, additional human rights safeguards were nevertheless added to the Framework Decision.

The first one is found in the tenth recital of its preamble, which not only refers to the European Convention for the Protection of Human Rights and Fundamental Freedoms but also especially emphasises that this Framework Decision may not

> be interpreted as being intended to reduce or restrict fundamental rights or freedoms such as the right to strike, freedom of assembly, of association or of expression, including the right of everyone to form and to join trade unions with others for the protection of his or her interests and the related right to demonstrate.[146]

If it is regrettable that this provision did not make it to the core of the text and remained a preambular provision, the second paragraph of the first article defining the terrorist offence mitigates this shortcoming by reminding that the Framework Decision does not affect the obligations of the member states to respect fundamental rights.

The third and final safeguard is a declaration that the Council issued following concerns raised by the European Parliament, non-governmental organisations, and academics about the fact that the Framework Decision could be construed as enabling member states to incriminate demonstrators on terrorism charges. The declaration seeks to prevent the potentially detrimental

144 Council Framework Decision of 13 June 2002 on Combating Terrorism (n 135) (Preamble).
145 Council Framework Decision of 13 June 2002 on Combating Terrorism (n 135) (Preamble).
146 Council Framework Decision of 13 June 2002 on Combating Terrorism (n 135) (Preamble).

effects of the Framework Decision on human rights defenders.[147] It more specifically clarifies that the Framework Decision should not be construed as an invitation to categorise as terrorists those who have fought to preserve or restore democratic values, as was the case in some member states during World War II. It also warns against categorising those using their right to freedom of expression as terrorists, even if they commit offence while exercising this right.[148] This declaration, created with the freedom fighters of World War II in mind, does not facilitate the application of the Framework Decision.[149] Peers points out in this respect that it reignited the debate over the 'just war' principle,[150] which is precisely the moral and political issue the Framework Decision had eliminated. While the Framework Decision invalidated the legitimacy of actions against the state, this declaration reintroduced the notion that some political crimes might be justified under specific circumstances. However, in practice, the complications arising from this declaration remain hypothetical, largely because its legal status and implications are unclear, and because the CJEU does not recognise such declarations related to Community law as having binding effect.[151]

Criticisms of the Framework Decision on its potential effects on fundamental rights

Despite the additional human rights safeguards it contained, the Framework Decision generated considerable criticism, with three main points standing out.

The first main criticism concerned the way in which the Framework Decision was adopted, which did not allow a healthy democratic process to take place. In a biting opinion attached to an European Parliament (EP) report on the Framework Decision on Combating Terrorism, some Members of the European Parliament (MEPs) warned that the adoption of the Framework Decision did not allow the democratic process to follow its normal course because of the climate or urgency surrounding its adoption, which allowed the adoption of a definition of terrorism dangerously threatening human rights and the rule of law. MEPs were more specifically concerned about the fact that the Framework Decision had been adopted under unprecedented time pressure, that it did not allow adequate preparations, and that it proposed a definition of terrorism opening the way to arbitrary law enforcement. MEPs

147 J. Monar, 'Justice and Home Affairs' [2002] *JCMS.* 121, 130.

148 European Council, Outcome of Proceedings of 6 Dec 2001, Statement No 2 (Council Doc. 14845/1/02) 2001, 15, quoted in S. Peers, 'EU Responses to Terrorism' [2003] *ICLQ.* 227, 235–236.

149 B. Saul, *Defining Terrorism in International Law* (Oxford University Press, Oxford 2006) 89.

150 S. Peers (n 148) 236.

151 S. Peers (n 148) 236.

subscribing to this opinion were also worried that the decision would allow the criminalisation of democratic actions and would considerably extend the surveillance powers of the police and the possibilities for covert investigations. Declaring that this initiative was a legal catastrophe, the opinion denounced the impotence of lawmakers that led to the adoption of this initiative.[152] The accessory role of the EP in the adoption of the two Framework Decisions of 13 June 2002 was also criticised in a later minority opinion signed by Maurizio Turco, an Italian MEP, who pointed out that in the adoption process of the two Framework Decisions, the EP had been completely sidelined and that the Framework Decision as currently worded could do more damage to the principle of democracy and constitutional government than terrorism itself.[153] Accusations that a tool advertised to protect fundamental rights, democracy, and, more generally, common European values actually flouted most of them in the course of its own adoption did not provide reassurance against the potential hazard that such a tool could cause on these values, let alone its ability to protect them.

The second criticism concerned the definition of terrorism itself. While some commentators welcomed the definition as a necessary step,[154] human rights organisations viewed this definition as too broad[155] and therefore problematic for fundamental rights, despite the provisions seeking to protect them.[156] The EU Network of Independent Experts in Fundamental Rights (CFR-CDF) considered that the EU definition of terrorism could not satisfy the lawfulness requirement because of the lack of precision in the definition of the offence. The CFR-CDF deemed the provision aiming at safeguarding human rights in the preamble equally vague and therefore unable to alleviate the risks linked to the unclarity of the definition of terrorism. As for the fundamental rights safeguards that the Council declaration seeking to protect those who fight for democratic values was supposed to provide, it was said to

152 European Parliament, Report 1. On the Commission proposal for a Council Framework Decision on Combatting Terrorism (COM(2001)521-C5-0452/2001–2001/0217(CNS)) 2. On the Commission proposal for a Council Framework Decision on the European arrest warrant and the Surrender Procedures Between the Member States (COM(2001)552-C5–0453/2001–2001/0215(CNS)) (A5–0397/2001) 2001, 53.

153 European Parliament, Report 1. On the Commission proposal for a Council Framework Decision on Combatting Terrorism (COM(2001)521-C5–0452/2001–2001/0217(CNS)) 2. On the Commission proposal for a Council Framework Decision on the European arrest warrant and the Surrender Procedures Between the Member States (COM(2001)552-C5–0453/2001–2001/0215(CNS)) (A5–0397/2001) 2001, 8.

154 E. Dimitriu, 'The E.U.'s Definition of Terrorism: The Council Framework Decision on Combating Terrorism' [2004] *Ger. Law J.* 585, 602.

155 Amnesty International EU Office, 'Human Rights Dissolving at the Borders? Counter-Terrorism and EU Criminal Law' [2005] 10.

156 O. Bures, 'EU Counterterrorism Policy: A Paper Tiger?' [2006] *Terror Polit. Violenc.* 57, 67.

only add to the confusion by going in another direction than the Framework Decision.[157]

The fallouts of the Framework Decision were a third source of concern. Peers noted in this respect that besides the specific crimes anti-terror legislations criminalise, one should be especially wary of the special investigative powers that these legislations grant to the states in order to combat terrorism.[158] In this respect, the Framework Decision came with a copious amount of measures.[159] Peers reported that measures aimed at tackling terrorism as worded in the Framework Decision started being adopted as early as December 2001 – *i.e. before* the formal adoption of the Framework Decision – despite ongoing concerns and reservations from the European Parliament on the definition of terrorism as worded in the Framework Decision and despite the fact that the second reading opinion of the European Parliament was only issued in February 2002.[160] These measures not only evaded parliamentary and judicial scrutiny thanks to a strategic selection of legal basis, but by copying the definition of terrorism as drafted in the Framework Decision instead of making a cross-reference to it, Peers further noted that they circumvented the clauses protecting human rights that the Framework Decision contained.[161] The Framework Decision also led to a cascade of very far-reaching measures, many of which were initiated by the Spanish presidency.[162] These measures, derived from the (not even yet adopted) Framework Decision, often bypassed the fundamental rights safeguards that were included in the Framework Decision itself. In an earlier version of one of these measures on the exchange of information, the Spanish presidency went as far as assimilating protestors at European summits and other similar events as a 'cat's paw' for terrorist organisations and accordingly sought to target them in the proposal.[163] Peers commented in this respect that this suggestion was so inconsistent with

157 EU Network of Independent Experts in Fundamental Rights (CFR-CDF), 'The Balance Between Freedom and Security in the Response by the European Union and its Member States to the Terrorist Threats' (Statewatch 2003) <http://www.statewatch.org/media/documents/news/2003/apr/CFR-CDF.ThemComment1.pdf> accessed 10 July 2019.
158 S. Peers (n 148) 237.
159 Council Common Position of 27 December 2001 on Combating Terrorism 2001/930/CFSP [2001] OJ L 344; Council Common Position of 27 December 2001 on the Application of Specific Measures to Combat Terrorism 2001/931/CFSP [2001] OJ L 344; Council Regulation No 2580/2001 of 27 December 2001 on Specific Restrictive Measures Directed Against Certain Persons and Entities with a View to Combating Terrorism [2001] OJ L 344; Council Decision of 27 December 2001 Establishing the List Provided for in Article 2(3) of Council Regulation No 2580/2001 on Specific Restrictive Measures Directed Against Certain Persons and Entities with a View to Combating Terrorism 2001/927/EC [2001] OJ L 344, quoted in S. Peers (n 148) 227–243.
160 S. Peers (n 148) 237.
161 S. Peers (n 148) 237.
162 S. Peers (n 148) 240–242.
163 S. Peers (n 148) 242.

the declaration attached to the Framework Decision that it was suggested either because of the uncertainty surrounding the legal value of the declaration or because of sheer contempt for it.[164] The final version eventually erased that reference to protestors, but the rapidity of how the definition of terrorism gave way to abusive interpretations of the Framework Decision's definition of 'terrorism' remains compelling. As a result, despite the Framework Decision's existing and supposedly robust provisions for safeguarding human rights, Peers questioned whether fundamental rights, such as freedom of assembly and expression, would be fully respected after the adoption of the Framework Decision in a context in which destabilisation and propaganda were targeted by member states.[165]

The 2008 amendments of the Framework Decision and its repeal by the 2017 directive on combatting terrorism

The 2002 Framework Decision on Combating Terrorism was amended in 2008 and repealed in 2017 by a directive aimed at dealing with foreign fighters.[166] With the Treaty of Lisbon having come into effect in the meantime, the directive was adopted under the co-decision procedure, involving the European Parliament as a co-legislator and subjecting the tool to judicial scrutiny by the Court of Justice, which made it less problematic than the 2002 Framework Decision in terms of democratic and judicial accountability.

The 2008 amendment was made to align the 2002 Framework Decision with the 2005 CoE Convention on the Prevention of Terrorism that criminalised public provocation, recruitment, and training for terrorism when done intentionally and unlawfully.[167] The amended Framework Decision inluded those crimes to the list of acts to be criminalised by the 2002 Framework Decision, as well as the aiding, abetting, inciting, or attempts to commit offences listed in articles 2 and 3 of the 2002 Framework Decision.[168] It also made specific mention of the fact that the latter did not affect the obligation of EU member states to safeguard freedom of expression and, in particular, of the press (and other media) in the application of the Framework Decision.[169]

164 S. Peers (n 148) 242.
165 S. Peers (n 148) 242–243.
166 Directive (EU) 2017/541 of the European Parliament and of the Council of 15 March 2017 on Combating Terrorism and Replacing Council Framework Decision 2002/475/JHA and Amending Council Decision 2005/671/JHA [2017] OJ L 88 (Preamble).
167 Council Framework Decision 2008/919/JHA of 28 November 2008 Amending Framework Decision 2002/475/JHA on Combating Terrorism [2008] OJ L 330 (Preamble).
168 Council Framework Decision 2008/919/JHA of 28 November 2008 Amending Framework Decision 2002/475/JHA on Combating Terrorism [2008] OJ L 330 (Preamble) (Art. 1).
169 Council Framework Decision 2008/919/JHA of 28 November 2008 Amending Framework Decision 2002/475/JHA on Combating Terrorism [2008] OJ L 330 (Preamble) (Art. 2).

As for the 2017 Directive that repealed the 2002 Framework Decision, it essentially reproduced the definition of terrorism drawn in 2002, along with its associated ambiguities, with two notable exceptions. First, it added illegal system and data interference (as referred to in EU tools on the matter) in specific cases to the list of terrorist offences. Second, it expanded the list of prohibited weapons to include certain types that were not covered by the 2002 Framework Decision.[170] The Directive, mirroring the CoE Convention of 2005 on the Prevention of Terrorism and its additional Protocol of 2015 (both implementing United Nations Security Council (UNSC) resolutions),[171] criminalises – but does not define as terrorist – the following offences: public provocation to commit a terrorist offence (article 5), recruitment for terrorism (article 6), providing training for terrorism (article 7), receiving training for terrorism (article 8), travelling for the purpose of terrorism (article 9), organising or otherwise facilitating travelling for the purpose of terrorism (article 10), and terrorism financing (article 11), as well as other offences related to terrorist activities (article 12). The Directive further regulates the use of investigative tools and confiscation (article 20) as well as measures the states can take against public provocation content online (article 21). Because it seeks to criminalise pre-emptive actions potentially leading to terrorism, the range of criminalisation of actions in the Directive is much wider than before. The clause protecting fundamental rights was therefore strengthened and incorporated into the core of the text, becoming a self-standing article. This article references article 6 of the Treaty on the European Union and specifically highlights the particularly vulnerable rights of the press and media.[172]

Given the context in which this Directive was adopted – namely European citizens travelling to war zones, particularly in Syria and Iraq, and posing a significant security threat upon their return[173] – the EU and its member states aimed to prevent such behaviour from occurring in the first place. However, pre-emptive security strategies come with controversial practices.[174] If this was already true for the 2002 Framework Decision on Combating Terrorism, it was all the more applicable to this Directive whose main purpose is prevention.

170 Directive (EU) 2017/541 of the European Parliament and of the Council of 15 March 2017 on Combating Terrorism and Replacing Council Framework Decision 2002/475/JHA and Amending Council Decision 2005/671/JHA (n 166) (Art. 3).

171 Council of Europe, Explanatory Report to the European Convention on the Prevention of Terrorism (2005) 2.

172 Directive (EU) 2017/541 of the European Parliament and of the Council of 15 March 2017 on Combating Terrorism and Replacing Council Framework Decision 2002/475/JHA and Amending Council Decision 2005/671/JHA (n 166) (Art. 23).

173 European Commission, Explanatory Memorandum of the Proposal for a Directive of the European Parliament and of the Council on Combating Terrorism and Replacing Council Framework Decision 2002/475/JHA on Combating Terrorism (COM(2015) 625 final) 2015, 2.

174 M. Goede, 'The Politics of Preemption and the War on Terror in Europe' [2008] *Eur. J. Int. Relat.* 161, 162.

Murphy pointed out in this respect that the shift operated in the EU towards the criminalisation of pre-emptive actions has enhanced systems of social control to a point where they are not compliant with legal principles anymore but can still be sanctioned as lawful by courts.[175] It is therefore unfortunate that the tools adopted as part of EU counterterrorism measures did not come with a denunciation clause as the one found in the CoE Conventions or the Aznar Protocol and the European arrest warrant, which give the possibility to suspend the application of those tools to states for which article 7 of the Treaty on the European Union (TEU) has been triggered. Cooperation in criminal matters, including for counterterrorism purposes, should not be a loyalty test of democratic solidarity among EU member states, which authors such as Guittet argue that they consistently have been.[176]

Conclusion

The Spanish campaign to pursue ever more cooperation at the EU level, driven by its fight against the ETA, proved to be largely successful. Spanish authorities managed to eliminate the right to asylum in the European Union for EU citizens and redefine the EU agenda on counterterrorism at the centre of which they put the automaticity of extradition.[177] The New York attacks helped advance this objective, as they enabled EU member states to overcome old rivalries and feuds by focusing on common efforts towards combatting terrorism.[178] The 9/11 attacks underscored the imperative of combating terrorism, thereby diminishing the relevance and applicability of the political offence exception clause. In this context, the fight against terrorism shifted the role of human rights in criminal cooperation; previously, human rights protections justified and facilitated such cooperation. After the attacks, however, human rights were seen as obstacles to cooperation, and limiting them was framed as necessary to safeguard citizens from the greater threat of terrorism.[179] At the EU level, the political offence exception has thus been abolished, and extradition has been streamlined to a point of near automaticity. The Framework Decision on Combating Terrorism further reframed the political intent of crimes as a terrorist intent and doing so reversed the relation of EU criminal law to political offences.

From the abolition of the right to asylum for EU citizens to the near automaticity of extradition that removed most barriers to surrender, Spain's ambition to enhance the EU counterterrorism framework effectively materialised. However, the existence of these new tools, regardless of their binding

175 C. Murphy, 'The legal Response to Terrorism of the European Union and Council of Europe' in B. Saul (ed), *Research Handbook on International Law and Terrorism* (Edward Elgar Publishing, 2014) 693.
176 E.-P. Guittet (n 13) 8–9.
177 E.-P. Guittet (n 13) 8–9.
178 E.-P. Guittet (n 13) 4–5.
179 E.-P. Guittet (n 13) 14.

nature, still does not guarantee that executing member states will comply with them if they see reasons not to. A case in point lies in the latest extradition request for Garcia and Moreno. As soon as the Framework Decision on the EAW entered into force in 2004, Spanish authorities issued another warrant for the surrender of Garcia and Moreno.[180] This time, Belgian judicial authorities had little choice but to grant the surrender, as neither the fact that the couple had become Belgian nor the long-gone political offence exemption could prevent it.[181] However, they once again declined the surrender, citing the statute of limitations under Belgian law and adopting a broad interpretation of Belgium's jurisdiction based on the active personality principle, enabled by the couple's prior naturalisation.[182] This episode therefore shows that regardless of the claimed need to further counterterrorism cooperation, forced solidarity does not work.

Bibliography

Legislation and official publications

European Union

Consolidated Version of the Treaty on the Functioning of the European Union - PROTOCOLS - Protocol (No. 24) on Asylum for Nationals of Member States of the European Union [2008] OJ C 115.

Convention Drawn up on the Basis of Article K.3 of the Treaty on European Union, on Simplified Extradition Procedure Between the Member States of the European Union [1995] OJ C 78.

Convention Drawn up on the Basis of Article K.3 of the Treaty on European Union, Relating to Extradition Between the Member States of the European Union [1996] OJ C 313.

Council Common Position of 27 December 2001 on the Application of Specific Measures to Combat Terrorism 2001/931/CFSP [2001] OJ L 344.

Council Common Position of 27 December 2001 on Combating Terrorism 2001/930/CFSP [2001] OJ L 344.

Council Decision of 27 December 2001 Establishing the List Provided for in Article 2(3) of Council Regulation No 2580/2001 on Specific Restrictive Measures Directed Against Certain Persons and Entities with a View to Combating Terrorism 2001/927/EC [2001] OJ L 344.

Council Framework Decision of 13 June 2002 on Combating Terrorism 2002/475/JHA [2002] OJ L 164.

Council Framework Decision of 13 June 2002 on the European Arrest Warrant and the Surrender Procedures Between Member States 2002/584/JHA [2002] OJ L 190.

Council of the European Union, Avis Concernant l'Entrée en Vigueur de la Convention de 1996 Relative à l'Extradition 2019/C 329/02 [2019] OJ C 329/2.

180 Interview with Paul Bekaert (n 15).

181 J. Kwik, 'Not without a Fight: Moreno-Garcia and the Tug-of-War of Extradition' [2016] 2–4.

182 J. Kwik, 'Not without a fight: Moreno-Garcia and the Tug-of-War of Extradition' [2016] 3.

Council Regulation No 2580/2001 of 27 December 2001 on Specific Restrictive Measures Directed Against Certain Persons and Entities with a View to Combating Terrorism [2001] OJ L 344.

Directive (EU) 2017/541 of the European Parliament and of the Council of 15 March 2017 on Combating Terrorism and Replacing Council Framework Decision 2002/475/JHA and Amending Council Decision 2005/671/JHA [2017] OJ L 88.

European Commission, Communication from the Commission to the Council and the European Parliament – Mutual recognition of Final Decisions in Criminal Matters (COM(2000) 495 final) 2000.

European Commission, Europe Must Have Common Instruments to Tackle Terrorism (IP/01/1284) 2001.

European Commission, Explanatory Memorandum of the Proposal for a Council framework Decision on Combating Terrorism COM/2001/0521 final - CNS 2001/0217 [2001] OJ C 332E.

European Commission, Explanatory Memorandum of the Proposal for a Directive of the European Parliament and of the Council on Combating Terrorism and Replacing Council Framework Decision 2002/475/JHA on Combating Terrorism (COM(2015) 625 final) 2015.

European Commission, Report from the Commission based on Article 11 of the Council Framework Decision of 13 June 2002 on combating terrorism (COM(2004) 409 final) 2004.

European Council, Madrid European Council 15–16 December 1995 Presidency Conclusions (1995).

European Council, Outcome of Proceedings of 6 Dec 2001, Statement No 2 (Council Doc. 14845/1/02) 2001.

European Council, Tampere European Council 15–16 October 1999 Presidency Conclusions (1999).

European Parliament, Report 1. On the Commission proposal for a Council Framework Decision on Combatting Terrorism (COM(2001)521-C5–0452/2001–2001/0217(CNS)) 2. On the Commission proposal for a Council framework decision on the European arrest warrant and the Surrender Procedures Between the Member States (COM(2001)552-C5–0453/2001–2001/0215(CNS)) (A5–0397/2001) 2001.

European Parliament, Resolution on the European Judicial Area (Extradition) [1982] OJ C 238.

European Parliament, Resolution on the Extradition of Two Presumed ETA Militants [1996] OJ C 65.

European Parliament, Resolution on Terrorism and its Effects on Security in Europe [1994] OJ C 91.

European Union, Convention Relating to Extradition Between the Member States of the European Union – Explanatory Report [1997] OJ C 191.

Treaty on European Union (Consolidated Version) - Treaty of Maastricht [1992] OJ C 325/5.

Council of Europe

Council of Europe, Explanatory Report to the European Convention on the Prevention of Terrorism (2005).

Books

Bossong R., *The Evolution of EU Counter-Terrorism: European Security Policy After 9/11* (Routledge, London and New York 2013).

Bot S., *Le Mandat d'Arrêt Européen* (Éditions Larcier, Brussels 2009).
Guittet E.-P., *Counter-Terror by Proxy: The Spanish State's Illicit War with ETA* (Manchester University Press, Manchester 2021).
Jannin L., Meneghini M., Pauti C., Poupet R. and Moderne F., *Le Droit d'Asile en Europe: Étude Comparée* (L'Harmattan, Paris 1999).
Jansson J., *Terrorism, Criminal Law and Politics. The Decline of the Political Offence Exception to Extradition* (Routledge, Abingdon, New York 2020).
Saul B., *Defining Terrorism in International Law* (Oxford University Press, Oxford 2006).
Shearer I. A., *Extradition in International Law* (Manchester University Press, Manchester 1971).
Willems A., *The Principle of Mutual Trust in EU Criminal Law* (Hart Publishing, Oxford, Dublin 2021).

Journal articles

Bigo D., 'La Mondialisation de l'(In)sécurité? Réflexions sur le Champ des Professionnels de la Gestion des Inquiétudes et Analytique de la Transnationalisation des Processus d'(In)sécurisation' [2005] *C&C (Online)*. 1.
Bures O., 'EU Counterterrorism Policy: A Paper Tiger?' [2006] *Terror Polit. Violenc.* 57.
Dimitriu E., 'The E.U.'s Definition of Terrorism: The Council Framework Decision on Combating Terrorism' [2004] *Ger. Law J.* 585.
Goede M., 'The Politics of Preemption and the War on Terror in Europe' [2008] *Eur. J. Int. Relat.* 161.
Guild E. and Garlick M., 'Refugee Protection, Counter-Terrorism, and Exclusion in the European Union' [2011] *RSQ*. 63.
Guild E. and Zwaan K., 'Does Europe Still Create Refugees? Examining the Situation of the Roma' [2014] *QLJ*. 141.
Guittet E.-P., '"Ne Pas Leur Faire Confiance Serait Leur Faire Offense". Antiterrorisme, Solidarité Démocratique et Identité Politique' [2006] *C&C (Online)*. 1.
Guittet E.-P., 'Political Identity and Democratic Solidarity After 9/11: The Spanish Case' [2004] *Altern. Global Local Polit.* 441.
Kaunert C. and Lénoard S., 'The Collective Securitization of Terrorism in the European Union' [2019] *WEP*. 261.
Mégie A., 'Généalogie du Champ de la Coopération Judiciaire Européenne' [2006] *C&C (Online)*. 1.
Mitsilegas V., 'The Limits of Mutual Trust in Europe's Area of Freedom, Security and Justice: From Automatic Inter-State Cooperation to the Slow Emergence of the Individual' [2012] *YEL*. 319.
Monar J., 'Justice and Home Affairs' [2002] *JCMS*. 121.
Nowell-Smith H., 'Behind the Scenes in the Negotiations of EU Criminal Justice Legislation' [2012] *NJECL*. 381.
Peers S., 'EU Responses to Terrorism' [2003] *ICLQ*. 227.
Plachta M., 'European Arrest Warrant: Revolution in Extradition' [2003] *Eur. J. Crime Crim. Law & Crim. Just.* 178.
Spencer J. R., 'The European Arrest Warrant' [2004] *Camb. Yearb. Eur. Leg. Stud.* 201.
Top S., 'Prosecuting Political Dissent: Discussing the Relevance of the Political Offence Exception in EU Extradition Law in Light of the Catalan Independence Crisis' [2021] *NJECL*. 107.
van der Wilt H., 'The Political Offence Exception in Extradition Law: An Antidote to Prefixed Ideas about Political Integration in Europe' [1997] *MJECL*. 25.
Vermeulen G., 'EU Conventions Enhancing and Updating Traditional Mechanisms for Judicial Cooperation in Criminal Matter' [2006] *Int'l Rev. Penal Law*. 59.

Vermeulen G. and Vander Beken T., 'New Conventions on Extradition in the European Union: Analysis and Evaluation' [1997] *Penn. St. Int'l Law Rev.* 265.

Weyembergh A. and Bribosia E., 'Extradition et Asile: Vers un Espace Judiciaire Européen?' [1997] *RBDI.* 69.

Book chapters

Guittet E.-P., 'L'Imposition de l'Agenda Politique Espagnol à l'Europe de l'Antiterrorisme' in D. Bigo, L. Bonelli & T. Deltombe (eds), *Au Nnom du 11 Septembre . . . Les Démocraties à l'Épreuve de l'Antiterrorisme* (La Découverte, 2008).

Heiberg M., 'ETA: Euskadi "ta Askatasuna"' in M. Heiberg, B. O'Leary & J. Tirman (eds), *Terror, Insurgency, and the State: Ending Protracted Conflicts* (University of Pennsylvania Press, 2007).

Murphy C., 'The Legal Response to Terrorism of the European Union and Council of Europe' in B. Saul (ed), *Research Handbook on International Law and Terrorism* (Edward Elgar Publishing, 2014).

Reports

Amnesty International EU Office, 'Human Rights Dissolving at the Borders? Counter-Terrorism and EU Criminal Law' [2005].

Landgren K., 'Deflecting International Protection by Treaty: Bilateral and Multilateral Accords on Extradition, Readmission and the Inadmissibility of Asylum Requests' [1999] UNHCR, New Issues in Refugee Research, Working Paper No. 10.

Online resources

CVCE, 'The Third Pillar of the European Union: Justice and Home Affairs' (CVCE) <https://www.cvce.eu/en/education/unit-content/-/unit/02bb76df-d066-4c08-a58a-d4686a3e68ff/9370a173-d882-4484-974a-f4002c3bd17a> accessed 21 April 2021.

Encyclopedia Britannica, 'Jose Maria Aznar' (Encyclopedia Britannica 2019) <https://www.britannica.com/biography/Jose-Maria-Aznar> accessed 2 July 2019.

EU Network of Independent Experts in Fundamental Rights (CFR-CDF), 'The Balance Between Freedom and Security in the Response by the European Union and its Member States to the Terrorist Threats' (Statewatch 2003) <http://www.statewatch.org/media/documents/news/2003/apr/CFR-CDF.ThemComment1.pdf> accessed 10 July 2019.

European Union, 'Convention on Extradition Between Member States' (European Union 2005) <https://eur-lex.europa.eu/legal-content/EN/TXT/?uri=LEGISSUM:l14015b> accessed 27 June 2019.

Journal Officiel du Grand-Duché de Luxembourg, 'Convention Établie sur la Base de l'Article K.3 du Traité sur l'Union Européenne, Relative à l'Extradition Entre les États Membres de l'Union Européenne, Faite à Dublin, le 27 Septembre 1996 - Entrée en Vigueur' (Legilux 2019) <http://legilux.public.lu/eli/etat/leg/div/2019/08/07/a714/jo> accessed 12 February 2021.

Willems A., 'The Extradition Saga Continues: Is the Latest Ruling a Win for Puigdemont, Spain, or for Mutual Trust?' (EUROPP blog - LSE 2018) <http://blogs.lse.ac.uk/europpblog/2018/07/18/the-extradition-saga-continues-is-the-latest-ruling-a-win-for-puigdemont-spain-or-for-mutual-trust/> accessed 23 October 2018.

Interviews

Interview with Claude Debrulle, Honorary General Director of the Former Directorate General on Legislation at the Belgian Ministry of Justice (Walloon Brabant, 15 April 2014).

Interview with Paul Bekaert, Lawyer of Luis Moreno Ramajo and Raquel Garcia Arranz (Tielt, 29 November 2018).

Interview with Paul Rietjens, Former Advisor in the Personal Office of the Belgian Minister of Foreign Affairs (Online, 12 December 2021).

Other resources

Kwik J., 'Not without a Fight: Moreno-Garcia and the Tug-of-War of Extradition' [2016].

5 Catalan independence crisis

Understanding the reaction of the Spanish government to Catalan claims of a fight for national liberation

The Catalan independence referendum of 1 October 2017

On 1 October 2017, Catalan separatists did something that was deemed quasi-impossible in today's Europe: they tried to create a new state within European borders by calling a referendum on independence. The turnout on 1 October 2017 was evaluated at 43%, and the results of the referendum favoured independence at 90.18%: 8% of voters voted against independence, and 2% left the ballot blank.[1] The Catalan[2] hopes to form a new state, however, rapidly deflated in the weeks following the referendum. Carles Puigdemont, the Catalan president at the time, declared independence on 10 October only to immediately suspend it;[3] days later, Spanish authorities triggered article 155 that suspended the Statute of Autonomy of Catalonia, enabling them to impose direct rule on Catalonia, and eventually called early elections in Catalonia in December 2017;[4] Puigdemont and his ministers left the country to seek refuge abroad, triggering a series of European and international arrest warrants against them; and those who had remained in Spain were immediately arrested for prosecution. Since then, the independence process has been completely halted, and the people identified as having closely or remotely contributed to it sentenced.[5] In more recent years, sentenced leaders have been pardoned; the Spanish criminal code has been overhauled in a way directly affecting crimes for which Catalan leaders were sentenced; and a new amnesty law targeting those involved in the independence process has been adopted. In

1 N. Marty, *Comprendre la Crise Catalane* (Cairn, France 2019) 115.

2 It is acknowledged that Catalans are Spaniards, but, in the following chapters, the two will be opposed for purposes of clarity and convenience. Equally, the word *Catalans* is used to refer to Catalan separatist authorities, and the word *Spain* is used to refer to Spanish authorities.

3 El Defensor de les Persones (Catalan Ombudsman), 'The Violation of Fundamental Rights and Freedoms Arising from the Criminal Justice Reaction Following October 1, and Application of the Article 155 of the Spanish Constitution' [2018] 9.

4 D. Cetrà and M. Harvey, 'Explaining Accommodation and Resistance to Demands for Independence Referendums in the UK and Spain' [2019] *Nations Natl.* 607, 613.

5 Parliamentary Assembly of the Council of Europe, Should Politicians be Prosecuted for Statements Made in the Exercise of Their Mandate? (Draft Resolution) 2021,18.

DOI: 10.4324/9781003425847-5

the latest regional elections of May 2024, independentists lost their majority in Catalonia, effectively bringing an end to the independence process initiated in 2017.[6]

The project to achieve independence was put in motion on 6 September 2017, when the Catalan Parliament adopted law 19/2017 consecrating the Catalan people sovereign. The law in turn led to the adoption of decree 139/2017 by the Catalan government, calling a referendum on self-determination to be held on 1 October 2017. Despite the Spanish Constitutional Court suspending the law passed on 6 September the following day for further review, Catalan leaders proceeded with organising the referendum.[7] On 8 September, the Catalan Parliament thus passed a law to regulate the transition to independence in case the referendum results favoured that outcome.[8] In response, central authorities launched Operation Anubis, a judicial and police operation aimed at thwarting the referendum;[9] financial audits from central authorities multiplied to ensure that no state fund was used for the organisation of the referendum; criminal prosecutions were launched against members of the Catalan Parliament and government; the superior prosecutor of Catalonia was seized to guarantee the prosecution of all civil servants participating in the organisation of the referendum; the judiciary authorised the closure of all public websites supporting or enabling the referendum; and 6000 Guardia Civil members and policemen were deployed to assist the 5000 local policemen already stationed in Catalonia. Overall, the bill for the Interior Ministry for the mobilisation of security forces was more than €87 million.[10]

In light of all these measures, Catalan separatists contend that the fact that the referendum was able to take place on 1 October was a miracle that was only made possible thanks to the great mobilisation of the Catalan people and grass-roots movements.[11] From the secret transportation of ballot boxes to voting centres to hackers organising themselves to counter what was described as cyber warfare against the Catalan separatist project, or the physical mobilisation of the population passively obstructing the passage of police forces in premises where the referendum was held, the mobilisation of the civilian population was described as instrumental to the effective organisation of the referendum. The Catalan media and people used their smartphones to record

6 Generalitat de Catalunya, '12 M 2024 - Eleccions al Parlament de Catalunya' (GenCat 2024) <https://resultats.eleccionsparlament.cat/ca/inici> accessed 20 June 2024.

7 N. Marty (n 1) 105.

8 M. Guidi and M. Casula, 'The Europeanisation of the Catalan Debate' in C. Closa, C. Margiotta & G. Martinico (eds), *Between Democracy and Law: The Amorality of Secession* (Routledge, 2020) 186.

9 N. Marty (n 1) 107.

10 N. Marty (n 1) 106–107, 117.

11 N. Marty (n 1) 109; R. Botran, 'Civil Society Mobilisation from Below' in I. Bernat & D. Whyte (eds), *Building a New Catalonia: Self-Determination and Emancipation* (Pollen Edicions, 2019) 171–174.

violent police interventions. These images circulated around the globe and sparked immediate global outrage at Spanish authorities.[12]

The sheer number of people on the streets ensuring that the referendum could take place was advanced by Catalan separatist leaders as a clear token of the legitimacy of Catalan independence referendum.[13] Catalan leaders emphasised that the mass mobilisations leading up to the referendum were particularly significant because they arose spontaneously from civil society, despite reported constant harassment from Spanish authorities.[14] People from all walks of life – bakers, butchers, mechanics, doctors, teachers, and others – peacefully came together to help their neighbours vote. According to Catalan leaders, the scale of this mobilisation was so vast that it dispelled any doubts about the legitimacy of the entire process.[15] This massive movement of civil disobedience was thus said to have once and for all anchored the sovereignty process in popular powers and made it an indisputable political process.[16] On top of the scale of the disobedience, its peacefulness was hailed by many pro-independence activists as additional evidence of the democratic and legitimate nature of the referendum, which has often been contrasted with the heavy police violence on the day of the referendum.[17]

Alleging a Catalan fight for national liberation from a Spanish state with strong ties to its Francoist past

Overall, Catalan separatists framed their whole endeavour as a fight for national liberation[18] articulated around the idea that Spain robs them.[19] This justification takes its source in a variety of resentments that are all rooted in a distant past. Susana Narotzky refers to this set of arguments put forward by Catalans to further their cause as historical grievances that she contends are linked to institutional and fiscal inequity and identity.[20] These grievances pertain to the fact that Catalans believe that Franco's legacy is still very much alive today in Spanish

12 N. Marty (n 1) 109–114.

13 C. Puigdemont, *La Crise Catalane. Une Opportunité pour l'Europe. Conversation avec Olivier Mouton* (Racine, Tielt 2018) 10.

14 C. Puigdemont, *La Crise Catalane. Une Opportunité pour l'Europe: Conversation avec Olivier Mouton* (Racine, Tielt 2018) 10–11.

15 C. Puigdemont, *La Crise Catalane. Une Opportunité pour l'Europe: Conversation avec Olivier Mouton* (Racine, Tielt 2018) 156.

16 B. Salellas and G. Serra, 'Necessary Disobedience' in I. Bernat & D. Whyte (eds), *Building a New Catalonia: Self-Determination and Emancipation* (Pollen Edicions, 2019) 166–167.

17 S. Narotzky, 'Evidence Struggles: Legality, Legitimacy and Social Mobilizations in the Catalan Political Conflict' [2019] *IJGLS.* 31, 56–57.

18 P. Wagner, 'Towards a Conceptual History of the Present: Democracy, Rights, and Freedom in the Recent Catalan Conflict' [2018] *Soc. Sci. Inf.* 588, 595–596.

19 C. García, 'The Power of Myths and Storytelling in Nation Building: The Campaign for the Independence of Catalonia from Spain (2012–2015)' [2018] *CJC.* 281, 283.

20 S. Narotzky (n 17) 33.

society. Catalan separatists indeed argue that the transition period after the dictatorship failed to exfoliate the country from all remnants of the dictatorship, leading some to even talk of 'postfacism' today in Spain. The term *postfascism*[21] is often used to refer to the situation in which many people occupying elite positions in the cultural, economic, and institutional spheres at the time of Franco still occupy them today and thereby ensure continuity of the regime in terms of occupation of critical societal positions. As a result, the need to debunk the myth of an exemplary Spanish transition to democracy is presented as paramount to understanding the position of oppression and injustice in which Catalan independentists argue they are today.[22] They contend that unlike countries like Italy and Portugal, which prosecuted and sentenced all persons serving in the fascist regime (which allowed for a clear-cut transition to democracy), fascism still lingers in Spain due to a policy of amnesty adopted in 1977 to absolve all political prisoners, those fighting *against* and *for* Franco alike, to enable a peaceful and inclusive transition to democracy.[23] According to authors like Bernat and Whyte, this means that there has not been a large-scale purge of supporters of – and, perhaps more importantly, of criminals working for – Franco in Spain who were all incorporated into the new regime, without having to renounce to any of their former commitments.[24]

This persistent Francoist heritage is said to be transversal to Spanish society, affecting the cultural and economic, as well as institutional, spheres.[25] Of particular interest to this book are the claims that the whole institutional architecture of the country has been modelled by Franco and has remained almost untouched since then. One example of this is that the current Audiencia Nacional in Spain, the Court that famously sought the prosecution of Catalan separatists in the trial following the referendum, is strikingly similar (identical, some contend)[26] to Franco's Public Order Tribunal, a Court known to

21 Many authors have used this term to denounce many practices, but it was most thoroughly explained by Ignasi Bernat and David Whyte in their book *Building a New Catalonia. Self-Determination and Emancipation* cited later and to which this chapter regularly refers. The book indeed voices arguments that are representative of the position of many authors from a large spectrum of political leanings. It should, however, be noted that the book has a clear political stance that should not be overlooked. Indeed, almost all its contributors are CUP members. The CUP, Popular Unity Candidacy, is a pro-independence anti-capitalist party active in Catalonia.

22 B. Serra i Puig, 'The Post-Dictatorship Transition Years: The Lessons to be Learned from Deceit' in I. I. Bernat & D. Whyte (eds), *Building a New Catalonia. Self-Determination and Emancipation* (Pollen Edicions, 2019) 83.

23 I. Bernat and D. Whyte, 'Catalonia, Postfascism and Popular Sovereignty' in I. Bernat & D. Whyte (eds), *Building a New Catalonia: Self-Determination and Emancipation* (Pollen Edicions, 2019) 26 & 45.

24 N. Marty (n 1) 49.

25 I. Bernat and D. Whyte (n 23) 23–70.

26 C. Ponsatí, 'Political Conflict in Catalonia and the Limits of Spanish Democracy' in B. De Wever, I. Ferreras & P. Van Parijs (eds), *Multi-level Nationalism? The Catalan Question and its Lessons for Belgium and for Europe* (Re-Bel Initiative, 2018) 29.

have been established at the time of the dictatorship to handle political dissent and crimes. The judicial proceedings against Catalans held at the Audiencia Nacional are considered particularly problematic because the process for selecting judges for Spain's highest courts, including the Audiencia Nacional, is described as highly political, with judges being partially appointed by government bodies.[27] Puigdemont decried, in this regard, the appointment of Judge Llarena, the judge repeatedly issuing European arrest warrants against members of the Catalan government in exile, as being utterly political.[28]

On top of this, during the trial, the Spanish Supreme Court allowed VOX, a far right-wing party, described as neo-Francoist[29] or proto-fascist,[30] to participate in the proceedings in the Catalan trial as part of the Acusación Popular (allowing individuals or an entity to prosecute someone for a criminal offence, based on grounds of public interest, even if they are not personally impacted by that offence)[31] and interrogate defendants during the trial.[32] All of this would be surprising, according to Catalan commentators, if only the foundational text of the country, the Constitution, was itself neutral. They argue that one cannot expect Courts to be neutral when the text they are protecting is not. They indeed view the Spanish Constitution – and legal framework in general – as being the Trojan horse of Spanish nationalism.[33] Commentators indeed contend that the text barricaded the principle of the indissoluble unity of the Spanish nation (article 2) behind military protection of this unity (article 8)[34] and an especially difficult amendment procedure (making it impossible to change both articles 2 and 8 or any article of the Constitution for that matter).[35]

The negotiation of the Constitution took place during a period of great political tension, as it was adopted against the backdrop of Spain's democratic transition following 40 years of dictatorship. As Nicolas Marty describes it, the Constitution is a 'redemption' text designed to overcome political deadlocks in

27 I. Bernat and D. Whyte (n 23) 47–48.
28 C. Puigdemont (n 13) 53.
29 C. Puigdemont, 'Spain's Imprisonment of Catalan Leaders is a Desperate Move that Will Backfire' (The Guardian 2019) <https://www.theguardian.com/commentisfree/2019/oct/14/spain-imprisonment-catalan-leaders-supreme-cout-jailed-nine?CMP=fb_gu&fbclid=IwAR3wDHXOSpJnZJGMil8KlUjQACxu5T21gjS7yM9NvIQVplyXhvJyrBQY8h> accessed 18 March 2020.
30 J. Luis Martí, 'Politics and Criminal Law: The Trial against the Catalan Independence Leaders' (Verfassungsblog 2019) <https://verfassungsblog.de/politics-and-criminal-law-the-trial-against-the-catalan-independence-leaders/> accessed 7 May 2022.
31 Supreme Court, Judgment No. 459/2019 (14 October 2019) 3.
32 Supreme Court, Judgment No. 459/2019 (14 October 2019) 3.
33 C. Puigdemont (n 13) 61.
34 Of note, the military had supported the Franco regime. P. Anderson, 'Decentralisation at a Crossroads: Spain, Catalonia and the Territorial Crisis' [2020] *Ethnoplitics.* 342, 344.
35 H. López Bofill, 'Hubris, Constitutionalism, and "the Indissoluble Unity of the Spanish Nation": The Repression of Catalan Secessionist Referenda in Spanish Constitutional Law' [2019] *Int. J. Const. Law.* 943, 943–956.

the aftermath of the civil war.[36] Different groups representing different interests sat together at the negotiation table to adopt a text that would be acceptable to all.[37] Crucially, the Constitution refers to nationalities and regions to which it gives the possibility to create regional autonomies without, however, going as far as federalism.[38] Catalans and Basques initially wanted to be recognised as nations, but this was unacceptable to the other groups. In the end, all sides settled on the term *nationality*, which recognises the particular historical, linguistic, and cultural heritage of Catalans, Basques, and Galicians, without, however, offering additional or different legal rights to the ones of the regions.[39] The latter can also choose to go in the direction of either a very advanced or a simple autonomy, just as nationalities do.[40] The Constitution is, to this day, considered an extremely ambiguous text, torn between centralist and autonomist ambitions, and is the focus of intense academic scrutiny.[41]

Authors like Bofill argue in this respect that the compromise on the Constitution might have felt as if it was willingly granted, as reminded by opponents of independence, but it was not. He indeed recalls that, at that time, the military was passive-aggressively threatening to organise another *coup d'état*. In this tensed climate, some of its organs took the liberty of directly drafting certain passages of the Constitution and self-proclaim as guardian of the indissoluble unity of the country (inserted in article 8).[42] The Constitution is thus said to have been adopted in a rather uneven playing field to establish and secure Spanish domination over other nationalities in Spain.[43] It is described as the tool that entrenched the process of centralisation, further cementing the already existing sense of alienation experienced by Catalans within the Spanish political system.[44] The Constitutional Court has equally been under fire during the Catalan process for becoming increasingly politicised and acting as the armed wing of the government, most notably when it issued severe sentences resulting in the continued incarceration of pro-independence political and civil society leaders arrested following the 2017 referendum.[45] The Constitution and the Courts are thus criticised for being politicised, with the latter accused of perpetuating political prosecutions through the same – but allegedly only rebranded – judicial instances.

36 Translation of the author. N. Marty (n 1) 57.
37 Translation of the author. N. Marty (n 1) 57.
38 N. Marty (n 1) 58.
39 N. Marty (n 1) 59. It should be noted in this respect that neither the term *nationality* nor the term *region* is defined in the Constitution. P. Anderson (n 34) 346.
40 N. Marty (n 1) 59.
41 P. Anderson (n 34) 344.
42 H. López Bofill (n 35) 952–959.
43 H. López Bofill (n 35) 946.
44 A. Wagner, J. Marin and D. Kroqi, 'The Catalan Struggle for Independence and the Role of the European Union' [2019] *RSPP.* 787, 791–792.
45 P. Anderson (n 34) 349.

Reclaiming political power: Spanish centralisation strategy and Catalan inalienable right to self-determination

According to Catalans, the historical oppression that they endure is not merely a persistent remnant of the past whose effects are still felt today. They indeed contend that it is also the result of an active and very contemporary campaign to absorb and suppress Catalan political power. Some argue in this regard that central authorities have deployed a subtle policy of re-centralisation under the impetus of the Partido Popular (PP), which had the ambition to equalise the powers enjoyed by the four historic regions and level off their statuses, which greatly frustrated autonomous communities.[46] Subordinating Catalonia to the central power is thus still an ambition of Spanish central authorities,[47] according to Catalan separatists who contend that their Statute of Autonomy is merely a certificate of good conduct for Spanish authorities rather than a real and honest attempt at granting autonomy to a region whose particular heritage is recognised and respected. For Catalan separatists, it is precisely the fact that they were, on paper, granted a voice but felt like they were never heard that frustrated them and sparked calls for independence. They officially have autonomy and therefore can decide in a lot of policy areas on their own, but they say many of their decisions and claims are invalidated, so their autonomy feels like a smokescreen.

Faced with their inability to negotiate a legal referendum or have the one they organised recognised, Catalans invoked their right to self-determination, grounded in international law.[48] As Wagner pointed out on this point, the Catalan discourse gradually shifted over time. While Catalan leaders initially sought an agreement enabling them to hold a referendum, they later asserted their more unilateral 'right to decide', or the 'right to self-determination'.[49] This right, according to them, derives from the fact that Catalans form a sort of permanent minority that has been oppressed, subordinated, and marginalised over centuries.[50] Referring to the example of the ruling of the International Court of Justice for Kosovo, Catalan separatists underscore their right to declare independence unilaterally as well as Spain's obligation to recognise it as part of the its obligation to comply with the international treaties to which it took.[51] Some contend, however, that the right to self-determination is not applicable *per se* as a universal right but presupposes that the claimants are part of a former colony.[52] While Catalans argue that Spain did invade Catalonia at the beginning of the

46 S. Balfour, 'The Catalan and Spanish crisis: A European Perspective' (EUROPP blog - LSE 2018) <https://blogs.lse.ac.uk/europpblog/2018/07/03/the-catalan-and-spanish-crisis-a-european-perspective/> accessed 6 May 2020.

47 A. Wagner, J. Marin and D. Kroqi (n 44) 791.

48 S. Narotzky (n 17) 46.

49 P. Wagner (n 18) 608.

50 S. Narotzky (n 17) 50.

51 C. Puigdemont (n 13) 182.

52 D. Muro, 'The Still Birth of the Catalan Republic' [2018] *Curr. Hist.* 83, 83.

18th century, others find it hard to accept Catalonia as a 'Spanish colony' in the same way as Cuba or the Philippines were.[53] Because of their identity, Catalans may feel that they are on a separate path from the rest of Spain,[54] but opponents to the idea of the Catalan right to self-determination categorically defend that the conditions to invoke the right to self-determination are not fulfilled in Spain because Catalonia is part of decentralised democratic system that not only protects minority rights but that also affords a high degree of self-determination to Catalans allowing them to protect their language and culture.[55] In addition, cases like the one of Kosovo, which unilaterally declared independence and was recognised by other countries, very often invoked by Catalans, are usually perceived as historical exceptions rather than replicable models in democratic contexts.[56] The main problem thus remains the recognition of Catalans as a separate and oppressed 'people' who would have an inalienable right to self-determination.[57]

The PP's traditional anti-devolution stance

If the Catalan discourse on independence radicalised in the years leading up to the referendum, The PP, which was in power in Spain at the time of the 2017 independence referendum, has never been much of a party comfortable with the idea of devolution.[58] Its dislike of the system of regional governments in Spain as well as its long-standing undercover strategies to recentralise it are public knowledge.[59] The last few years alone provide many examples of this. For instance, when Kosovo declared its right to self-determination and subsequent independence in 2008, the PP (in the opposition at the time) strongly opposed any formal recognition of the country out of fear that the Kosovan example would set a precedent and inspire autonomous regions in Spain to do the same.[60] Equally, the PP has been known to use budgetary leverage, especially in the aftermath of the 2008 crisis, to eviscerate self-government by increasing the dependence of autonomous regions to central authorities for access to funds.[61] Another example includes that of the adoption of an Organic

53 N. Marty (n 1) 189–190.
54 N. Marty (n 1) 189–190.
55 P. Wagner (n 18) 602.
56 D. Muro (n 52) 83.
57 S. Narotzky (n 17) 50.
58 M. Grau Creus, 'A Step Backwards or a Step Forwards? The Politics and Policies of Decentralization under the Governments of the Partido Popular' [2005] *South Eur. Soc. Politics.* 263, 263–279.
59 D. Gardner, 'Autonomy under Fire' (Financial Times 2012) <https://www.orwellfoundation.com/wp-content/uploads/2013/03/Autonomy-under-fire.pdf> accessed 4 May 2022.
60 E. Johansson-Nogués, 'The Kosovo Juggling Act? Zapatero's Delicate Balance Act between Spanish Constraints and European Imperatives' in E. Barbé (ed), *Spain in Europe 2004–2008* (Observatory of European Foreign Policy, 2008) 2.
61 D. Gardner (n 59).

Law in 2013 by the Rajoy government for the Improvement of Educational Quality, which was normally a devolved power. Enacted on the basis of article 150(3) of the Constitution allowing central authorities to adopt laws in areas normally under the competence of autonomous communities when considered necessary for the general interest, the law aimed to reduce the number of classes taught in linguistic immersion in autonomous communities. Its ultimate goal was to standardise education in Spain by increasing the power of the Ministry of Education at the expense of the autonomous communities. The education minister was not shy to acknowledge, in this respect, that the law was designed to hispanicise Catalan students.[62] Similar examples showing the PP's willingness to recentralise governance abound. The PP governments of José Maria Aznar and Mariano Rajoy in particular have been described as especially prone to pushing for uniformity and Spanish nationalism when in power.[63]

Besides the generally unfavourable stance of the PP towards regional aspirations, the political climate ahead of the 2015 general elections was not particularly conducive to dialogue with Catalan authorities on their local ambitions. The ruling PP had been under increased pressure about its economic and social policies marked by strict austerity measures.[64] If macroeconomic indicators seemed to point to promising results under the PP, discontent grew among the population as unemployment rates soared and that important budget cuts were made in the health, education, and social sectors.[65] Major corruption scandals affecting the traditional political parties (PP and the Partido Socialista Obrero Español [PSOE]) and even the king further fuelled discontent regarding the political establishment and opened the way to news parties like Podemos and Ciudadanos to surge and gain momentum in Spain.[66] The question of regional separatism coming on top of all this thus added further complexity to an already tensed political climate. Ahead of the 2015 general elections, both the PP and the PSOE were thus very aware of the fact that appearing too eager to make concessions to Catalans would plummet their electoral score.[67] The results of the 2015 elections not only reflected the general discontent and fragmentation among the Spanish population, it also changed the traditional two-party system with smaller satellite parties, to a truly multiparty one.[68] Although the PP won the elections, it lost its governing

62 P. Anderson (n 34) 347.

63 P. Anderson (n 34) 345.

64 I. Medina and P. Correa, 'The 2015 Spanish Election: The Times They Are a' Changing' [2016] *Reg. Fed. Stud.* 407, 408.

65 T. D. Lancaster, 'The Spanish General Elections of 2015 and 2016: A New Stage in Democratic Politics?' [2017] *West Eur. Politics.* 919, 922–923.

66 T. D. Lancaster, 'The Spanish General Elections of 2015 and 2016: A New Stage in Democratic Politics?' [2017] *West Eur. Politics.* 919, 922–923.

67 N. Marty (n 1) 99.

68 T. D. Lancaster (n 65) 926.

majority and ascended to power with the lowest winning margin ever documented in contemporary Spanish history.[69] The Rajoy government could thus only deal with day-to-day business until it secured a more comfortable majority at the snap elections of 2016.[70] The mounting pressure on the Catalan side for the organisation of an independence referendum took place against this general background in which the Catalan question served as an important point of positioning and self-definition for all political parties. Accordingly, after his re-election in June 2016, Rajoy was not inclined to make any concessions to Catalan leaders on their referendum on independence.[71]

Violation of the Constitution and the Spanish legal framework at large

Once the referendum took place, the strategy of the Rajoy government was to treat the issue as a purely legal one, which enabled it to disengage from any potential political resolution of the crisis.[72] The way Spanish authorities saw it, the political process could only take place in a democratic framework respectful of the rule of law.[73] Any political endeavour aspiring to legality and legitimacy needed to be in line with the Spanish legal framework. The Catalan referendum process, however, was organised in sheer violation of the Spanish Constitution, and this in multiple ways.

First and foremost, the Constitution ensures and protects the indissoluble unity of the Spanish Nation (art. 2), which Catalan separatist authorities openly sought to dissolve. Second, the text of the Constitution explicitly states that 'the Spanish people' are the subjects of national sovereignty (art. 1.2) and does not recognise Catalans as a separate nation.[74] As a result, Catalans do not hold a special right to make decisions independently from the rest of the Spanish people on their constitutional future.[75] So if there ever was going to be a legal referendum on the Catalan independence, it would have been merely consultative and organised on a national basis – rather than just in Catalonia – because the sovereignty belongs to the Spanish people – of which the Catalan nationality is only a part.[76] As previously outlined, this distinction about nation and nationality was a point of contention at the time of the negotiation of the Spanish Constitution in 1978. Catalans and Basques initially

69 T. D. Lancaster (n 65) 926.
70 N. Marty (n 1) 99.
71 N. Marty (n 1) 100–102.
72 D. Cetrà and M. Harvey (n 4) 607.
73 H. López Bofill (n 35) 945.
74 D. Cetrà and M. Harvey (n 4) 616.
75 D. Cetrà, E. Casanas-Adam and M. Tarrega, 'The 2017 Catalan Independence Referendum: A Symposium' [2018] *Scot. Aff.* 126, 131.
76 D. Cetrà, E. Casanas-Adam and M. Tarrega, 'The 2017 Catalan Independence Referendum: A Symposium' [2018] *Scot. Aff.* 126, 131.

wanted to be recognised as nations but were eventually only granted the status of nationality. The latter meant that their particular historical, linguistic and cultural heritage was recognised but that they did not derive any special rights from it other than the ones they already enjoyed from their recognition as autonomous regions.[77] Accordingly, the Rajoy government considered that the matter of Catalonia or the Basque Country potentially becoming independent one day was actually resolved in 1978.

Furthermore, Catalan authorities were said to have breached the Statute of Autonomy of Catalonia. Doing so, they dashed, according to Spanish authorities, any possibility of peaceful dialogue. Indeed, because of the special status that Catalans enjoy as an autonomous region, Spanish authorities considered that the Constitution offers a democratic framework where regional aspirations can be expressed and democratically discussed.[78] Catalan leaders indeed tried to negotiate a legal referendum, but when they did not obtain it, they organised it unilaterally.[79] They are thus said to have betrayed their mandate and breached the Statute of Autonomy whose very existence is made possible by the Constitution allowing them to run the region in relative autonomy.[80]

A fourth argument advanced by the PP was the one of the violations of the civil rights of a large portion of Catalan citizens who did not wish the referendum to take place. Indeed, Garicano pointed out that the Catalan government's public opinion centre recorded in 2019 that 41.2% of Catalans shared they felt as Spanish as they felt Catalan and that only 20.1% said they only felt Catalan (the rest being divided among those feeling mostly Spanish, mostly Catalan or only Spanish).[81] This referendum was thus, according to Madrid, pushed by the Catalan nationalist machine that swept all dissenting views before it and, on the way, violated the civil rights of the entire Catalan population. With their referendum, they were thus said to have hijacked the right of the whole Catalan population to political and legal stability and security for their own political ambition. In addition, many commentators pointed out the Catalan referendum did not have procedural guarantees,[82] so even the civic rights of those who voted and wished for it to take place were not properly secured.

In any case, and this was the fifth argument of Spanish authorities, the autonomous regions do not have a mandate to organise referenda. In theory, the Spanish Constitution allows for the organisation of referenda to consult

77 N. Marty (n 1) 57–59.
78 N. Marty (n 1) 101–102.
79 N. Marty (n 1) 101–102.
80 N. Marty (n 1) 126.
81 L. Garicano, 'Europe Should Commend Catalan Convictions' (Politico 2019) <https://www.politico.eu/article/europe-should-commend-catalan-convictions-separatist-catalan-leaders/> accessed 19 February 2020. Not to mention that the rest of Spain was very much opposed to the referendum. N. Marty (n 1) 120.
82 S. Narotzky (n 17) 46.

all citizens on political matters of particular importance.[83] However, this is an exclusive competence of the central state, and these referenda are meant to be merely consultative.[84] The current legal framework does not entitle autonomous communities to hold them and even less so when they do not include the whole Spanish population. Some argued, however, that setting up a legal framework to enable Catalans to organise this referendum would have in fact been possible. For instance, a temporary transfer of state competence to the autonomous region, as was done for Scotland in 2014, could have been considered.[85] Alternatively, Madrid could have granted an express authorisation to exceptionally hold a regional consultation instead of a national one.[86] None of these alternatives, however, would have changed the fact that the referendum would have been consultative and not binding,[87] especially given that the recent jurisprudence of the Spanish Constitutional Court has not supported this kind of initiative. It famously ruled in 2008 that the Basque Country could not organise a consultation on self-determination because it would require a reform of the Constitution.[88] It has stuck to this position since then in successive rulings.[89]

In addition to the fact that the referendum itself was unconstitutional, Spanish authorities argue that the process leading to it was also in breach of the Spanish legal framework. This argument refers more specifically to the two laws adopted on 6 and 8 September 2017 that, respectively, enabled the organisation of the referendum and regulated the transition to independence in case of a positive result in the referendum. These acts of disobedience were all the more serious to Spanish authorities that they had gone through a similar process three years earlier. In 2014, Arthur Mas, the then president of the Autonomous Community of Catalonia, also tried to establish a legal framework for the right of the Catalan people to decide on their future. At the time, the Catalan Parliament had adopted a law on non-referendum popular consultations and other forms of civic participation.[90] Mas had also signed a decree calling for the organisation of the consultation, and the central government

83 A. Garrido Muñoz, 'Catalan Independence in the Spanish Constitution and Courts' (Oxford Constitutional Law) <https://oxcon.ouplaw.com/page/Catalan-independence/catalan-independence-in-the-spanish-constitution-and-courts> accessed 19 February 2020.
84 D. Cetrà, E. Casanas-Adam and M. Tarrega (n 75) 132.
85 D. Cetrà and M. Harvey, 'Explaining Accommodation and Resistance to Demands for Independence Referendums in the UK and Spain' [2019] *Nations Natl.* 607, 617.
86 D. Cetrà, E. Casanas-Adam and M. Tarrega (n 75) 132.
87 D. Cetrà and M. Harvey (n 85) 616.
88 D. Cetrà and M. Harvey (n 85) 616.
89 See, for instance, Constitutional Court, Judgment No. 42/2014 (25 March 2014), Constitutional Court, Judgment No. 31/2015 (25 February 2015), and Constitutional Court, Judgment No. 117/2017 (7 October 2017) (related to the Catalan independence process).
90 Law 10/2014 on Popular Non-Referendum and Other Forms of Citizen Participation (26 September 2014).

had, that time too, deemed the law illegal and had suspended it.[91] The consultation nevertheless took place and Mas, as well as other civil society members and civil servants, were prosecuted for disobedience, embezzlement, prevarication, and usurpation.[92] If the Spanish government had been more lenient towards Catalan separatists on that occasion, it did not indulge this kind of anti-constitutional behaviour a second time.[93] It should however be noted that the organisation of an illegal referendum is not a criminal offence in Spain. It was decriminalised in 2005 by Organic Law 2/2005 whose preamble states that the principles of minimal intervention and proportionality are central to the application of criminal law and that other means of control of legality exist in the Spanish legal framework.[94]

Critics of the use of criminal law by the Spanish judiciary to prosecute Catalan leaders thus contend that the court used other (and heavier) charges (such as rebellion, punishable by 30 years) so as to revive the previous crime of illegal organisation of a referendum (which carried a lighter sentence of 3–5 years).[95] The Supreme Court, however, retorted that the organisation of a referendum that was *explicitly prohibited by Court rulings* was not covered by the Organic Law 2/2005 decriminalising the organisation of an illegal referendum.[96] It thus went on to consider the charges of rebellion, sedition, misappropriation of public funds, disobedience, and criminal organisation.[97] Since the 2019 trial, the criminal code has been reformed. Changes include an abolition of the crime of sedition and important changes in the crime of misappropriation of public funds. The following outlines the charges and associated sentences as they stood at the time of the trial in October 2019.

Rebellion (first charge against Catalan separatists)

The first and most contentious charge put forward for separatists who stood trial before the Supreme Court was the one of rebellion. The use of this charge shocked for many reasons, including the fact that it was last applied in the trial of a leader involved in the failed 1981 military coup.[98] The level and capacity for violence were thus different this time, and the use of this charge for what was considered to be a mostly peaceful crime raised concerns. Eventually, this charge was dropped. Although the judges overseeing the case deliberated

91 N. Marty (n 1) 92.
92 N. Marty (n 1) 93.
93 D. Cetrà, E. Casanas-Adam and M. Tarrega (n 75) 128.
94 Organic Law 2/2005, Amendment of the Criminal Code (22 June 2005).
95 Parliamentary Assembly of the Council of Europe (n 5) 20.
96 Supreme Court, Judgment No. 459/2019 (n 31) 339.
97 Supreme Court, Judgment No. 459/2019 (n 31) 1.
98 J. Faus and J. Elías Rodríguez, 'Catalan Leaders Go on Trial in Madrid over Independence Bid' (Reuters 2019) <https://www.reuters.com/article/us-spain-politics-catalonia/catalan-leaders-go-on-trial-in-madrid-over-independence-bid-idUSKCN1Q01LD> accessed 11 May 2022.

that violence (not only physical but also psychological) did take place, they considered that the level of violence was not enough to constitute an act of rebellion.[99] They also contemplated that the acts of violence that took place in the 20 September–1 October 2017 period were not instrumental in enabling a real secession.[100] Rather, it was considered to be a leverage for Catalan leaders to force Spanish authorities to sit at the table with Catalan separatists and negotiate a way to independence.[101]

Sedition (second charge against Catalan separatists)

With the offence of rebellion dropped, Catalan leaders were eventually charged with sedition. Although the 2022 reform of the criminal code has erased this crime that is now englobed by the less serious offence of aggravated form of public disorder, as previously stated, the following will present the rationale of the Court in 2019 regarding this charge.[102] At the time of the Catalan trial in 2019, the offences of rebellion and sedition were very much linked in Spanish law and were even presented as alternatives to one another.[103] The key difference between the two offences lied in their targets: rebellion is aimed at core elements of the constitutional system, such as the Constitution, the Crown, the legislative chambers, national territorial integrity, and others.[104] In contrast, the crime of sedition was concerned with obstructing the legislative, governmental, or judicial will. This referred more specifically to hindering the application of laws, the performance of duties by government officials, corporate authorities, or civil servants, as well as the execution and fulfilment of their orders, administration or legal resolutions.[105] Regardless of whether violence was used (although the latter is constitutive of the offence in the case of rebellion), the two had different aims. One is an attack against the core, essential elements that constitute the state, the other was an aggravated form of obstruction to its normal functioning. This also explained their locations in different titles of the criminal code. The crime of rebellion is indeed found in Title XXI of the penal code, covering crimes against the Constitution whereas sedition was in Title XXII on crimes against the public order. The notion of public order, as defined by the Supreme Court, is more than a situation of public calm or peace. It rather refers to one of institutional order, meaning

99 Supreme Court, Judgment No. 459/2019 (n 31) 261.
100 Supreme Court, Judgment No. 459/2019 (n 31) 263.
101 Supreme Court, Judgment No. 459/2019 (n 31) 265.
102 Organic Law 14/2022, on the Transposition of European Directives and Other Provisions for the Adaptation of Criminal Legislation to the Legal System of the European Union, and Reform of Crimes against Moral Integrity, Public Disorder and Smuggling of Dual-Use Weapons (22 December 2022).
103 Supreme Court, Judgment No. 459/2019 (n 31) 270.
104 Supreme Court, Judgment No. 459/2019 (n 31) 270.
105 Supreme Court, Judgment No. 459/2019 (n 31) 270.

that public institutions and services are able to carry out their work and fulfil their purpose normally.[106] The difference between public order and public peace was elaborated by the Court in a ruling issued in 2010. In that ruling, and drawing from previous jurisprudence on the matter,[107] the Court established that while public order refers to the good functioning of public institutions and services, public peace is linked to a general situation of peaceful and collective cohabitation conducive to citizens enjoying their rights, and more specifically their fundamental rights.[108]

The Court further stated in the 2019 ruling pertaining to the case of Catalan leaders that sedition implied active behaviour, meaning that it was not mere disobedience; it entailed a collective uprising and resistance.[109] Sedition, according to the Supreme Court judges, usually took place as a succession of actions, rather than as one simple offence. In that sense, the Court explained, sedition was usually a compound offence.[110] Each of the acts leading to it did not need to constitute an offence *per se*; it was their aggregation that made up the offence of sedition. As aforesaid, these aggregated actions needed to be aimed at (but not necessarily result in)[111] undermining the effectiveness of laws or obstructing the execution of orders or resolutions by public officials. The collective movement necessary for sedition needed not a physical presence of its members that could equally seek to achieve their aim via any means that modern information society offers.[112] The fact that people gathered and assembled was not an offence. The offence occurred, according to the Court, when the actions were not only turbulent and public but also involved forceful or unlawful means. The Court further noted that their goal was to generate a situation in which laws were not followed or the effectiveness of judicial or administrative orders was obstructed.[113]

In the 2019 ruling, the Supreme Court overall aligned its interpretation of the offence of sedition to the one it had previously adopted on 10 October 1980. In the latter case, the Court had ruled that the offence of sedition involved, first, a collective and tumultuous uprising that sought to hamper the normal functioning of public institutions and services. Second, the Court had emphasised that sedition also included an element of intent, in the sense that the offence was committed with the aim of achieving certain objectives, regardless of whether these came to fruition.[114] In addition, the

106 Supreme Court, Judgment No. 459/2019 (n 31) 270–271.
107 Supreme Court, Judgment No. 865/2011 (20 July 2011); Supreme Court, Judgment No. 987/2009 (13 October 2009) and Supreme Court, Judgment No. 1622/2001 (21 September 2001).
108 Supreme Court, Judgment No. 1154/2010 (12 January 2010).
109 Supreme Court, Judgment No. 459/2019 (n 31) 273.
110 Supreme Court, Judgment No. 459/2019 (n 31) 274.
111 Supreme Court, Judgment No. 459/2019 (n 31) 276–277.
112 Supreme Court, Judgment No. 459/2019 (n 31) 274.
113 Supreme Court, Judgment No. 459/2019 (n 31) 274.
114 Supreme Court, Judgment No. 1049 (10 October 1980).

Court further clarified at the time that sedition entailed an element of force that could be construed as either the use of violent (psychological or physical) methods or the use of methods outside legal channels.[115]

In the case at hand, the adoption of 139/2017 and 19/2017 by the Catalan Parliament (later quashed by the Constitutional Court) was interpreted as a clear sign of the ambition of Catalan leaders to repeal the legislation in force. The Court criticised the secessionists for undermining the constitutional pact[116] and attempting to establish a parallel legal framework in rupture with the existing state structure.[117] Beyond the clear intent to defy the legal framework and disobey the Constitutional Court, the Supreme Court pointed to the events of the referendum day and the period leading up to it, starting on 20 September 2017. During this time, police officers were prevented from enforcing the law by large groups of people who opposed them, albeit non-violently. This, according to the Supreme Court, unmistakably demonstrated that the offence of sedition had occurred. According to the judges handling the case, the mere inability of police officers to enforce the law was sufficient to qualify the offence as sedition. They explained that the right to protest did not extend to physically obstructing law enforcement from executing a court order, particularly on such a large scale that it affected the entire autonomous region.[118] In this case, they said the judiciary's authority was suspended and overridden by the will of the organisers and their supporters, who imposed the referendum by force.[119] The Court further outlined that the criminal behaviours of those who committed the offence of sedition were not alleviated by reports of violent incidents involving the police. These excesses were tried in another Court and did not interfere with the decision made in this ruling.[120]

Misappropriation of public funds (third charge against Catalan separatists)

To make this mass-scale sedition possible, Catalan leaders were accused of having committed an aggravated form of misappropriation of public funds. As for the crime of sedition, this charge also underwent important changes in the 2022 reform of the criminal code, but the following outlines its use in the 2019 trial. This charge was motivated in this case by the fact that Catalan leaders were accused of having used public money to organise the referendum.[121] Since the reform of the criminal code in 2015, the offence of misuse of public funds not only applied to traditional misappropriation or theft but also to

115 Supreme Court, Judgment No. 459/2019 (n 31) 276.
116 Supreme Court, Judgment No. 459/2019 (n 31) 238.
117 Supreme Court, Judgment No. 459/2019 (n 31) 238.
118 Supreme Court, Judgment No. 459/2019 (n 31) 277.
119 Supreme Court, Judgment No. 459/2019 (n 31) 277.
120 Supreme Court, Judgment No. 459/2019 (n 31) 278.
121 Supreme Court, Judgment No. 459/2019 (n 31) 279.

"malfeasance in the use of public funds" at the time of the trial.[122] In a ruling issued in 2019, the Court found that the revised classification of misappropriation outlawed the actions of public authorities or officials who, by violating their duties of faithfulness and loyalty and abusing their position, harmed public property. This new classification was thus said to be broader than the previous definition of misappropriation, as it encompassed not only theft but also other misconducts, such as the unauthorised assumption of obligations.[123]

Catalan leaders were thus accused of gross disloyal misconduct, as well as of having used public resources (human, material, and technological) for the organisation of the referendum.[124] The Court finally noted that the offences of sedition and misuse of public funds were interrelated. This was because sedition entailed some of its constitutive elements to take place outside of legal channels and that is what embezzlement was. The offences of sedition and embezzlement thus not only shared their purpose in this case, but the latter fuelled the former.[125]

Disobedience (fourth charge against Catalan separatists)

Of the 12 defendants who had remained in Spain and who stood trial before the Supreme Court, three were sentenced for the offence of disobedience. The Court considered that because Catalan leaders had ignored the repeated warnings of the Constitutional Court to abstain from implementing parliamentary resolutions and orders that had been quashed and/or suspended by the Constitutional Court, they were guilty of disobedience.[126]

The Court clarified, in this regard, that disobedience does not necessarily entail active insubordination. Disobedience can equally arise when a person displays a repeated and clear inaction over time regarding an order[127] that eventually translates into a refusal to obey.[128] This refusal to comply with orders or juridical decisions does not require, according to the Court, a hierarchical relationship between the body from which the order emanates and the body refusing to observe the order. The Court had already established in previous rulings that disobedience can also occur in the case of a refusal to comply with judicial decisions,[129] which is what happened in the Catalan case.[130]

122 Supreme Court, Judgment No. 459/2019 (n 31) 279–280.
123 Supreme Court, Judgment No. 281/2019 (30 May 2019).
124 Supreme Court, Judgment No. 459/2019 (n 31) 281.
125 Supreme Court, Judgment No. 459/2019 (n 31) 285.
126 Supreme Court, Judgment No. 459/2019 (n 31) 286.
127 Supreme Court, Judgment No. 459/2019 (n 31) 286.
128 Supreme Court, Judgment No. 485/2002 (14 June 2002); Supreme Court, Judgment No. 1203/1997 (11 October 1997).
129 Supreme Court, Judgment No. 177/2017 (22 March 2017); Supreme Court, Judgment No. 722/2018 (23 January 2018); Supreme Court, Judgment No. 80/2006 (6 February 2006); Supreme Court, Judgment No. 263/2001 (24 February 2001).
130 Supreme Court, Judgment No. 459/2019 (n 31) 287.

Criminal organisation (fifth charge against Catalan separatists)

Despite the organised and concerted efforts of Catalan separatist leaders to make the referendum possible – as put forward by a class action that argued that the organisation of the referendum followed a carefully designed two-year strategy that entailed the establishment of an organised and hierarchical group composed of a large number of persons all working together to achieve the goal of an illegal referendum,[131] the Court considered that the crimes committed by Catalan leaders did not amount to the offence of criminal organisation.

The Court indeed contemplated that the distribution of tasks and the organisation required for the holding of the referendum – although essential to the offence of criminal organisation – was not enough to consider that the offence qualified as one of criminal organisation. The Court further noted in this regard that the definition of the offence of sedition included a distinct criminal treatment for those who planned and prepared the sedition or were identified as their principal perpetrator.[132] It thus deemed that there was no factual basis to ground the claim of the constitution of a criminal organisation.[133]

In the end, Catalan leaders were thus found guilty of sedition, disobedience, and misappropriation of public funds and sentenced to prison terms ranging from 9 to 13 years, banned from public office for several years, and/or received fines.

Reflection on the PP's position

The ruling PP thus chose to engage as little as possible on the political front to handle the Catalan independence crisis and focused on the illegality of Catalan actions instead. It insisted that what Spanish authorities did was not to prosecute independentism *per se* but the illegal actions committed by Catalan separatists.[134] While it is true that Catalans broke the law and that all Spanish judicial authorities did was to prosecute illegal behaviours, the severity of the charges was still difficult to square for many observers.[135]

Some authors argue in this respect that the Spanish Constitution is not a mere legal text and that it is actually one of the only ways left for Spaniards to express their patriotism. In this sense, the Catalan independence process was more than a violation of the Spanish Constitution, it was a symbolic revolution that threatened the mental structures of the rest of the country wired around national unity and mono-nationalism. Nicolas Marty and Diego Muro speak

131 Supreme Court, Judgment No. 459/2019 (n 31) 288–289.

132 Supreme Court, Judgment No. 459/2019 (n 31) 290.

133 Supreme Court, Judgment No. 459/2019 (n 31) 290.

134 S. Cabanas Ansorena, 'Spain Isn't Imposing Excessive Punishment on Catalonia's Leaders. It's Enforcing the Law' (Foreign Policy 2019) <https://foreignpolicy.com/2019/11/14/spain-isnt-imposing-excessive-punishment-on-catalonias-leaders-its-enforcing-the-law/> accessed 24 February 2020; Parliamentary Assembly of the Council of Europe (n 5) 24.

135 Parliamentary Assembly of the Council of Europe (n 5) 14.

in this regard of 'constitutional patriotism'[136] in Spain. The concept is derived from Jürgen Habermas's vision of what is left of nationalism after the events of the end of the 19th and in the 20th century in Germany. Both argue that Spanish patriotism borrows its rationale from a theory of Habermas on German nationalism. As was the case for Germany, the years of the dictatorship largely tarnished Spanish nationalism.[137] Because of that, Muro argues that the 'ethnic' elements of Spanish nationalism (such as Castilian ethnocentrism and Catholicism) gave room to more 'civic' elements of nationalism (the 1978 Constitution) taking over, hence the idea of 'constitutional patriotism'.[138] According to these authors, the Spanish Constitution grew to be a way for Spaniards – and the PP specifically – to celebrate the Spanish culture and unity, while leaving aside the connotations associated to the years of Franco.[139] This would partly explain why the Spanish response was so violent when Catalan separatists breached the Constitution. It would also explain and resonate with the reaction of José María Aznar when Jean-Luc Dehaene, back in 1996, questioned the compatibility of the Aznar Protocol at the moment of its adoption with the international treaties on the right to asylum (discussed in Chapter 4). After the Catalan independence referendum, the PP-led Spanish government went as far as (unsuccessfully) trying to add offences against the public order and constitutional integrity of member states to the EU list of offences that do not require a double criminality check under the European arrest warrant scheme.[140]

The demise of the PP: an opportunity for the PSOE to shine

Although the PP managed to prevent a Catalan secession, the Catalan independence referendum nevertheless generated a full-scale constitutional crisis in Spain that undermined the PP's stance both nationally and internationally. At the international level, the violence of the police forces on the day of the referendum,[141] the heavy-handed use of criminal law to deal with what was widely considered a political crisis,[142] and the severity of the charges,[143] all led to intense debates that

136 N. Marty (n 1) 73.
137 N. Marty (n 1) 74.
138 D. Muro (n 52) 85.
139 N. Marty (n 1) 74.
140 N. Nielsen, 'No Chance of Expanding EU Warrant Crime List' (EU Observer 2017) <https://euobserver.com/justice/140218> accessed 14 May 2022.
141 N. Marty (n 1) 115; Amnesty International, 'Spain: Excessive Use of Force by National Police and Civil Guard in Catalonia' (Amnesty International 2017) <https://www.amnesty.org/en/latest/news/2017/10/spain-excessive-use-of-force-by-national-police-and-civil-guard-in-catalonia/> accessed 21 February 2020; Human Rights Watch, 'Spain: Police Used Excessive Force in Catalonia' (Human Rights Watch 2017) <https://www.hrw.org/news/2017/10/12/spain-police-used-excessive-force-catalonia> accessed 23 October 2018.
142 José Luis Martí (n 30); Parliamentary Assembly of the Council of Europe (n 5) 4.
143 United Nations Human Rights Office of the High Commissioner, 'UN Expert Urges Spain Not to Pursue Criminal Charges of Rebellion Against Political Figures in Catalonia' (United Nations Human Rights Office of the High Commissioner 2018) <https://

tarnished the PP's posture. At the national level, the catastrophic results of the PP at the snap elections of 21 December 2017 in Catalonia[144] – coupled with its unpopular austerity measures[145] and the major Gürtel corruption scandal implicating senior PP figures sentenced to as long as 37 years of prison[146] – seriously damaged the PP's reputation. This situation emboldened the Sanchez-led PSOE to oust Rajoy's government in a vote of non-confidence in June 2018, mere days after the *Gürtel* verdict.[147] The PSOE subsequently won the general elections of April 2019, and then again the ones of November 2019 after a failed attempt to form a coalition government following the April elections.[148] The PSOE victory paved the way to a new relationship between Catalan authorities and the central government. Upon his election, Pedro Sanchez declared that he would put an end to the nefarious cycle of the government exacerbating the problems with Catalonia.[149] The PSOE had indeed condemned the PP for their antagonising response to the Catalan crisis. Even if Pedro Sanchez was also opposed to the Catalan referendum, he had called on Mariano Rajoy to adopt a more conciliatory approach on this issue, accusing him of jeopardising the national unity with his confrontational attitude.[150]

A seemingly more agreeable PSOE to regional separatism: extending an olive branch to Catalan separatists

The PSOE has indeed traditionally been more accommodating to Catalan demands. Although the party equally embraces constitutional patriotism, its vision

---

www.ohchr.org/en/press-releases/2018/04/un-expert-urges-spain-not-pursue-criminal-charges-rebellion-against> accessed 12 May 2022.

144 N. Marty (n 1) 133.

145 I. Medina and P. Correa (n 64) 408.

146 The Gürtel case refers to a major corruption scandal affecting high PP figures. It more specifically concerned the establishment by Fransisco Correa, a businessman with close ties to the PP, of a system of institutional corruption whereby Correa manipulated the granting of public contracts at every level (central, regional, local) through his close relations to eminent PP figures. Correa was sentenced to 51 years in prison, and other PP members were equally sentenced to long prison sentences of up to 37 years. S. Jones, 'Court Finds Spain's Ruling Party Benefited from Bribery Scheme' (The Guardian 2018) <https://www.theguardian.com/world/2018/may/24/court-finds-spain-ruling-party-pp-benefited-bribery-luis-barcenas> accessed 12 May 2022.

147 S. Jones, 'Mariano Rajoy Ousted as Spain Prime Minister' (The Guardian 2018) <https://www.theguardian.com/world/2018/jun/01/mariano-rajoy-ousted-as-spain-prime-minister> accessed 12 May 2022.

148 S. Jones, 'Spain Likely to Return to the Polls in November after Party Talks Fail' (The Guardian 2019) <https://www.theguardian.com/world/2019/sep/17/spain-braces-for-another-election-as-deadline-looms> accessed 12 May 2022.

149 S. Saeed, 'Spanish PM Sánchez Signals Softer Approach to Catalonia' (Politico 2018) <https://www.politico.eu/article/pedro-sanchez-spain-catalonia-signals-softer-approach-to-catalonia/> accessed 12 May 2022.

150 M. Guidi and M. Casula (n 8) 185.

of the Constitution is more evolutive than the one of the PP.[151] In 2003, for instance, the PSOE adopted the 'Declaration of Santillana' advocating for a plural, constitutional, and united Spain.[152] After his election as prime minister in 2019, Sanchez announced an upcoming revision of the Spanish criminal code to update it to modern needs.[153] The reformed criminal code was adopted in December 2022. The overhaul erased the crime of sedition, which was absorbed by the lesser crime of aggravated form of public disorder that carries a lower sentence and shorter ban on holding public office. Furthermore, the new crime of misuse of public funds now distinguishes between crimes committed for personal enrichment and those that do not. In both cases, the sentence is lower than before, and the ban on holding public office is equally shorter.[154]

Upon the victory of the PSOE at the general elections in November 2019, Sanchez also initiated a dialogue with Catalan authorities to start a reconciliation process.[155] The dialogue initially failed, as Sanchez's offer to increase investments in Catalonia did not meet the Catalan demands for an amnesty and a binding referendum on self-determination.[156] In another attempt at reaching out to Catalans, Sanchez issued pardons for nine Catalan separatists in prison. However, this measure only received a lukewarm welcome as it failed to satisfy Catalan hardliners who wanted a full amnesty.[157] The PSOE subsequently found itself in a delicate situation in which it was under fire both from right-wing political parties who accused it of selling out to Catalans for political support in parliament and from Catalan separatists who accused Sanchez of paying lip service to promises of true dialogue where Catalan demands would be seriously

151 A. Fernandez Garcia and M. Petithomme, 'Nationalisme d'État aux Nationalismes Espagnols, la Réinvention de la "Nation" Espagnole Depuis la Transition Démocratique' in A. Garcia Herrero & M. Petithomme (eds), *Les nationalismes dans l'Espagne contemporaine (1975–2011): Compétition politique et identités nationales* (Armand Colin, 2012) 73.

152 A. Fernandez Garcia and M. Petithomme, 'Nationalisme d'État aux Nationalismes Espagnols, la Réinvention de la "Nation" Espagnole Depuis la Transition Démocratique' in A. Garcia Herrero & M. Petithomme (eds), *Les nationalismes dans l'Espagne contemporaine (1975–2011): Compétition politique et identités nationales* (Armand Colin, 2012) 73.

153 PSOE, 'Sánchez Plantea Revisar el Delito de Rebellion para Adecuarlo al Desafío Secesionista' (PSOE) <https://www.psoe.es/actualidad/noticias-actualidad/sanchez-plantea-revisar-el-delito-de-rebelion-para-adecuarlo-al-desafio-secesionista/> accessed 25 January 2020.

154 Organic Law 14/2022 (n 102).

155 Reuters, 'Spain's Sanchez Promises Dialogue on Catalonia if Wins Confirmation Vote' (Reuters 2019) <https://www.reuters.com/article/us-spain-politics-catalonia-idUSKBN1YL1GY> accessed 12 May 2022.

156 G. Hedgecoe, 'Catalan Independence Talks are Back – and the Stakes are High for PM Sánchez' (Politico 2021) <https://www.politico.eu/article/catalonia-independence-spain-prime-minister-pedro-sanchez/> accessed 12 May 2022.

157 S. Jones, 'Spanish Government Pardons Nine Jailed Catalan Leaders' (The Guardian 2021) <https://www.theguardian.com/world/2021/jun/22/spanish-government-pardons-nine-jailed-catalan-leaders> accessed 12 May 2022.

considered.[158] Eventually, the Catalan demands for a law on amnesty were granted by the PSOE-led government following the 2023 general elections. In those elections, the PP regained in popularity and recovered its position as the first party in the country with 33% of the votes and 136 seats at the Congress of Deputies out of 350. However, failing to form a government, the PP cleared the way for the PSOE, which managed to secure the support of smaller parties (including Junts per Catalunya, the independentist party of former Catalan president and leader of the independence process Carles Puigdemont) to reach the 176 seats Sanchez needed for his absolute majority. In exchange for the independentists' support and in view of overcoming the constitutional crisis with Catalans, Sanchez accepted to pass the previously requested controversial law granting amnesty to Catalan separatists, which was widely criticised by right-wing parties who accused him of jeopardising the rule of law for his own political gain.[159] The law, narrowly passed by the Spanish Parliament in May 2024, eliminated criminal, administrative, and financial liability for Catalan separatists involved in the 2014 consultation and the 2017 independence process for actions conducted between 1 November 2011 and 13 November 2023 in pursuit of independence. However, it excluded crimes of treason and particularly heinous crimes, such as crimes leading to death, torture, racist crimes, or crimes based on discrimination, terrorism, and other similar crimes, from its scope.[160]

At the international level, Sanchez's approach to the Catalan question was incontrovertibly more in line with what the international community had called for, that is de-escalating tensions and dealing with the crisis on a political level rather than a judicial one. Sanchez seemed to have been mindful of international calls as his pardons came a day after the CoE Parliamentary Assembly Committee on Legal Affairs adopted a resolution calling on Spain to reassess its response to the Catalan crisis by establishing a dialogue with Catalan separatists, refraining from using criminal law to deal with what it essentially considered to be a political crisis, considering pardoning Catalan leaders in jail without expecting them to renounce their political convictions,

158 S. Jones, 'Spanish Government Pardons Nine Jailed Catalan Leaders' (The Guardian 2021) <https://www.theguardian.com/world/2021/jun/22/spanish-government-pardons-nine-jailed-catalan-leaders> accessed 12 May 2022.

159 La Moncloa, 'Pedro Sánchez is Sworn in as President of the Government of Spain with an Absolute Majority' (La Moncloa 2023) <https://www.lamoncloa.gob.es/lang/en/presidente/news/Paginas/2023/20231116_investiture-session.aspx#:~:text=The%20Plenary%20of%20the%20Lower,in%20favour%20and%20171%20against> accessed 20 June 2024; N. Torbisco Casals and N. Krisch, 'The Spanish Amnesty, the Conflict with Catalonia, and the Rule of Law' (Verfassunsblog 2024) <https://verfassungsblog.de/the-spanish-amnesty-the-conflict-with-catalonia-and-the-rule-of-law/> accessed 26 June 2024; Reuters, 'Spanish Socialists and Catalan Junts Reach Deal for Government Support, Amnesty' (Reuters 2023) <https://www.reuters.com/world/europe/spanish-socialists-reach-deal-with-catalan-junts-government-support-tve-2023–11–09/> accessed 20 June 2024.

160 Organic Law 1/2024, on Amnesty for Institutional, Political and Social Normalisation in Catalonia (14 March 2024).

reforming its offences of rebellion and sedition so that they could not be used to recriminalise the (decriminalised) organisation of an illegal referendum, and dropping the extradition requests and remaining prosecutions for lower-raking officials.[161]

If the PSOE appears to be more agreeable on the Catalan question, its more inclusive approach should not, however, be conflated with one of agreement with the Catalan separatist project. The PSOE has indeed been quite clear in the past on the fact that it would not agree to a referendum on independence.[162] A scandal revealed by Citizen Lab alleged that, under PSOE leadership, the Spanish National Intelligence Center used Pegasus spyware to spy on Catalan leaders, suggesting the PSOE's cautiousness and suspicion toward the separatist movement.[163] Furthermore, recent PSOE history includes the setting up of the state-sponsored terrorist group of GAL death squads to combat Basque terrorism in the 1980s.[164] So if the PSOE seems indeed more amenable than the PP on the Catalan question, it has its own record of brutal repression of regional separatism. Anderson notes, in this respect, that centralisation strategies have been put in place both by the PSOE and the PP alike over the years.[165] The PSOE thus does not seem to have a substantially different approach from the PP to Catalan separatism as it does to Catalan separatists. Its goal seems to be similar to that of the PP, that is Spanish unity and even a possible centralisation. Therefore, the smaller concessions made to Catalan leaders do not actually steer the PSOE away from its main goal, which is territorial integrity and the respect of the Spanish Constitution.[166]

Conclusion

Against the converging centralising strategies of both the PP and the PSOE, Catalan separatists framed their endeavour as a fight for national liberation, denouncing the structural domination of which they argue they have been the victims. The message they put forward is that while Catalonia has never stopped upholding the ideals and applied the standards of democratic states, Spain silently sunk into (post)fascism and deceived everyone with the myth

161 Parliamentary Assembly of the Council of Europe (n 5) 4.

162 EuroEFE, 'Spanish PM: Socialists Will "Never" Endorse Catalonia Independence Vote' (Euractiv 2021) <https://www.euractiv.com/section/politics/news/spanish-pm-socialists-will-never-endorse-catalonia-independence-vote/> accessed 12 May 2022.

163 J. Scott-Railton, E. Campo, B. Marczak, B. Abdul Razzak, S. Anstis, G. Böcü, S. Solimano and R. Deibert, 'CatalanGate - Extensive Mercenary Spyware Operation against Catalans Using Pegasus and Candiru' (Citizenlab 2022) <https://citizenlab.ca/2022/04/catalangate-extensive-mercenary-spyware-operation-against-catalans-using-pegasus-candiru/> accessed 13 May 2022.

164 E.-P. Guittet, '"Ne Pas Leur Faire Confiance Serait Leur Faire Offense". Antiterrorisme, Solidarité Démocratique et Identité Politique' [2006] *C&C (Online)*. 5.

165 P. Anderson (n 34) 347.

166 P. Anderson (n 34) 350–351.

of a successful democratic transition. They therefore justified the legitimacy of their project by their willingness to create a real democracy as opposed to what they described as a postfascist Spain. The massive and spontaneous mobilisation of Catalan citizens to ensure the conduct of the referendum was further evidence, according to Catalan separatist leaders, of the legitimacy of the independence process.

In the direct aftermath of the referendum, the PP-led government reacted strongly. It first triggered article 155, thereby recalling some of the previously devolved powers to be taken over by the corresponding central service. It also deployed a heavy police presence and subsequently judicialised the process. Insisting on the fact that the Catalan crisis was a domestic issue, the PP framed the crisis as one of illegality, which enabled it to circumvent the question of the potential legitimacy of the Catalan aspirations altogether. The charges brought forward against Catalan leaders were described as overly severe and included rebellion, sedition, misappropriation of public funds, disobedience, and criminal organisation. Catalan separatists tried by the Supreme Court were eventually convicted on charges of sedition, disobedience, and misappropriation of public funds with sentences ranging from 9 to 13 years. When the PSOE rose to power in 2019, it adopted a more assuaging stance rooted in dialogue. After taking office, the PSOE-led government indeed sought to de-escalate the conflict and restore the divide between the autonomous community and central authorities. It did so by initiating a political dialogue, issuing pardons to sentenced separatists, overhauling its criminal code, and eventually adopting an amnesty law for Catalan separatists. Notwithstanding this seemingly more compromising stance, the PSOE shares the objective of keeping a strong central state with the PP.

Bibliography

Legislation, cases, official publications

Council of Europe

Parliamentary Assembly of the Council of Europe, Should Politicians be Prosecuted for Statements Made in the Exercise of Their Mandate? (Draft Resolution) 2021.

Spain

Constitutional Court, Judgment No. 31/2015 (25 February 2015).
Constitutional Court, Judgment No. 42/2014 (25 March 2014).
Constitutional Court, Judgment No. 117/2017 (7 October 2017).
El Defensor de les Persones (Catalan Ombudsman), 'The Violation of Fundamental Rights and Freedoms Arising from the Criminal Justice Reaction Following October 1, and Application of the Article 155 of the Spanish Constitution' [2018].
Law 10/2014 on Popular Non-Referendum and Other Forms of Citizen Participation (26 September 2014).
Organic Law 1/2024, on Amnesty for Institutional, Political and Social Normalisation in Catalonia (14 March 2024).

Organic Law 2/2005, Amendment of the Criminal Code (22 June 2005).
Organic Law 14/2022, on the Transposition of European Directives and Other Provisions for the Adaptation of Criminal Legislation to the Legal System of the European Union, and Reform of Crimes against Moral Integrity, Public Disorder and Smuggling of Dual-Use Weapons (22 December 2022).
Supreme Court, Judgment No. 80/2006 (6 February 2006).
Supreme Court, Judgment No. 177/2017 (22 March 2017).
Supreme Court, Judgment No. 263/2001 (24 February 2001).
Supreme Court, Judgment No. 281/2019 (30 May 2019).
Supreme Court, Judgment No. 459/2019 (14 October 2019).
Supreme Court, Judgment No. 485/2002 (14 June 2002).
Supreme Court, Judgment No. 722/2018 (23 January 2018).
Supreme Court, Judgment No. 865/2011 (20 July 2011).
Supreme Court, Judgment No. 987/2009 (13 October 2009).
Supreme Court, Judgment No. 1049 (10 October 1980).
Supreme Court, Judgment No. 1154/2010 (12 January 2010).
Supreme Court, Judgment No. 1203/1997 (11 October 1997).
Supreme Court, Judgment No. 1622/2001 (21 September 2001).

Books

Marty N., *Comprendre la Crise Catalane* (Cairn, France 2019).
Puigdemont C., *La Crise Catalane. Une Opportunité pour l'Europe. Conversation avec Olivier Mouton* (Racine, Tielt 2018).

Journal articles

Anderson P., 'Decentralisation at a Crossroads: Spain, Catalonia and the Territorial Crisis' [2020] *Ethnoplitics*. 342.
Cetrà D., Casanas-Adam E. and Tarrega M., 'The 2017 Catalan Independence Referendum: A Symposium' [2018] *Scot. Aff.* 126.
Cetrà D. and Harvey M., 'Explaining Accommodation and Resistance to Demands for Independence Referendums in the UK and Spain' [2019] *Nations Natl.* 607.
García C., 'The Power of Myths and Storytelling in Nation Building: The Campaign for the Independence of Catalonia from Spain (2012–2015)' [2018] *CJC*. 281.
Grau Creus M., 'A Step Backwards or a Step Forwards? The Politics and Policies of Decentralization under the Governments of the Partido Popular' [2005] *South Eur. Soc. Politics*. 263.
Guittet E.-P., '"Ne Pas Leur Faire Confiance Serait Leur Faire Offense". Antiterrorisme, Solidarité Démocratique et Identité Politique' [2006] *C&C (Online)*.
Lancaster T. D., 'The Spanish General Elections of 2015 and 2016: A New Stage in Democratic Politics?' [2017] *West Eur. Politics*. 919.
López Bofill H., 'Hubris, Constitutionalism, and "the Indissoluble Unity of the Spanish Nation": The Repression of Catalan Secessionist Referenda in Spanish Constitutional Law' [2019] *Int. J. Const. Law*. 943.
Medina I. and Correa P., 'The 2015 Spanish Election: The Times They Are a' Changing' [2016] *Reg. Fed. Stud.* 407.
Muro D., 'The Still Birth of the Catalan Republic' [2018] *Curr. Hist.* 83.
Narotzky S., 'Evidence Struggles: Legality, Legitimacy and Social Mobilizations in the Catalan Political Conflict' [2019] *IJGLS*. 31.
Wagner A., Marin J. and Kroqi D., 'The Catalan Struggle for Independence and the Role of the European Union' [2019] *RSPP*. 787.

Wagner P., 'Towards a Conceptual History of the Present: Democracy, Rights, and Freedom in the Recent Catalan Conflict' [2018] *Soc. Sci. Inf.* 588.

Book chapters

Bernat I. and Whyte D., 'Catalonia, Postfascism and Popular Sovereignty' in I Bernat & D. Whyte (eds), *Building a New Catalonia: Self-Determination and Emancipation* (Pollen Edicions, 2019).

Botran R., 'Civil Society Mobilisation from Below' in I. Bernat & D. Whyte (eds), *Building a New Catalonia: Self-Determination and Emancipation* (Pollen Edicions, 2019).

Fernandez Garcia A. and Petithomme M., 'Nationalisme d'État aux Nationalismes Espagnols, la Réinvention de la "Nation" Espagnole Depuis la Transition Démocratique' in A. Garcia Herrero & M. Petithomme (eds), *Les nationalismes dans l'Espagne contemporaine (1975–2011): Compétition politique et identités nationales* (Armand Colin, 2012).

Guidi M. and Casula M., 'The Europeanisation of the Catalan Debate' in C. Closa, C. Margiotta & G. Martinico (eds), *Between Democracy and Law: The Amorality of Secession* (Routledge, 2020).

Johansson-Nogués E., 'The Kosovo Juggling Act? Zapatero's Delicate Balance Act between Spanish Constraints and European Imperatives' in E. Barbé (ed), *Spain in Europe 2004–2008* (Observatory of European Foreign Policy, 2008).

Ponsatí C., 'Political Conflict in Catalonia and the Limits of Spanish Democracy' in B. De Wever, I. Ferreras & P. Van Parijs (eds), *Multi-level Nationalism? The Catalan Question and its Lessons for Belgium and for Europe* (Re-Bel Initiative, 2018).

Salellas B. and Serra G., 'Necessary Disobedience' in I. Bernat & D. Whyte (eds), *Building a New Catalonia: Self-Determination and Emancipation* (Pollen Edicions, 2019).

Serra i Puig B., 'The Post-Dictatorship Transition Years: The Lessons to be Learned from Deceit' in I. I. Bernat & D. Whyte (eds), *Building a New Catalonia: Self-Determination and Emancipation* (Pollen Edicions, 2019).

Online resources

Amnesty International, 'Spain: Excessive Use of Force by National Police and Civil Guard in Catalonia' (Amnesty International 2017) <https://www.amnesty.org/en/latest/news/2017/10/spain-excessive-use-of-force-by-national-police-and-civil-guard-in-catalonia/> accessed 21 February 2020.

Balfour S., 'The Catalan and Spanish crisis: A European Perspective' (EUROPP blog - LSE 2018) <https://blogs.lse.ac.uk/europpblog/2018/07/03/the-catalan-and-spanish-crisis-a-european-perspective/> accessed 6 May 2020.

Encina C. G., 'Whither Spain? The July 2023 General Election Results and Beyond' (Center for Strategic and International Studies 2023) <https://www.csis.org/analysis/whither-spain-july-2023-general-election-results-and-beyond> accessed 20 June 2024.

European Network of Councils for the Judiciary, 'Members – Spain - Factsheet' (European Network of Councils for the Judiciary) <https://www.encj.eu/images/stories/pdf/factsheets/cgpj_spain.pdf> accessed 7 May 2022.

Garrido Muñoz A., 'Catalan Independence in the Spanish Constitution and Courts' (Oxford Constitutional Law) <https://oxcon.ouplaw.com/page/Catalan-independence/catalan-independence-in-the-spanish-constitution-and-courts> accessed 19 February 2020.

Generalitat de Catalunya, '12 M 2024 - Eleccions al Parlament de Catalunya' (GenCat 2024) <https://resultats.eleccionsparlament.cat/ca/inici> accessed 20 June 2024.

Human Rights Watch, 'Spain: Police Used Excessive Force in Catalonia' (Human Rights Watch 2017) <https://www.hrw.org/news/2017/10/12/spain-police-used-excessive-force-catalonia> accessed 23 October 2018.

La Moncloa, 'Pedro Sánchez is Sworn in as President of the Government of Spain with an Absolute Majority' (La Moncloa 2023) <https://www.lamoncloa.gob.es/lang/en/presidente/news/Paginas/2023/20231116_investiture-session.aspx#:~:text=The%20Plenary%20of%20the%20Lower,in%20favour%20and%20171%20against> accessed 20 June 2024.

Luis Martí J., 'Politics and Criminal Law: The Trial against the Catalan Independence Leaders' (Verfassungsblog 2019) <https://verfassungsblog.de/politics-and-criminal-law-the-trial-against-the-catalan-independence-leaders/> accessed 7 May 2022.

PSOE, 'Sánchez Plantea Revisar el Delito de Rebellion para Adecuarlo al Desafío Secesionista' (PSOE) <https://www.psoe.es/actualidad/noticias-actualidad/sanchez-plantea-revisar-el-delito-de-rebelion-para-adecuarlo-al-desafio-secesionista/> accessed 25 January 2020.

Scott-Railton J., Campo E., Marczak B., Abdul Razzak B., Anstis S., Böcü G., Solimano S. and Deibert R., 'CatalanGate - Extensive Mercenary Spyware Operation against Catalans Using Pegasus and Candiru' (Citizenlab 2022) <https://citizenlab.ca/2022/04/catalangate-extensive-mercenary-spyware-operation-against-catalans-using-pegasus-candiru/> accessed 13 May 2022.

Torbisco Casals N. and Krisch N., 'The Spanish Amnesty, the Conflict with Catalonia, and the Rule of Law' (Verfassunsblog 2024) <https://verfassungsblog.de/the-spanish-amnesty-the-conflict-with-catalonia-and-the-rule-of-law/> accessed 26 June 2024.

United Nations Human Rights Office of the High Commissioner, 'UN Expert Urges Spain Not to Pursue Criminal Charges of Rebellion Against Political Figures in Catalonia' (United Nations Human Rights Office of the High Commissioner 2018) <https://www.ohchr.org/en/press-releases/2018/04/un-expert-urges-spain-not-pursue-criminal-charges-rebellion-against> accessed 12 May 2022.

Newspaper articles

Ara, "We'll Control the Second Chamber from Behind the Scenes': Cosidó's Text Justifying the PP's Pact with the PSOE on the GCJ' (Ara 2018) <https://en.ara.cat/misc/control-the-justifying-psoe-gcj_1_2711425.html> accessed 7 May 2022.

Cabanas Ansorena S., 'Spain Isn't Imposing Excessive Punishment on Catalonia's Leaders. It's Enforcing the Law' (Foreign Policy 2019) <https://foreignpolicy.com/2019/11/14/spain-isnt-imposing-excessive-punishment-on-catalonias-leaders-its-enforcing-the-law/> accessed 24 February 2020.

EuroEFE, 'Spanish PM: Socialists Will "Never" Endorse Catalonia Independence Vote' (Euractiv 2021) <https://www.euractiv.com/section/politics/news/spanish-pm-socialists-will-never-endorse-catalonia-independence-vote/> accessed 12 May 2022.

Faus J. and Elías Rodríguez J., 'Catalan Leaders Go on Trial in Madrid Over Independence Bid' (Reuters 2019) <https://www.reuters.com/article/us-spain-politics-catalonia/catalan-leaders-go-on-trial-in-madrid-over-independence-bid-idUSKCN1Q01LD> accessed 11 May 2022.

Gardner D., 'Autonomy under Fire' (Financial Times 2012) <https://www.orwell-foundation.com/wp-content/uploads/2013/03/Autonomy-under-fire.pdf> accessed 4 May 2022.

Garicano L., 'Europe Should Commend Catalan Convictions' (Politico 2019) <https://www.politico.eu/article/europe-should-commend-catalan-convictions-separatist-catalan-leaders/> accessed 19 February 2020.

Hedgecoe G., 'Catalan Independence Talks are Back – and the Stakes are High for PM Sánchez' (Politico 2021) <https://www.politico.eu/article/catalonia-independence-spain-prime-minister-pedro-sanchez/> accessed 12 May 2022.

Jones S., 'Court Finds Spain's Ruling Party Benefited from Bribery Scheme' (The Guardian 2018) <https://www.theguardian.com/world/2018/may/24/court-finds-spain-ruling-party-pp-benefited-bribery-luis-barcenas> accessed 12 May 2022.

Jones S., 'Mariano Rajoy Ousted as Spain Prime Minister' (The Guardian 2018) <https://www.theguardian.com/world/2018/jun/01/mariano-rajoy-ousted-as-spain-prime-minister> accessed 12 May 2022.

Jones S., 'Spain Likely to Return to the Polls in November after Party Talks Fail' (The Guardian 2019) <https://www.theguardian.com/world/2019/sep/17/spain-braces-for-another-election-as-deadline-looms> accessed 12 May 2022.

Jones S., 'Spanish Government Pardons Nine Jailed Catalan Leaders' (The Guardian 2021) <https://www.theguardian.com/world/2021/jun/22/spanish-government-pardons-nine-jailed-catalan-leaders> accessed 12 May 2022.

Nielsen N., 'No Chance of Expanding EU Warrant Crime List' (EU Observer 2017) <https://euobserver.com/justice/140218> accessed 14 May 2022.

Puigdemont C., 'Spain's Imprisonment of Catalan Leaders is a Desperate Move that Will Backfire' (The Guardian 2019) <https://www.theguardian.com/commentisfree/2019/oct/14/spain-imprisonment-catalan-leaders-supreme-cout-jailed-nine?CMP=fb_gu&fbclid=IwAR3wDHXOSpJnZJGMil8KlUjQACxu5T21gjS7yM9NvIQVplyXhvJyrBQY8h> accessed 18 March 2020.

Reuters, 'Spain's Sanchez Promises Dialogue on Catalonia if Wins Confirmation Vote' (Reuters 2019) <https://www.reuters.com/article/us-spain-politics-catalonia-idUSKBN1YL1GY> accessed 12 May 2022.

Reuters, 'Spanish Socialists and Catalan Junts Reach Deal for Government Support, Amnesty' (Reuters 2023) <https://www.reuters.com/world/europe/spanish-socialists-reach-deal-with-catalan-junts-government-support-tve-2023–11–09/> accessed 20 June 2024.

Saeed S., 'Spanish PM Sánchez Signals Softer Approach to Catalonia' (Politico 2018) <https://www.politico.eu/article/pedro-sanchez-spain-catalonia-signals-softer-approach-to-catalonia/> accessed 12 May 2022.

6 Between a rock and a hard place

EU member states in the Catalan independence crisis and the crisis of the European arrest warrant system

First wave of European arrest warrants (2017)

In the immediate aftermath of the referendum on independence, Carles Puigdemont, the Catalan President at the time, and members of his government fled in self-imposed exile to Brussels. In the months that followed, two other Catalan politicians followed suit and went to Switzerland. The exile of Catalan separatist leaders internationalised the domestic constitutional crisis that Spanish authorities had sought to resolve domestically. This strategy to internationalise the crisis was designed by Gonzalo Boye, one of the Spain-based lawyers of members of the Catalan government in exile, who wanted to contrast what he viewed as a biased and unfair judicial proceeding against Catalan leaders in Spain to the fair treatment they would get abroad.[1] Accordingly, when EU and CoE member states received the Spanish extradition requests, Catalan exiles played the card of voluntary cooperation by spontaneously turning themselves in to judicial authorities and declaring in foreign newspapers that they did not fear justice from fair judicial systems.[2]

The first wave of European arrest warrants directly followed the declaration of independence. After Puigdemont declared independence on 27 October 2017, he left the country together with six members of his government.

1 Interview with Paul Bekaert, Lawyer of Carles Puigdemont, Lluis Puig and Clara Ponsatí (when in Belgium) (Tielt, 29 November 2018); J.-P. Stroobants, 'En Belgique, la Défence des Ex-Ministres Catalans Dénonce "un Procès Politique" de Madrid' (Le Monde 2017) <https://www.hvlaw.eu/sites/default/files/online/news/presse/Le_Monde_15-11-2017.pdf> accessed 27 March 2020; S. Oliveira, 'Jaume Alonso-Cuevillas' (Catalonia Today 2019) <https://www.cataloniatoday.cat/article/1552272-jaume-alonso-cuevillas.html> accessed 27 March 2020; L. Andersen, 'Puigdemont's Defence Team Set to Play the "Political Trial" Card' (The Brussels Time 2017) <https://www.brusselstimes.com/all-news/belgium-all-news/44994/puigdemont-s-defence-team-set-to-play-the-political-trial-card/> accessed 27 March 2020.

2 S. Jones and J. Rankin, 'Ex-Catalan Leader Appears Before Belgian Authorities Over Arrest Warrant' (The Guardian 2019) <https://www.theguardian.com/world/2019/oct/18/ex-catalan-leader-carles-puigdemont-belgian-authorities-arrest-warrant> accessed 14 April 2020; L. Brooks, 'Ex-Catalan Minister Vows to Fight "Politically Motivated" Extradition' (The Guardian 2019) <https://www.theguardian.com/world/2019/nov/14/ex-catalan-minister-clara-Ponsatí -vows-to-fight-politically-motivated-extradition> accessed 25 March 2020.

DOI: 10.4324/9781003425847-6

They arrived in Brussels on 29 October 2017. The next day, Spain's public prosecutor charged Puigdemont and his ministers with rebellion, sedition, embezzlement, prevarication, and disobedience to authority. Two of the exiles returned to appear before the court as soon as the charges were filed. On 3 November, Spanish judge Lamela issued European arrest warrants against all Catalan exiles in Belgium.[3] To oppose their surrender, Catalan exiles invoked the fact that the dual criminality principle could not be upheld and that there was a risk of human rights violations.[4] On 5 December, Judge Llarena of the Spanish Supreme Court withdrew all the warrants not only because of the apparent willingness of Catalan members in exile to return to Spain but also, according to commentators like Auke Willems, because of the first hearing in a Belgian court, where the defence of Catalan exiles unsettled the Spanish Court.[5] The latter argued that if the Catalan leaders returned voluntarily, the proceedings against all Catalan suspects, both those in exile and those who remained in Spain, could be conducted jointly and uniformly. However, if Belgium denied part of the request, this would not be possible. In addition, Judge Llarena also contended that this situation would disadvantage those still in Spain, as they could be subject to more thorough investigations than those who had left the country.[6]

Second wave of European and international arrest warrants (2018)

On 23 March 2018, Llarena re-issued European arrest warrants against Catalan exiles in the European Union for rebellion and embezzlement. In the meantime, however, Clara Ponsatí, one of the exiled Catalan politician, had moved to Scotland, and Carles Puigdemont had travelled to Germany. The

3 Comunicación Poder Judicial, 'La Juez Lamela Dicta Órdenes Europeas de Detención Contra el Expresidente de la Generalitat Carles Puigdemont y Cuatro Exconsellers Por los Delitos de Rebelión, Sedición, Malversación, Prevaricación y Desobediencia a la Autoridad' (Poder Judicial 2017) <https://www.poderjudicial.es/cgpj/en/Judiciary/National-High-Court/Pressroom/Press-Releases/La-juez-Lamela-dicta-ordenes-europeas-de-detencion-contra-el-expresidente-de-la-Generalitat-Carles-Puigdemont-y-cuatro-exconsellers> accessed 20 May 2022.

4 Interview with Paul Bekaert (n 1).

5 A. Willems, 'Understanding Spain's Decision to Revoke the European Arrest Warrant for Carles Puigdemont'(EUROPPblog-LSE2017)<https://blogs.lse.ac.uk/europpblog/2017/12/12/understanding-spains-decision-to-revoke-the-european-arrest-warrant-for-carles-puigdemont/> accessed 7 April 2020.

6 Comunicación Poder Judicial, 'El Magistrado del Tribunal Supremo Pablo Llarena Deja sin Efecto las Euro-órdenes contra Puigdemont y los Exconsellers que se Encuentran en Bélgica' (Poder Judicial 2017) <https://www.poderjudicial.es/portal/site/cgpj/menuitem.65d2c4456b6ddb628e635fc1dc432ea0/?vgnextoid=dda146a5fd320610VgnVCM1000006f48ac0aRCRD&vgnextchannel=3f99c38cb605c210VgnVCM100000cb34e20aRCRD&vgnextfmt=default&vgnextlocale=es_ES> accessed 7 April 2020.

others remained in Belgium. As the investigations progressed,[7] Llarena also sent out an international extradition warrant for Marta Rovira, a member of the Parliament of Catalonia and leader of the left-wing and pro-independence Esquerra Republicana party who had fled to Switzerland. However, no international warrant was issued for Anna Gabriel, another member of the Catalan Parliament of the Popular Unity Candidacy Party, who had also fled to Switzerland, although a national arrest warrant remained in force against her.[8] This second wave of warrants was said to follow the finalisation of the preparation of the trial where final charges were laid out.[9] However, accounts of the Citizen Lab suggest otherwise as they confirm that the spyware used on Catalan leaders mentioned in the previous chapter also took place outside of Spain, namely in Belgium, Germany, and Switzerland. There would therefore be a case to argue that the extradition orders were connected to the intelligence collected by the spyware on the movements of Catalan leaders, considering Belgium's track record of not extraditing separatists to Spain.[10] This second warrant was denied by the Belgian Court because it was not accompanied by a conform Spanish arrest warrant.[11] This decision greatly upset Judge Llarena, who publicly called it unacceptable.[12] His irritation with these refusals stemmed from his repeated

7 Comunicación Poder Judicial, 'El Magistrado del Tribunal Supremo Pablo Llarena Amplía su Investigación a Artur Mas, Marta Rovira, Anna Gabriel y Otras Tres Personas. El Juez Ha Notificado un Auto en el Que les Comunica la Existencia del Procedimiento y los Derechos que les Asisten' (Poder Judicial 2017) <https://www.poderjudicial.es/cgpj/en/Judiciary/Pressroom/News-archive/El-magistrado-del-Tribunal-Supremo-Pablo-Llarena-amplia-su-investigacion-a-Artur-Mas--Marta-Rovira--Anna-Gabriel-y-otras-tres-personas> accessed 21 May 2022.

8 Comunicación Poder Judicial, 'El Juez del Tribunal Supremo Pablo Llarena Acuerda la Prisión Provisional Incondicional de Turull, Rull, Romeva, Bassa y Forcadell por Riesgo de Fuga y de Reiteración Delictiva' (Poder Judicial 2018) <https://www.poderjudicial.es/cgpj/en/Judiciary/Pressroom/News-archive/El-juez-del-Tribunal-Supremo-Pablo-Llarena-acuerda-la-prision-provisional-incondicional-de-Turull--Rull--Romeva--Bassa-y-Forcadell> accessed 20 May 2022.

9 Interview with Paul Bekaert, Lawyer of Carles Puigdemont, Lluis Puig and Clara Ponsatí (when in Belgium) (Online, 1 November 2019).

10 J. Scott-Railton, E. Campo, B. Marczak, B. Abdul Razzak, S. Anstis, G. Böcü, S. Solimano and R. Deibert, 'CatalanGate - Extensive Mercenary Spyware Operation against Catalans Using Pegasus and Candiru' (Citizenlab 2022) <https://citizenlab.ca/2022/04/catalangate-extensive-mercenary-spyware-operation-against-catalans-using-pegasus-candiru/> accessed 13 May 2022.

11 Parquet de Bruxelles, 'Communiqué de Presse – Mandats d'Arrêts Européens Émis par l'Espagne' (Ministère Public 2018) <https://www.om-mp.be/fr/article/communique-presse-mandats-arret-europeens-emis-espagne-2> accessed 20 May 2022.

12 Comunicación Poder Judicial, 'El Juez del Tribunal Supremo Pablo Llarena Rechaza la Entrega de Carles Puigdemont Solo por el Delito de Malversación. El Magistrado Destaca la "Falta de Compromiso" del Tribunal Alemán que Decidió sobre la Euroorden Dictada contra el Expresidente de la Generalitat' (Poder Judicial 2018) <https://www.poderjudicial.es/cgpj/es/Poder-Judicial/Tribunal-Supremo/Noticias-Judiciales/El-juez-del-Tribunal-Supremo-Pablo-Llarena-rechaza-la-entrega-de-Carles-Puigdemont-solo-por-el-delito-de-malversacion> accessed 20 May 2022.

efforts to emphasise the supposedly automatic nature of the European arrest warrant scheme, which he reminded is based on the principle of mutual recognition.[13] The German warrant was accepted but only for the charge of embezzlement, not for rebellion, which the Court rejected on grounds of lack of dual criminality. This latter decision is analysed in greater detail in a later section of this chapter. As for Swiss authorities, they declared, days before receiving an extradition request for Marta Rovira, that extradition would not be possible if it appeared that the prosecution was motivated by political reasons.[14] A few months earlier, amidst rumours that Spain would issue an international extradition warrant against Anna Gabriel in February of the same year, Folco Galli, the spokesperson of the Swiss Federal Office for Justice, had already made a similar declaration, saying that her extradition would most probably be rejected as the crimes for which she was charged were likely to be political.[15] In light of all this, Spanish judicial authorities withdrew all European and international arrest warrants on 19 July 2018.[16]

Third wave of European arrest warrants (2019–present)

On 14 October 2019, the Spanish Supreme Court gave its long-awaited verdict on the trial of Catalan separatists.[17] Llarena feared in this respect that if mere threats of indictment had led Puigdemont to flee, actual convictions could motivate him to seek refuge in a non-EU country, where cooperation would be even more challenging. Reminding that mutual trust governs relations among EU member states and that the European arrest warrant scheme is supposed to facilitate and streamline extradition processes among these member state who all freely entered this commitment, Llarena issued a new European arrest warrant against Carles Puigdemont for charges of sedition and embezzlement.[18] Puigdemont presented himself to the Belgian police on

13 Comunicación Poder Judicial, 'El Juez del Tribunal Supremo Pablo Llarena Rechaza la Entrega de Carles Puigdemont Solo por el Delito de Malversación. El Magistrado Destaca la "Falta de Compromiso" del Tribunal Alemán que Decidió sobre la Euroorden Dictada contra el Expresidente de la Generalitat' (Poder Judicial 2018) <https://www.poderjudicial.es/cgpj/es/Poder-Judicial/Tribunal-Supremo/Noticias-Judiciales/El-juez-del-Tribunal-Supremo-Pablo-Llarena-rechaza-la-entrega-de-Carles-Puigdemont-solo-por-el-delito-de-malversacion> accessed 20 May 2022.

14 CPE-N Commissions de Politique Extérieure, 'Communiqué de Presse – La Protection des Intérêts Économiques Extérieurs de la Suisse à l'Ordre du Jour' (Assemblée fédérale – le Parlement Suisse 2018) <https://www.parlament.ch/press-releases/Pages/mm-apk-n-2018-04-17.aspx> accessed 20 May 2022.

15 A. Harari, 'La Suisse N'Expulsera pas L'Indépendantiste Catalane Anna Gabriel' (Le Temps 2018) <https://www.letemps.ch/suisse/suisse-nexpulsera-lindependantiste-catalane-anna-gabriel> accessed 17 December 2019.

16 Comunicación Poder Judicial (n 12).

17 Supreme Court, Judgment No. 459/2019 (14 October 2019).

18 Comunicación Poder Judicial, 'El Juez Llarena Dicta Orden Europea e Internacional de Detención contra Puigdemont por Delitos de Sedición y Malversación. El Auto Señala

17 October and was released on the condition that he does not leave the country and remains reachable.[19]

The European arrest warrant against Puigdemont was followed, on 5 November 2019, by European and international arrest warrants (in case one or all of them left the European Union)[20] against Antoni Comín, Clara Ponsatí, and Lluis Puig, respectively, for charges of sedition and embezzlement, sedition, and embezzlement and disobedience.[21] Although Catalan leaders in self-imposed exile were not tried *in absentia*, Llarena considered that the sentence validated the indictment and reinforced suspicions of actual criminality.[22] Following the receipt of the warrant by Belgian authorities, Puig and Comín presented themselves to the police on 7 November and were released after a court hearing on the same day on the same conditions as Puigdemont, that is that they do not leave the country and remain reachable.[23]

Before Spain issued those European Arrest Warrants, however, Puigdemont, Comín, and Ponsatí were elected as MEPs at the European elections

que la Sala Segunda del Tribunal Supremo ha Dictado hoy la Sentencia que Pone Término al Proceso Respecto de los Acusados Enjuiciados' (Poder Judicial 2019) <https://www.poderjudicial.es/cgpj/es/Causa-especial-20907-2017/Ultimas-Noticias/El-juez-Llarena-dicta-orden-europea-e-internacional-de-detencion-contra-Puigdemont-por-delitos-de-sedicion-y-malversacion> accessed 21 May 2022.

19 Parquet de Bruxelles, 'Press Release – European Arrest Warrant Issued by Spain' (Ministère Public 2019) <https://www.om-mp.be/fr/node/2254> accessed 21 May 2022.

20 Comunicación Poder Judicial, 'El Juez del Tribunal Supremo Pablo Llarena Emite Euroórdenes contra los Exconsellers Catalanes Comin, Ponsatí y Puig. Las Órdenes Internacionales se han Enviado a Interpol para la Detención a Efectos Extradicionales en el Caso de que Estos Procesados se Localicen en un País que no Pertenezca a la UE' (Poder Judicial 2019) <https://www.poderjudicial.es/cgpj/es/Causa-especial-20907-2017/Ultimas-Noticias/El-juez-del-Tribunal-Supremo-Pablo-Llarena-emite-euroordenes-contra-los-exconsellers-catalanes-Comin--Ponsati-y-Puig> accessed 21 May 2022.

21 Comunicación Poder Judicial, 'El Juez del Tribunal Supremo Pablo Llarena Emite Euroórdenes contra los Exconsellers Catalanes Comin, Ponsatí y Puig. Las Órdenes Internacionales se han Enviado a Interpol para la Detención a Efectos Extradicionales en el Caso de que Estos Procesados se Localicen en un País que no Pertenezca a la UE' (Poder Judicial 2019) <https://www.poderjudicial.es/cgpj/es/Causa-especial-20907-2017/Ultimas-Noticias/El-juez-del-Tribunal-Supremo-Pablo-Llarena-emite-euroordenes-contra-los-exconsellers-catalanes-Comin--Ponsati-y-Puig> accessed 21 May 2022.

22 Comunicación Poder Judicial, 'El Juez del Tribunal Supremo Pablo Llarena Emite Euroórdenes contra los Exconsellers Catalanes Comin, Ponsatí y Puig. Las Órdenes Internacionales se han Enviado a Interpol para la Detención a Efectos Extradicionales en el Caso de que Estos Procesados se Localicen en un País que no Pertenezca a la UE' (Poder Judicial 2019) <https://www.poderjudicial.es/cgpj/es/Causa-especial-20907-2017/Ultimas-Noticias/El-juez-del-Tribunal-Supremo-Pablo-Llarena-emite-euroordenes-contra-los-exconsellers-catalanes-Comin--Ponsati-y-Puig> accessed 21 May 2022.

23 Parquet de Bruxelles, 'Communiqué de Presse – Bruxelles – Mandats d'Arrêts Européens Émis par l'Espagne' (Ministère Public 2019) <https://www.om-mp.be/fr/article/communique-presse-bruxelles-mandats-arret-europeens-emis-espagne> accessed 21 May 2022.

of May 2019.[24] This event momentarily set their path on different tracks than the ones of Lluis Puig. The European elections indeed raised the question of the immunity of MEP-elects, which circled back to the issue of the surrender of the exiles who had been elected at the European Parliament. It started with the case of Oriol Junqueras, the vice-president of Catalonia at the time of the referendum, who had remained in Spain. On 2 November 2017, Junqueras was arrested and put in preventive detention, where he remained until his pardon after the trial.[25] Despite being in prison, Junqueras ran for the European Parliament elections of 2019. He won a seat as an MEP on 26 May 2019, together with Carles Puigdemont and Antoni Comín (both in Belgium since 2017). The Spanish electoral commission validated this result.[26] After the election, however, the Spanish Supreme Court did not allow Junqueras to leave prison to take his oath of allegiance to the Spanish Constitution at the electoral commission, a compulsory requirement under Spanish law to become a Spanish MEP.[27] Equally, Comín and Puigdemont, both in Brussels, were also unable to take their seats because they needed to travel to Spain to take their oath. The electoral commission insisted in this respect that they needed to come in person and that a notarised declaration would not suffice. Because they feared being arrested upon their arrival, they did not go.[28] As a result, the Spanish central electoral commission did not transfer any of their names to the European Parliament, and they were all barred from taking their seats.[29]

24 Ponsatí was awarded a seat slightly later following the United Kingdom's exit from the European Union and the subsequent redistribution of British seats to remaining member states. S. Carrell, 'Extradition Case against Catalan MEP Suspended in Scotland' (The Guardian 2020) <https://www.theguardian.com/uk-news/2020/mar/05/clara-Ponsatí-extradition-case-against-catalan-mep-suspended-in-scotland> accessed 15 May 2020.

25 United Nations Working Group on Arbitrary Detention, 'Opiniones Aprobadas por el Grupo de Trabajo Sobre la Detención Arbitraria en su 84o Período de Sesiones (24 de Abril a 3 de Mayo de 2019). Opinión núm. 6/2019, Relativa a Jordi Cuixart I Navarro, Jordi Sánchez I Picanyol y Oriol Junqueras I Vies (España). A/HRC/WGAD/2019/6' (OHCHR 2019) <https://www.ohchr.org/Documents/Issues/Detention/Opinions/Session84/A_HRC_WGAD_2019_6.pdf> accessed 24 April 2020; United Nations Human Rights Office of the High Commissioner, 'High Commissioner's Global Update of Human Rights Concerns' (United Nations 2018) <https://www.ohchr.org/en/NewsEvents/Pages/DisplayNews.aspx?NewsID=22772&LangID=E> accessed 13 May 2020; Cardiff EDC, 'Case C-502/19, Junqueras Vies' (European Sources Online 2019) <https://www.europeansources.info/record/case-c-502-19-junqueras-vies/> accessed 13 May 2020.

26 Cardiff EDC (n 25).

27 Oriol Junqueras Vies [19 December 2019] Case C-502/19. EU:C:2019:1115, 10.

28 P. Van Elsuwege, 'Empty Seats in the European Parliament: What about EU Citizenship?' (Verfassungsblog 2019) <https://verfassungsblog.de/empty-seats-in-the-european-parliament-what-about-eu-citizenship/> accessed 14 May 2020.

29 P. Van Elsuwege, 'Empty Seats in the European Parliament: What about EU Citizenship?' (Verfassungsblog 2019) <https://verfassungsblog.de/empty-seats-in-the-european-parliament-what-about-eu-citizenship/> accessed 14 May 2020.

Junqueras, in Spain but unable to leave prison to go to the Spanish Electoral Commission to get his accreditation, brought an action before the Spanish Supreme Court, claiming he had immunity under the Protocol on the privileges and immunities of the European Union. The Supreme Court consequently introduced a preliminary ruling procedure before the CJEU on the question of his immunity.[30] In the preliminary ruling procedure, the Supreme Court inquired whether the immunity attached to the role of MEP started at the moment of one's election as MEP or only after full accreditation was granted. According to Spanish law, the privileges – and therefore the immunity – that come with the role of MEP start only *after* one officially becomes MEP. This means that elected members must first appear before the electoral commission to swear allegiance to the Spanish constitution before they can officially take their seat as MEP.[31] The Spanish concern regarding Junqueras was to keep him on the territory to ensure the proper conduct of the criminal trial before he could get any form of immunity or leave the territory.[32]

On 19 December 2019, however, the CJEU ruled that the immunity attached to the position of MEP actually takes effect at the moment of the election as MEP, that Junqueras should be released and that, if the Spanish Supreme Court considered he should not benefit from that immunity, it should request the European Parliament to waive it.[33] That is exactly what the Court did, although it did not release Junqueras. Insisting on the duty of loyal cooperation of the European Parliament with national jurisdictional bodies applying EU law, the Court introduced a formal request to waive the immunity not only of Junqueras but of all prosecuted Catalans who became MEPs. The Court argued that the criminal charges brought against these people pertained to crimes they had committed long before their election at the European Parliament and that, therefore, the prosecutions were not intended to prevent them from conducting their activities as MEPs. The Supreme Court further argued that Parliamentary immunity should not be used to avoid criminal responsibilities for actions conducted outside the person's mandate as MEP. Such a use of the immunity attached to the role of MEP, it added, would jeopardise the principle of equality before the law and the right to good administration of

30 Comunicación Poder Judicial, 'El Tribunal Supremo Activa el Trámite para Plantear una Cuestión Prejudicial al TJUE Sobre el Alcance de la Inmunidad en Relación con Oriol Junqueras. La Sala Mantiene la Situación de Prisión del Exvicepresidente de la Generalitat y Deja en Suspenso su Recurso contra la Denegación del Permiso Extraordinario para Acudir a la Junta Electoral Central' (Poder Judicial 2019) <https://www.poderjudicial.es/cgpj/en/Judiciary/Supreme-Court/Pressroom/Press-Archive/El-Tribunal-Supremo-activa-el-tramite-para-plantear-una-cuestion-prejudicial-al-TJUE-sobre-el-alcance-de-la-inmunidad-en-relacion-con-Oriol-Junqueras> accessed 22 May 2022.

31 La Ley Orgánica 5/1985, de Régimen Electoral General of 19 June 1985 (20 June 1985) (Art. 224).

32 Oriol Junqueras Vies (n 27) 11.

33 Oriol Junqueras Vies (n 27) 24.

justice within a reasonable time.[34] Although Puigdemont and Comín were not involved in the legal proceeding concerning Junqueras, the CJEU decision applied *mutatis mutandis* to their situation.[35]

Of crucial importance in the decision of the European Parliament on the immunity of Catalan exiles was the issue of *fumus persecutionis*, pertaining to elements suggesting that the legal proceeding was initiated to hamper the political activity of the MEP.[36] In other words, the European Parliament was expected to adjudicate on potential political persecution exerted by Spain on Catalan MEPs as regards their political mandate. This situation was thus exceptional both because of the content of the vote and because the decision was political rather than judicial. On 9 March 2021, in accordance with the Spanish argumentation, the European Parliament voted to waive the immunity of Catalan leaders because it considered that Spanish judicial authorities could not possibly be trying to hinder the activities of Catalan MEPs at the European Parliament for the simple reason that the crimes for which the waivers were requested took place well before the elections took place and that the election of Puigdemont, Comín, and Ponsatí as MEPs was merely hypothetical at the time.[37] Following

34 Comunicación Poder Judicial, 'El Instructor de la Causa del "Procés" en el Tribunal Supremo Pide al Parlamento Europeo que Suspenda la Inmunidad de Carles Puigdemont y Antoni Comín y Ratifica la Orden de Detención en Territorio Español. El magistrado Pablo Llarena Señala que la Inmunidad no Sería Aplicable en España al Estar ya Procesados y que no se Requeriría Suplicatorio' (Poder Judicial 2020) <https://www.poderjudicial.es/cgpj/es/Causa-especial-20907-2017/Archivo-de-resoluciones/2020/-El-instructor-de-la-causa-del--proces--en-el-Tribunal-Supremo-pide-al-Parlamento-Europeo-que-suspenda-la-inmunidad-de-Carles-Puigdemont-y-Antoni-Comin-y-ratifica-la-orden-de-detencion-en-territorio-espanol> accessed 22 May 2022; Comunicación Poder Judicial, 'El Presidente del TS Remite al del Parlamento Europeo la Solicitud de Suplicatorio de Clara Ponsatí' (Poder Judicial 2020) <https://www.poderjudicial.es/cgpj/en/Judiciary/Supreme-Court/Pressroom/Press-Archive/El-presidente-del-TS-remite-al-del-Parlamento-Europeo-la-solicitud-de-suplicatorio-de-Clara-Ponsati> accessed 22 May 2022.

35 P. Van Elsuwege (n 28).

36 European Parliament, Request for Waiver of the Immunity of Carles Puigdemont i Casamajó. European Parliament Decision of 9 March 2021 on the Request for Waiver of the Immunity of Carles Puigdemont i Casamajó (2020/2024(IMM)), (P9_TA(2021)0059) 2021; European Parliament, Request for Waiver of the Immunity of Antoni Comín i Oliveres. European Parliament Decision of 9 March 2021 on the Request for Waiver of the Immunity of Antoni Comín i Oliveres (2020/2025(IMM)), (P9_TA(2021)0060) 2021; European Parliament, Request for Waiver of the Immunity of Clara Ponsatí Obiols. European Parliament Decision of 9 March 2021 on the Request for Waiver of the Immunity of Clara Ponsatí Obiols (2020/2031(IMM)), (P9_TA(2021)0061) 2021.

37 European Parliament, Request for Waiver of the Immunity of Carles Puigdemont i Casamajó. European Parliament Decision of 9 March 2021 on the Request for Waiver of the Immunity of Carles Puigdemont i Casamajó (2020/2024(IMM)), (P9_TA(2021)0059) 2021; European Parliament, Request for Waiver of the Immunity of Antoni Comín i Oliveres. European Parliament Decision of 9 March 2021 on the Request for Waiver of the Immunity of Antoni Comín i Oliveres (2020/2025(IMM)), (P9_TA(2021)0060) 2021; European Parliament, Request for Waiver of the Immunity of Clara Ponsatí Obiols. European Parliament

the vote on the immunity of Catalan MEPs, the latter tried to regain immunity several times. They first sought to annul the decision to waive the immunity and, on two occasions, requested the General Court to impose interim measures to suspend the waiver due to the imminent risk of surrender to Spain.[38] The General Court initially rejected these requests twice[39] but ultimately approved them on appeal on 24 May 2022.[40] In the summer of 2023, the General Court of the European Union finally rejected the request for annulment, thereby lifting the immunity of Catalan MEPs.[41] At the time of writing, this decision is under appeal at the General Court, and the ruling is pending.[42]

The second application for interim measures, submitted before the General Court's decision, came after Puigdemont's arrest in Italy on 23 September 2021, pursuant to a European arrest warrant against him.[43] This arrest was directly linked to the European arrest warrant against Lluis Puig previously mentioned. Lluis Puig had not become an MEP, like his colleagues, so he was not concerned by the questions linked to a potential immunity. This meant that the European arrest warrant targeting him was still applicable. Belgian judicial authorities, however, rejected the warrant, arguing that the Supreme Court lacked the authority to issue a European arrest warrant for Lluis Puig. They contended that a Catalan court should handle the case and that Puig's fundamental rights, including the right to a fair trial, were at risk.[44]

Decision of 9 March 2021 on the Request for Waiver of the Immunity of Clara Ponsatí Obiols (2020/2031(IMM)), (P9_TA(2021)0061) 2021.

38 Tribunal de L'Union Européenne, Le Vice-Président du Tribunal de l'Union Européenne Suspend Provisoirement la Levée de l'Immunité Parlementaire de MM. Carles Puigdemont i Casamajó et Antoni Comín i Oliveres ainsi que de Mme Clara Ponsatí i Obiols (Communiqué de Presse No. 91/21) 2021.

39 Tribunal de L'Union Européenne, Le Vice-Président du Tribunal de l'Union Européenne Rejette la Demande de Suspension de la Levée de l'Immunité Parlementaire de MM. Carles Puigdemont i Casamajó et Antoni Comín i Oliveres ainsi que de Mme Clara Ponsatí i Obiols (Communiqué de Presse No. 141/21) 2021; General Court of the European Union, The Vice-President of the General Court of the European Union Refuses the New Request for the Suspension of Waiver of the Parliamentary Immunity of Mr Carles Puigdemont i Casamajó, Mr Antoni Comín i Oliveres and Ms Clara Ponsatí i Obiols (Press release No. 213/21) 2021.

40 Order of the Vice-President of the Court of 24 May 2022, Carles Puigdemont i Casamajó and Others v. European Parliament (Appeal – Interim Relief – Institutional Law – Members of the European Parliament – Privileges and Immunities – Waiver of the Parliamentary Immunity of a Member of the Parliament – Prima Facie Case – Impartiality of the Rapporteur When Examining the Request for Waiver of Parliamentary Immunity – Urgency – European Arrest Warrant – Alert on Persons Wanted for Arrest for Surrender Purposes – Exercise of the Mandate of a Member of the Parliament – Balance of Interests) EU:C:2022:413.

41 Puigdemont i Casamajó et Comín i Oliveres [5 July 2023] Case T115/20. EU:T:2023:372.

42 Puigdemont i Casamajó and Others v. Parliament [22 December 2023] C-572/23 P.

43 General Court of the European Union (n 39).

44 Comunicación Poder Judicial, 'El Instructor de la Causa del "Procés" Plantea Cuestión Prejudicial al TJUE Sobre la Euroorden' (Poder Judicial 2021) <https://www.poderjudicial.es/cgpj/en/Judiciary/Supreme-Court/Pressroom/Press-Archive/El-instructor-de-la-causa-del--proces--plantea-cuestion-prejudicial--al-TJUE-sobre-la-euroorden> accessed 24 May 2022.

The Public Prosecutor's appeal against this decision was unsuccessful.[45] The Spanish Supreme Court consequently introduced a preliminary ruling question on the compatibility of this decision with EU law, which automatically suspended the criminal proceeding in Spain. This not only impacted Puig but also all other Catalan exiles targeted by a European arrest warrant as part of that criminal proceeding.[46] As a result, when Puigdemont was arrested in Italy, although the Spanish judiciary contended that the Italian Court should hand him back to Spain,[47] the surrender procedure was in fact suspended until the CJEU ruled on the preliminary ruling.[48] On 31 January 2023, the CJEU issued its decision on the matter and sided with cooperation, although it recognised the latter can be restricted in cases of serious risks of human rights violation. The ruling is analysed in a further section of this chapter.

At the time of writing, the third wave of European arrest warrants was also the last one. On 12 January 2023, following the reform of the Spanish criminal code, Judge Llarena withdrew the European and international arrest warrants against Puigdemont, Comín, Ponsatí, Puig, and Rovira. Those initially indicted for sedition were eventually charged with disobedience. The charge of embezzlement was maintained.[49] Following the lifting of immunity for Catalan MEPs in January 2023, no new European arrest warrant requests were issued. Judge Llarena decided to wait because the exiled MEPs could appeal the General Court's decision (which they did), potentially allowing them to seek precautionary measures that would temporarily restore their immunity.[50]

45 Comunicación Poder Judicial, 'El Instructor de la Causa del "Procés" Plantea Cuestión Prejudicial al TJUE Sobre la Euroorden' (Poder Judicial 2021) <https://www.poderjudicial.es/cgpj/en/Judiciary/Supreme-Court/Pressroom/Press-Archive/El-instructor-de-la-causa-del--proces--plantea-cuestion-prejudicial--al-TJUE-sobre-la-euroorden> accessed 24 May 2022.

46 Tribunal de L'Union Européenne (n 39).

47 Comunicación Poder Judicial, 'El Juez Confirma al Tribunal Italiano que la Euroorden contra Puigdemont Está Vigente y que no ha Sido Suspendida por el Planteamiento de la Cuestión Prejudicial. El Magistrado del Tribunal Supremo Remite Información Complementaria a Eurojust para Clarificar el Estado de la Causa y Reclamar la Entrega del Detenido a la Justicia Española' (Poder Judicial 2021) <https://www.poderjudicial.es/cgpj/en/Judiciary/Pressroom/News-archive/El-juez-confirma-al-tribunal-italiano-que-la-euroorden-contra-Puigdemont-esta-vigente-y-que-no-ha-sido-suspendida-por-el-planteamiento-de-la-cuestion-prejudicial> accessed 2 June 2022

48 General Court of the European Union (n 39).

49 Comunicación Poder Judicial, 'El Instructor de la Causa del Procés en el TS Aplica la Derogación del Delito de Sedición a Carles Puigdemont y Acuerda su Procesamiento por Desobediencia y Malversación. El Magistrado Pablo Llarena Considera que Los Hechos no Encajan en el Delito de Desórdenes Públicos y que la Reforma Legal Ofrece "un Contexto Cercano a la Despenalización"' (Poder Judicial 2023) <https://www.poderjudicial.es/cgpj/es/Poder-Judicial/Tribunal-Supremo/Oficina-de-Comunicacion/Archivo-de-notas-de-prensa/El-instructor-de-la-causa-del-proces-en-el-TS-aplica-la-derogacion-del-delito-de-sedicion-a-Carles-Puigdemont-y-acuerda-su-procesamiento-por-desobediencia-y-malversacion> accessed 15 July 2024.

50 Comunicación Poder Judicial, 'El Instructor de la Causa del "Procés" en el Tribunal Supremo Resolverá sobre la Euroorden contra Carles Puigdemont Cuando el TJUE se

Equally, no new requests were made after the CJEU's decision on the Puig case in July 2023. A year later, in the European elections of June 2024, only Comín renewed his mandate. Puigdemont and Ponsatí decided to focus on political life at the Catalan level ahead of the local elections of June 2024.[51] In 2024, Spain passed an amnesty law, and on 1 July 2024, the Supreme Court ruled that although the amnesty covered the offence of disobedience, it did not apply to the embezzlement of public funds that occurred during the independence process. This was because the law included two exceptions that applied in this case: the embezzlement was committed for personal gain, and it affected the financial interests of the EU. Llarena therefore declared that the national arrest warrants against Puigdemont, Comín, and Puig for the crime of embezzlement remained in force. He did not, however, re-issue European or international extradition warrants for those remaining in exile.[52]

In parallel to the proceedings linked to the trial of the independence process itself (that resulted in the 14 October 2019 ruling outlined in the previous chapter), a new wave of exiles followed the beginning of criminal proceedings against Puigdemont and Rubén Wagensberg, the deputy of the Catalan Parliament. Puigdemont and Wagensberg faced charges of terrorism due to their involvement in the 'Tsunami Democratic' movement. The latter concerned a protest that erupted at El Prat airport following the 14 October 2019 ruling of the Supreme Court on the independence process. Protestors gathered with false plane tickets and boarding passes in view of disrupting air traffic. They were accused of having thrown dangerous items, such as inflammable items, fire extinguishers, glass, metal carts, or luggage, to police forces to prevent their restoring order. They were also alleged to have attacked and damaged public and police buildings. In this process, Puigdemont was charged with being aware of and participating in meetings of this organised group that aimed to undermine the constitutional order, destabilise

---

Pronuncie sobre Eventuales Medidas Cautelares' (Poder Judicial 2023) <https://www.poderjudicial.es/cgpj/es/Poder-Judicial/Tribunal-Supremo/Oficina-de-Comunicacion/Archivo-de-notas-de-prensa/El-instructor-de-la-causa-del--proces--en-el-Tribunal-Supremo-resolvera-sobre-la-euroorden-contra-Carles-Puigdemont-cuando-el-TJUE-se-pronuncie-sobre-eventuales-medidas-cautelares> accessed 15 July 2024.

51 F. Heller, 'Carles Puigdemont Établit son "Quartier Général" Politique en France' (Euractiv 2024) <https://www.euractiv.fr/section/elections/news/puigdemont-sets-up-political-headquarters-in-france/> accessed 16 July 2024; T. Partal, 'Clara Ponsatí: "We Want to Be the Backbone of the Independence Process"' (VilaWeb 2024) <https://www.vilaweb.cat/noticies/clara-ponsati-we-want-to-be-the-backbone-of-the-independence-process/> accessed 16 July 2024.

52 Comunicación Poder Judicial, 'El Tribunal Supremo Declara no Amnistiado el Delito de Malversación de Caudales Públicos en la Causa del "Procés". El Magistrado Pablo Llarena Mantiene las Órdenes Nacionales de Detención contra Carles Puigdemont, Antoni Comín y Lluís Puig' (Poder Judicial 2024) <https://www.poderjudicial.es/cgpj/es/Poder-Judicial/Tribunal-Supremo/Oficina-de-Comunicacion/Archivo-de-notas-de-prensa/El-Tribunal-Supremo-declara-no-amnistiado-el-delito-de-malversacion-de-caudales-publicos-en-la-causa-del--proces-> accessed 15 July 2024.

democratic institutions, and obstruct public authorities. His involvement in meetings prior to the group's formation and his support for its activities led the Criminal Chamber of the Supreme Court to regard him as the leader and intellectual author of the group, attributing significant influence and control over its actions to him. Rubén Wagensberg was in turn suspected of being the real face behind a pseudonym publishing official statements of the movement.[53] As part of this process, no European or international arrest warrant was issued for Catalan exiles, but a European investigation order was issued for Puigdemont to provide a statement on the case.[54] Additionally, a request for judicial assistance to locate Marta Rovira, exiled in Switzerland, was issued to Switzerland. The Swiss Federal Department of Justice, however, refused the request because it considered that the dual criminality requirement could not be fulfilled and that the request for assistance concerned political rather than terrorist endeavours.[55] In July 2024, in an unexpected turn of event, the National Court (Audiencia Nacional) declared that the criminal proceedings concerning the *Tsunami Democratic* case were invalidated due to a procedural error and closed the case.[56]

Lawyers of Catalan exiles make the case for a political trial

When issuing European and international extradition warrants, Spanish judicial authorities were determined to prosecute the leaders of the illegal Catalan independence referendum domestically. They were optimistic that securing

53 Comunicación Poder Judicial, 'El Tribunal Supremo Abre Causa Penal por Delito de Terrorismo a Carles Puigdemont y al Diputado Wagensberg en el Caso de "Tsunami Democràtic"' (Poder Judicial 2024) <https://www.poderjudicial.es/cgpj/es/Poder-Judicial/Tribunal-Supremo/Oficina-de-Comunicacion/Archivo-de-notas-de-prensa/El-Tribunal-Supremo-abre-causa-penal-por-delito-de-terrorismo-a-Carles-Puigdemont-y-al-diputado-Wagensberg-en-el-caso-de--Tsunami-Democratic-> accessed 16 July 2024.

54 Comunicación Poder Judicial, 'El Tribunal Supremo Cita como Investigados a Carles Puigdemont y a Rubén Wagensberg para que Presten Declaración Voluntaria por Videoconferencia el Próximo Mes de Junio' (Poder Judicial 2024) <https://www.poderjudicial.es/cgpj/es/Poder-Judicial/Tribunal-Supremo/Oficina-de-Comunicacion/Archivo-de-notas-de-prensa/El-Tribunal-Supremo-cita-como-investigados-a-Carles-Puigdemont-y-a-Ruben-Wagensberg-para-que-presten-declaracion-voluntaria-por-videoconferencia-el-proximo-mes-de-junio> accessed 16 July 2024.

55 M. Sánchez Iranzo, 'Why Switzerland Has Again Slammed the Door on Spanish Judge García-Castellón. Switzerland Reiterates that the Democratic Tsunami Demonstrations Are not Terrorism and Refuses to Locate Marta Rovira' (El Nacional 2024) <https://www.elnacional.cat/en/politics/why-switzerland-slams-door-spanish-judge-garcia-castellon_1235613_102.html> accessed 16 July 2024.

56 Comunicación Poder Judicial, 'La Instructora del Caso "Tsunami Democràtic" en el Tribunal Supremo Acuerda el Archivo de la Causa en la que Investigaba a Puigdemont y Wagensberg. Tras la Decisión de la Audiencia Nacional de Invalidar las Diligencias Acordadas desde Julio de 2021' (Poder Judicial 2024) <https://www.poderjudicial.es/cgpj/fr/Pouvoir-Judiciaire/Tribunal-supreme/Salle-de-presse/Bibliotheque-de-communiques-de-presse/La-instructora-del-caso--Tsunami-Democratic--en-el-Tribunal-Supremo-acuerda-el-archivo-de-la-causa-en-la-que-investigaba-a-Puigdemont-y-Wagensberg> accessed 16 July 2024.

the return of the Catalan leaders would be a straightforward formality. This was, for example, visible in their insistence on the quasi-automatic nature of the European arrest warrant scheme and on the mutual recognition principle underlying it.[57] Many commentators, however, considered this repetitive use of the European arrest warrant scheme as an abuse of the European arrest warrant system. Although there is no limit on the number of times European arrest warrants can be issued for the same facts and individuals after previous warrants have been withdrawn, the persistence of the Spanish Court was said to betray the Spanish contempt for mutual respect and the right of other jurisdictions to freely decide rather than simply execute orders.[58] Paul Bekaert, the Belgian lawyer for Puigdemont, noted in this respect that the withdrawal and re-issuance of warrants based on the advancement of the procedure in Spain had no incidence on the decision of executing authorities to grant the surrender. The competent judge in the executing country just needed to ensure that the crimes for which the surrenders were requested were punishable under national law.[59] This was not new to the Spanish Supreme Court, which led Bekaert to contend that the repeated withdrawals and re-issuances of warrants were intended to create an atmosphere of intimidation for Catalan exiles.[60]

Olivier Peter, the lawyer representing Anna Gabriel, a Catalan MP who had fled to Switzerland, shared the same view. He reported that, in the aftermath of the exile of Anna Gabriel to Switzerland, Spanish authorities regularly declared in the press that they would request her extradition and that there

57 Comunicación Poder Judicial (n 12); Comunicación Poder Judicial (n 18); Comunicación Poder Judicial (n 44).

58 Ramon Tremosa i Balcells (ALDE), Josep-Maria Terricabras (Verts/ALE), Jordi Solé (Verts/ALE), Martina Anderson (GUE/NGL), José Bové (Verts/ALE), Bodil Valero (Verts/ALE), Igor Šoltes (Verts/ALE), Izaskun Bilbao Barandica (ALDE), Josu Juaristi Abaunz (GUE/NGL), Jill Evans (Verts/ALE), António Marinho e Pinto (ALDE), Bart Staes (Verts/ALE), Barbara Spinelli (GUE/NGL), Maria Lidia Senra Rodríguez (GUE/NGL) and Rolandas Paksas (EFDD) 1145474.EN, PE 617.651 Question for Written Answer E-000746/2018 to the Commission. Subject: Misuse of the European Arrest Warrant by Spain [2018]; A. Willems, 'Will Spain's Latest Attempt at Extraditing Carles Pugidemont Succeed' (EUROPP blog - LSE 2019) <https://blogs.lse.ac.uk/europpblog/2019/10/23/will-spains-latest-attempt-to-extradite-carles-puigdemont-succeed/#comments> accessed 25 May 2022; R. Bunche, 'Free Movement Threatened if European Arrest Warrant Abused' (EUobserver 2018) <https://euobserver.com/opinion/141498> accessed 25 May 2022; G. McPherson, 'VIDEO: St Andrews Professor Clara Ponsatí and Lawyer Address Catalonia Supporters Outside Court' (The Courrier 2018) <https://www.thecourier.co.uk/fp/news/politics/scottish-politics/654121/video-st-andrews-professor-clara-Ponsatí-and-lawyer-address-catalonia-supporters-outside-court/> accessed 27 March 2020; Interview with Paul Bekaert (n 9); J. Urías, 'Spain Has a Problem with Its Judiciary' (Verfassungsblog 2020) <https://verfassungsblog.de/spain-has-a-problem-with-its-judiciary/> accessed 15 April 2020.

59 Interview with Paul Bekaert (n 9).

60 Interview with Paul Bekaert (n 9).

was no reason for the Swiss authorities to reject it.[61] In reaction to that, the spokesperson of the Swiss Federal Office for Justice declared that the crimes for which Spain intended to request extraditions were in all likelihood political. In that case, Switzerland could not grant the extradition.[62] Following that declaration – and Olivier Peter links the two events – the rebellion charges were dropped in the Spanish prosecution and the remaining offence (disobedience) alone was not eligible for extradition anymore, as it did not reach the minimum threshold of possible sentence. Peter thus contends that dropping the charge of rebellion enabled Spanish authorities to renounce sending out the extradition request they had been promoting extensively in the media – one they were confident would succeed. This move, according to Peter, spared them the embarrassment of a potential refusal and, more importantly, the formal acknowledgement of the political nature of the crime.[63] The Swiss lawyer further adds that this was not the end of the Spanish manoeuvres to apprehend Gabriel. After Gabriel was identified in Switzerland, Spanish authorities decided to arrest Hervé Falciani, a whistle-blower sought by Switzerland who had been living in Spain for years. Peter claims that this move was an implied offer to exchange Falciani for Gabriel, although the Spanish foreign minister at the time explicitly denied any secret plot to swap Catalan exiles for Falciani.[64] The offer quickly expired, however, after the Swiss declaration. Falciani was released and the extradition procedure regarding the latter was terminated.[65]

The lawyers of Catalan exiles therefore argued that Spanish judicial and political authorities had fostered a climate of intimidation against Catalan exiles and condemned their actions as authoritarian. They further argued that Spain had judicialised a political debate that should have never been handled with criminal law[66] and that Catalan leaders in exile would not enjoy a fair trial because of the political nature of the trial. Christophe Marchand, for example, the lawyer of Catalan exiles Meritxell Serret and Antoni Comín at the time of these events, referred to declarations made by judges, prosecutors and their respective delegates, ministers, and members of Parliament, as well as to the speech of the king on the day of the referendum, to demonstrate that Catalan separatists had, in fact, already been condemned before trial and that they would not be

61 Interview with Olivier Peter, Lawyer of Anna Gabriel and Jordi Cuixart (Online, 11 November 2019).

62 A. Harari (n 15).

63 Interview with Olivier Peter (n 61).

64 SDA-ATS/ac, 'Catalan Crisis: Switzerland to Offer Good Offices but Not Interfere' (Swissinfo 2018) <https://www.swissinfo.ch/eng/politics/separatists-in-exile_catalan-crisis--switzerland-to-offer-good-offices-but-not-interfere-/44068630> accessed 25 May 2022.

65 Interview with Olivier Peter (n 61).

66 Interview with Paul Bekaert (n 1); J.-P. Stroobants (n 1); S. Oliveira (n 1); L. Andersen (n 1); ACN Barcelona, 'Wolfgang Schomburg: "This Was Never a Matter for Criminal Law"' (Catalan News 2018) <https://www.catalannews.com/society-science/item/wolfgang-schomburg-this-was-never-a-matter-for-criminal-law-2> accessed 27 March 2020; L. Brooks (n 2); G. McPherson (n 58).

afforded a genuine presumption of innocence if surrendered to Spain.[67] Lawyers also referenced international reports that highlighted general deficiencies in the functioning of Spain's judiciary[68] and expressed specific concerns about human rights in the prosecution and trial of Catalan leaders. This last concern actually stemmed from the UN working group on arbitrary detention[69] that showed great concern over the unjustified pre-trial detention of Catalan leaders in Spain and that urged the Spanish Court to release them. This call to release Catalan separatists was echoed by the United Nations Human Rights Office of the High Commissioner.[70] Similarly, International Trial Watch denounced the breach of several rights and legal principles in the conduct of the trial of Catalan leaders in Spain, therefore supporting the lawyers' argument about the breach of Catalan separatists' fundamental rights in Spain.[71] According to the lawyers of catalan exiles, these reports collectively provided solid evidence that the fundamental rights of their clients would be seriously jeopardised if they were returned to Spain.

Lawyers also criticised the politicisation of the Audiencia Nacional, the Supreme Court, and the Constitutional Court, and accused them of acting as enforcers of government decisions.[72] Taking the example of the trials against Basque activists, they argued that national minorities seeking independence in Spain have historically been particularly vulnerable to judicial injustices. Marchand specifically referred to the *Atutxa* case brought before the European Court of Human Rights in 2015 and concluded in 2017, where the Court recognised that Atutxa and the other defendants, all pursuing independence of the Basque region, did not enjoy their right to a fair trial.[73] One of the objectives of the Belgian legal team defending the Catalan exiles was therefore to draw parallels between the Basque case and the Catalan one, in order to establish a broader category of vulnerable groups composed of politicians seeking regional independence. They argued that these individuals were systematically denied the right to a fair trial within the Spanish legal system.[74] Accordingly, upon receipt of the first wave of warrants, Belgian lawyers of

67 Interview with Christophe Marchand, Lawyer of Antoni Comin and Meritxell Serret (Brussels, 1 October 2018).

68 GRECO, 'Fourth Evaluation Round: Corruption Prevention in Respect of Members of Parliament, Judges and Prosecutors' (Council of Europe 2018) <https://rm.coe.int/fourth-evaluation-round-corruption-prevention-in-respect-of-members-of/1680779c4d> accessed 15 April 2020.

69 United Nations Working Group on Arbitrary Detention (n 25).

70 United Nations Human Rights Office of the High Commissioner (n 25).

71 International Trial Watch – Catalan Referendum Case, 'Factual and Legal Assessment by International and National Observers of the Judgment Condemning Catalan Authorities and Social Leaders (SCJ 459/2019)' (International Trial Watch 2019) <https://internationaltrialwatch.org/wp-content/uploads/2019/11/POSICIONAMIENTO_SENTENCIA_12112019-ingles-carta.pdf> accessed 4 May 2020.

72 Interview with Olivier Peter (n 61).

73 Atutxa Mendiola and others v. Spain, Application No. 41427/14 (ECtHR 13/09/2017) 13.

74 Interview with Christophe Marchand (n 67).

Catalan exiles made declarations in the press saying that the judge would have to determine whether warrants had been issued for purposes of political persecution.[75] These remarks strongly aligned with later Swiss declarations, which also highlighted the potentially political nature of the prosecutions and of the offences in question.

No dual criminality (German reason to refuse the execution of the Spanish warrant)

Due to the political ramifications of the case, addressing the issue of Catalan exiles was a delicate task for judges in executing countries. None of them accepted the surrenders on the political charges of the cases. Three reasons were invoked to reject the surrenders on the political charges of the warrants: the absence of a domestic warrant supporting the European arrest one (first warrant), the lack of dual criminality (second warrant), and the lack of competence of the Spanish Supreme Court to issue the warrants (third warrant). The last two are scrutinised in further detail in the present and following sections, as they are based on an in-depth examination of the case.

As previously outlined, the Framework Decision on the European arrest warrant foresees 32 categories of offences for which the dual criminality principle shall not apply. The offences of sedition and rebellion, however, are not part of those exceptions, which means that the dual criminality principle can still be applied to those cases. As Anne Weyembergh pointed out, however, whereas the Framework Decision foresaw an optional application of the principle for offences not included in the list, many EU member states transposed it as a mandatory ground for refusal. Belgium and Germany are two of these member states.[76]

Upon the arrest of Puigdemont in Germany, the Schleswig-Holstein Higher Regional Court started by examining whether the acts for which his surrender was requested would also constitute a criminal offence under German law.[77] In this case, the offence of rebellion was most closely compared to the German offences of 'high treason against the federation' and 'breach of peace'. To determine whether the Spanish offence of rebellion was comparable to the German one of high treason, the Court relied on a previous case brought before the Federal Court of Justice pertaining to the eruption of violence during protests against the construction of the west runway of Frankfurt airport. The demonstrators were charged with coercion of constitutional bodies. Commentators like Stefan Braum argued in this respect that by choosing this case

75 L. Andersen (n 1); J.-P. Stroobants (n 1).

76 A. Weyembergh, 'The Puigdemont Case Exposes Challenges in the European Arrest Warrant' (CEPS 2017) <https://www.ceps.eu/wp-content/uploads/2017/12/Weyembergh_PuigdemontEAW.pdf> accessed 4 January 2021.

77 S. Braum, 'The Carles Puigdemont Case: Europe's Criminal Law in the Crisis of Confidence' [2018] *Ger. Law J.* 1349, 1352.

for comparison, the German Court actually set higher standards for the double criminality principle to be fulfilled because it meant that the discussions revolved around the interpretation of the notion of violence and the threshold required for it to lead to coercion. Indeed, this approach to high treason not only required violence but also necessitated an assessment of the intensity of the violence and of its ability to make constitutional bodies capitulate to the demands of protestors ('vis compulsiva').[78] This, according to Braum, created potentially excessive requirements in the examination of the applicability of the double criminality principle.[79] Indeed, reaching a level of violence enough to influence the action of the constitutional body is more difficult in cases of non-(physically) coercive means because of the assumption that constitutional bodies are more insulated to coercion and pressure than private individuals.[80] The German judge reported choosing to apply this more demanding requirement precisely for that reason. He also considered that in democratic societies, criminal law should be used as restrictively as possible in cases involving political conflicts.[81] In the end, the judge contemplated that the instances of collateral violence observed on the margins of the referendum were not enough to engender an immediate secession from Spain and therefore truly endanger the Spanish constitutional order. He stated that the referendum was rather leveraged by Puigdemont to further the negotiations between Madrid and Barcelona, and not to actually lead to immediate secession.[82] As a result, he considered that the level of force required to match the German offence of high treason was not met in the Catalan case because the independence could not have been achieved in this way.[83]

Regarding the possibility of matching the offence of rebellion to the one of 'breach of peace', the Court contemplated that the violence that took place during the referendum could not be imputed to Puigdemont. The Court indeed considered that Puigdemont was not the instigator of acts of violence because he did not have the intent to generate violence, as evidenced

78 S. Braum, 'The Carles Puigdemont Case: Europe's Criminal Law in the Crisis of Confidence' [2018] *Ger. Law J.* 1353.

79 S. Braum, 'The Carles Puigdemont Case: Europe's Criminal Law in the Crisis of Confidence' [2018] *Ger. Law J.* 1356.

80 S. Braum, 'The Carles Puigdemont Case: Europe's Criminal Law in the Crisis of Confidence' [2018] *Ger. Law J.* 1352–1353.

81 J. König, P. Meichelbeck and M. Puchta, 'The Curious Case of Carles Puigdemont – The European Arrest Warrant as an Inadequate Means with Regard to Political Offenses' [2021] *Ger. Law J.* 256, 263.

82 Press Secretary Frauke Holmer, 'Matter Carles Puigdemont: The Extradition for the Accusation of Embezzlement of Public Funds is Admissible; an Extradition for the Accusation of Rebellion is Inadmissible. Carles Puigdemont Remains Free' (Schleswig-Holsteinisches Oberlandesgericht 2018) <https://www.schleswig-holstein.de/DE/Justiz/OLG/Presse/PI/201806Puigdemontenglisch.html> accessed 10 April 2020.

83 Press Secretary Frauke Holmer (n 82).

by his repeated calls to keep the whole process peaceful. It also determined that Puigdemont could not be assumed to be in control of the violence or able to influence it since he did not have actual physical control over it.[84] As a result, the Court established that the dual criminality principle could not be satisfied in this case and rejected the surrender for the charge of rebellion. The surrender was, however, later authorised for the offence of embezzlement and only for that one.[85] The offence of corruption, subsuming the one of embezzlement, is indeed in the list of 32 categories of offences for which the dual criminality requirement is lifted in the Framework Decision on the European arrest warrant. As a result of the German decision, the Spanish judge withdrew all European and international arrest warrants against Catalan exiles because Spanish judicial authorities wanted to be able to prosecute Puigdemont and his ministers on the former charges as well.[86]

The Spanish response to the German argument

In response to the German ruling, the Second Chamber of the Spanish Supreme Court issued an order corroborating evidence of rebellion, stating that the secessionist process could not be compared to protests against the construction of a new wing at Frankfurt Airport.[87] The Court argued that, in the case of the Catalan independence referendum, secessionists meticulously planned and organised an unconstitutional referendum over the course of two years, adding that this effort undermined both the central and regional legal systems and flagrantly disregarded rulings from the Constitutional Court that had opposed the process.[88]

84 J. König, P. Meichelbeck and M. Puchta (n 81) 264.
85 J. König, P. Meichelbeck and M. Puchta (n 81) 264.
86 Comunicación Poder Judicial (n 6).
87 Comunicación Poder Judicial, 'El Tribunal Supremo Ratifica la Existencia de Indicios de Delito de Rebelión en la Actuación de los Dirigentes del "Procés" y Rebate los Argumentos del Tribunal Alemán. La Sala Cree que no es Razonable Equiparar lo Ocurrido en Cataluña con las Protestas contra la Ampliación de un Aeropuerto en Frankfurt' (Poder Judicial 2018) <https://www.poderjudicial.es/cgpj/en/Judiciary/Pressroom/News-archive/El-Tribunal-Supremo-ratifica-la-existencia-de-indicios-de-delito-de-rebelion-en-la-actuacion-de-los-dirigentes-del--proces--y-rebate-los-argumentos-del-tribunal-aleman> accessed 31 May 2022.
88 Comunicación Poder Judicial, 'El Tribunal Supremo Ratifica la Existencia de Indicios de Delito de Rebelión en la Actuación de los Dirigentes del "Procés" y Rebate los Argumentos del Tribunal Alemán. La Sala Cree que no es Razonable Equiparar lo Ocurrido en Cataluña con las Protestas contra la Ampliación de un Aeropuerto en Frankfurt' (Poder Judicial 2018) <https://www.poderjudicial.es/cgpj/en/Judiciary/Pressroom/News-archive/El-Tribunal-Supremo-ratifica-la-existencia-de-indicios-de-delito-de-rebelion-en-la-actuacion-de-los-dirigentes-del--proces--y-rebate-los-argumentos-del-tribunal-aleman> accessed 31 May 2022.

For the Spanish Supreme Court, the fact that those rebellious acts were conducted by those in power made the situation even more serious and reduced the requirement of recourse to violence. It also considered that, because of the sheer number of people who went to vote (2 million), the violence that occurred on the margins of the referendum was completely foreseeable.[89] In response to the German Court's argument that the violence on the day of the referendum did not sway the state's resolve, the Supreme Court countered by highlighting that the 6000 officers deployed to prevent the referendum were vastly outnumbered by the 2 million voters. Despite the efforts, the referendum went ahead, resulting in the organisers declaring Catalonia's independence. The Supreme Court further argued that had more police been involved, it could have led, in the words of the Court, to a 'massacre', and the German Court might then have considered issuing the European arrest warrant.[90] The Court overall doubted the argument put forward by the German Court according to which, if the same event had happened in Germany, it would have merely resulted in a symbolic conviction.[91]

In response to a prior request from the German Court for more information regarding the crime of embezzlement before making a formal decision on the request for surrender, Judge Llarena expressed his confidence that the German Court would ultimately extradite Puigdemont for rebellion. He argued that he could not believe the German criminal code did not include a similar offence.[92]

89 Comunicación Poder Judicial, 'El Tribunal Supremo Ratifica la Existencia de Indicios de Delito de Rebelión en la Actuación de los Dirigentes del "Procés" y Rebate los Argumentos del Tribunal Alemán. La Sala Cree que no es Razonable Equiparar lo Ocurrido en Cataluña con las Protestas contra la Ampliación de un Aeropuerto en Frankfurt' (Poder Judicial 2018) <https://www.poderjudicial.es/cgpj/en/Judiciary/Pressroom/News-archive/El-Tribunal-Supremo-ratifica-la-existencia-de-indicios-de-delito-de-rebelion-en-la-actuacion-de-los-dirigentes-del--proces--y-rebate-los-argumentos-del-tribunal-aleman> accessed 31 May 2022.

90 Comunicación Poder Judicial, 'El Tribunal Supremo Ratifica la Existencia de Indicios de Delito de Rebelión en la Actuación de los Dirigentes del "Procés" y Rebate los Argumentos del Tribunal Alemán. La Sala Cree que no es Razonable Equiparar lo Ocurrido en Cataluña con las Protestas contra la Ampliación de un Aeropuerto en Frankfurt' (Poder Judicial 2018) <https://www.poderjudicial.es/cgpj/en/Judiciary/Pressroom/News-archive/El-Tribunal-Supremo-ratifica-la-existencia-de-indicios-de-delito-de-rebelion-en-la-actuacion-de-los-dirigentes-del--proces--y-rebate-los-argumentos-del-tribunal-aleman> accessed 31 May 2022.

91 Comunicación Poder Judicial, 'El Tribunal Supremo Ratifica la Existencia de Indicios de Delito de Rebelión en la Actuación de los Dirigentes del "Procés" y Rebate los Argumentos del Tribunal Alemán. La Sala Cree que no es Razonable Equiparar lo Ocurrido en Cataluña con las Protestas contra la Ampliación de un Aeropuerto en Frankfurt' (Poder Judicial 2018) <https://www.poderjudicial.es/cgpj/en/Judiciary/Pressroom/News-archive/El-Tribunal-Supremo-ratifica-la-existencia-de-indicios-de-delito-de-rebelion-en-la-actuacion-de-los-dirigentes-del--proces--y-rebate-los-argumentos-del-tribunal-aleman> accessed 31 May 2022.

92 Comunicación Poder Judicial, 'El Juez Llarena Remite un Escrito a Alemania con Información Complementaria para la Entrega de Puigdemont y Otro a Bélgica por Puig, Comin y Serret. El

He insisted that the assessment of the dual criminality principle should be based on an evaluation of the facts and not the legal qualification attached to them.[93] When the German judge confirmed that the surrender would be denied for rebellion, however, Llarena denounced the lack of commitment of the German Court that he accused of having anticipated the outcome of a trial for which it had no jurisdiction. He further deplored the fact that the Court conducted a dual criminality check that exceeded what is normally expected from executing judicial authorities.[94] Additionally, Llarena noted that the German judge had identified certain formal requirements for executing the warrant under German law as unmet. However, the judge reached this conclusion without requesting further information from the Spanish judge on the matter. Llarena thus contended that, instead of assuming dual criminality could not be respected, the Court should have made a request for a preliminary ruling to the CJEU to ensure a uniform application of EU law on the dual criminality requirement, reminding in passing that the European arrest warrant should be based on mutual recognition and that its execution should be refused in exceptional circumstances only.[95]

Several commentators of the case shared Llarena's opinion.[96] Ruiz Yamuza, a Spanish judge, for instance, contended that Germany applied an excessively restrictive interpretation of the double criminality requirement in this case both in form and content. Indeed, German law not only transformed this optional ground for refusal into a compulsory one in its transposition of the Framework Decision on the European arrest warrant, but the German judge in charge of the case also sought to establish a very close correspondence between the German offences of high treason and rioting to the Spanish offence of rebellion,

---

Magistrado Expone que, de Acuerdo a las Reglas de la Orden Europea de Detención (OED), el Estado Requerido Sólo Podría Denegar la Entrega si los Hechos por los que se ha Emitido la Orden de Detención Europea No Son Constitutivos de Ningún Tipo de Infracción Penal en su Territorio' (Poder Judicial 2018) <https://www.poderjudicial.es/cgpj/en/Judiciary/Press-room/News-archive/El-juez-Llarena-remite-un-escrito-a-Alemania-con-informacion-complementaria-para-la-entrega-de-Puigdemont-y-otro-a-Belgica-por-Puig--Comin-y-Serret> accessed 31 May 2022.

93 Comunicación Poder Judicial, 'El Juez Llarena Remite un Escrito a Alemania con Información Complementaria para la Entrega de Puigdemont y Otro a Bélgica por Puig, Comin y Serret. El Magistrado Expone que, de Acuerdo a las Reglas de la Orden Europea de Detención (OED), el Estado Requerido Sólo Podría Denegar la Entrega si los Hechos por los que se ha Emitido la Orden de Detención Europea No Son Constitutivos de Ningún Tipo de Infracción Penal en su Territorio' (Poder Judicial 2018) <https://www.poderjudicial.es/cgpj/en/Judiciary/Press-room/News-archive/El-juez-Llarena-remite-un-escrito-a-Alemania-con-informacion-complementaria-para-la-entrega-de-Puigdemont-y-otro-a-Belgica-por-Puig--Comin-y-Serret> accessed 31 May 2022.

94 Comunicación Poder Judicial (n 12).

95 Comunicación Poder Judicial (n 12).

96 L. Bachmaier, 'European Arrest Warrant, Double Criminality and Mutual Recognition: A Much Debated Case' [2018] *EuCLR*. 152, 152–159; M. Muñoz de Morales Romero, 'Dual Criminality under Review: On the Puigdemont Case' [2018] *Eur. Crim. Law Rev*. 167, 167–175.

which the CJEU does not instruct.[97] The CJEU indeed ruled in the Grundza case that, in the assessment of the double criminality principle,

> there does not have to be an exact match between the constituent elements of the offence, as defined in the law of the issuing State and the executing State, respectively, or between the name given to or the classification of the offence under the national law of the respective States.[98]

The Court clarified in this respect that the role of the executing authorities is simply to verify whether the "*acts* concerned also constitute an *offence* under the law of the executing State, *whatever its constituent elements* or *however it is described*".[99] What the German Court did here, however, was to favour a more constricting view as to how the double criminality principle should be applied, namely that of assessing if and how the acts for which the European arrest warrant was issued would have been punished had they taken place in Germany, which opened the way to a more detailed analysis of the case. Ruiz Yamuza thus contended that the German judge should have been satisfied with the fact that the acts constituted an offence under Spanish law and that German law safeguards similar legal rights to those that Spain sought to protect through its surrender requests.[100] He therefore argued that the manner in which German judicial authorities handled the European arrest warrant request from the Spanish judicial authorities resembled how they would treat a request from a third country with which there was no mutual trust.[101]

Dual criminality in context: check as possible lack of trust

It is noteworthy that the dual criminality principle has been partially abolished in the European arrest warrant system to fully implement the principle of mutual trust. The dual criminality principle is indeed rooted in mistrust in the judicial system of other countries, as it requires a convergence of criminal laws for cooperation to take place. Mutual trust and recognition conversely seek to foster cooperation despite existing differences. The compatibility of the mutual recognition requirement with this principle of dual criminality has generated considerable academic debate over the years. At the institutional level, this issue is also discussed, but there is broad agreement on the overall need to promote mutual recognition. This is for example visible in the CJEU ruling on the *Grundza* case, where the Court reiterated that "the condition of double criminality is an exception to the general rule of recognition of judgments

97 F.-G. Ruiz Yamuza, 'CJEU Case Law on Double Criminality. The Grundza-Piotrowski Paradox? Some Notes Regarding the Puigdemont Case' [2019] *ERA Forum*. 465, 477.
98 Joszef Grundza [11 January 2017] Case C-289/15, EU:C:2017:4, para 48.
99 Joszef Grundza [11 January 2017] Case C-289/15, EU:C:2017:4, para. 47.
100 F.-G. Ruiz Yamuza (n 98) 477.
101 F.-G. Ruiz Yamuza (n 98) 478.

and enforcement of sentences".[102] More recently, in an own-initiative report of the European Parliament's Committee on Civil Liberties, Justice and Home Affairs (LIBE) on the implementation of the European arrest warrant, the rapporteur (Javier Zarzalejos, MEP from the European People's Party, European family to the Spanish PP to which Zarzalejos belong) proposed extending the list of 32 offences for which double criminality checks should not apply. He suggested that this list should include offences related to public order and the constitutional integrity of member states. The report also insisted on the importance of mutual recognition and on the need to interpret double criminality as restrictively as possible or bear the risk of undermining not only the European arrest warrant system but the EU system as a whole.[103]

In recent years, however, CJEU rulings have increasingly questioned blind trust in the fields of migration and cooperation in criminal matters. Initially, the CJEU issued isolated rulings in which it prioritised human right concerns over cooperation. These decisions have since multiplied, forming a significant body of jurisprudence.[104] As a result, some have argued that human rights protection has turned into a *de facto* ground for refusal to cooperate under primary EU law.[105] These developments were followed by the latest rule of conditionality mechanism adopted at the EU level that foresees the possibility to withhold parts of the EU budget in member states in breach of rule of law.[106] The debates surrounding the double criminality requirement thus take place within a wider discussion on mutual trust in the EU.[107] If mutual

102 Joszef Grundza (n 99) para 46.

103 European Parliament, Report on the Implementation of the European Arrest Warrant and the Surrender Procedures between Member States (2019/2207(INI)) Committee on Civil Liberties and Home Affairs, Rapporteur: Javier Zarzalejos RR\1220194EN.docx (PE655.688v02-00) 2020, 5 & 16.

104 See Aranyosi and Căldăraru, ML and Dorobantu on the risk of inhuman and degrading treatment; Minister for Justice and Equality and Openbaar Ministerie on the right to a fair trial in an independent tribunal. Eurojust, 'Case-Law by the Court of Justice of the European Union on the European Arrest Warrant' (Eurojust 2021) <https://www.eurojust.europa.eu/sites/default/files/assets/2021_12_08_cjeu_case_law_on_eaw.pdf> accessed 19 July 2024, 46.

105 European Parliament Research Service, European Arrest Warrant – Framework for Analysis and Preliminary Findings on its Implementation (PE 642.814) 2020, 8.

106 Regulation (EU, Euratom) 2020/2092 of the European Parliament and of the Council of 16 December 2020 on a General Regime of Conditionality for the Protection of the Union Budget [2020] OJ L 433I.

107 A non-exhaustive list of writings on this topic includes A. Willems, *The Principle of Mutual Trust in EU Criminal Law* (Hart Publishing, Oxford, Dublin 2021); E. Xanthopoulou, 'Mutual Trust and Rights in EU Criminal Law and Asylum Law: Three Phases of Evolution and the Uncharted Territory beyond Blind Trust' [2018] *CMLR*. 489, 489–509; V. Mitsilegas, 'The Limits of Mutual Trust in Europe's Area of Freedom, Security and Justice: From Automatic Inter-State Cooperation to the Slow Emergence of the Individual' [2012] *YEL*. 319, 319–372; S. Top and P. De Hert, 'Castano Avoids a Clash Between the ECtHR and the CJEU, but Erodes Soering. Thinking Human Rights Transnationally' [2020] *NJECL*. 52, 52–68; S. Carrera, E. Guild and N. Hernanz, 'Europe's Most Wanted? Recalibrating Trust

trust still remains the rule, the Court has nevertheless adopted an increasingly cautious approach on this point. In the case at hand, despite the supposedly automatic nature of the European arrest warrant, the fact that the German Court conducted such an in-depth assessment of the dual criminality requirement revealed the unease of the Court to surrender Puigdemont to Spain and even, according to some, an open lack of confidence that Puigdemont would enjoy a fair trial in Spain.[108]

No authority to issue a warrant (Belgian reason to refuse the execution of the Spanish warrant)

Equally linked to trust is the issue of whether the executing judicial authority recognises the competence of the issuing authority to issue a European arrest warrant. The recognition of an independent judicial authority and the conditions under which prosecutors are considered to be so is still a debated question on which the CJEU provides continuous guidance.[109] The core issue here – that particularly concerns prosecutors due to their role – is the one of the independence of the judiciary from executive powers.[110] The question of which judicial authority should be deemed competent to issue or execute a European arrest warrant is linked to the broader debate on the desirability and extent to which EU criminal law should be harmonised, considering its implications for state sovereignty and, more importantly, human rights.[111] There is thus a difficult balance to strike between the need to eliminate barriers to cooperation and the necessity of applying caution to avoid blind trust. It is indeed crucial to ensure that executing judicial authorities remain responsible,[112] particularly in the context of safeguarding human rights.[113]

On 7 August 2020, to the dismay of Spanish authorities, the Brussels Court of First Instance rejected the European arrest warrant the Spanish Supreme Court issued against Lluis Puig. The Court's decision was based on the determination that the Spanish Supreme Court lacked the competence to issue a European arrest warrant in this particular case. The Court asserted its jurisdiction to assess the competence of the Spanish Supreme Court to

in the European Arrest Warrant System' [2013] *CEPS Papers.* 1, 1–42; K. Lenaerts, 'La Vie Après L'Avis: Exploring the Principle of Mutual (Yet Not Blind) Trust' [2017] *CMLR.* 805, 805–840; S. Braum (n 77).

108 L. Foffani, 'The Case Puigdemont: The Stress-Test of the European Arrest Warrant' [2018] *Eur. Crim. Law Rev.* 196, 196–200.

109 European Parliament Research Service (n 106) 7.

110 European Parliament Research Service (n 106) 7–9.

111 European Parliament Research Service (n 106) 8.

112 A. Weyembergh, 'Transverse Report on Judicial Control in Cooperation in Criminal Matters. The Evolution from Traditional Judicial Cooperation to Mutual Recognition' in K. Ligeti (ed), *Toward a Prosecutor for the European Union, A Comparative Analysis* (Volume 1) (Hart Publishing, 2013) 102.

113 European Parliament Research Service (n 106) 8.

issue European arrest warrants in this case, relying on several grounds. It first referred to the CJEU's case law regarding which public prosecution services can be considered competent judicial authorities for the application of European arrest warrants; secondly, it invoked recitals 8 and 12 of the Framework Decision, which highlight the necessity for adequate control in the execution of European arrest warrants and the need to uphold fundamental rights; and, third, the Court referred to the case law of the European Court of Human Rights.[114] The decision of the Court to advance a lack of competence of the Spanish Supreme Court to issues a European arrest warrant in the case at hand was based on the opinion of the Working Group on Arbitrary Detention of the Human Rights Council of the United Nations General Assembly, the case law of the ECtHR, and provisions of Belgian and Spanish law.[115] Arguing that the Spanish Supreme Court was not competent to investigate the case of Puig and that the latter should be tried in a Catalan Court, the Belgian Court advanced that Puig's fundamental rights, and more specifically his right to the presumption of innocence, would be at risk if he was sent back to Spain.[116] This argument not only affected Puig but also challenged the entire judicial procedure in Spain, making it of significant interest to all Catalan exiles.

Spanish response to the Belgian argument

The Spanish Supreme Court, however, contested the Belgian Court's authority to assess the competence of the issuing authority under EU law. This decision, according to Llarena, contravened the principle of mutual recognition of judicial decisions. Reminding that no EU rule allowed executing judicial authorities to determine whether issuing judicial authorities were competent to send out a European arrest warrant request, Llarena claimed that the decision of Belgian authorities turned the principle of mutual trust into a principle

114 Opinion of Advocate General Richard de la Tour Delivered on 14 July 2022. Criminal Proceedings against Lluís Puig Gordi and Others. Request for a Preliminary Ruling from the Tribunal Supremo. Reference for a Preliminary Ruling – Area of Freedom, Security and Justice – Judicial Cooperation in Criminal Matters – European Arrest Warrant – Framework Decision 2002/584/JHA – Surrender Procedures between Member States – Conditions for Execution – Jurisdiction of the Issuing Judicial Authority – Second Paragraph of Article 47 of the Charter of Fundamental Rights of the European Union – Right of Access to a Tribunal Previously Established by Law – Possibility of Issuing a new European Arrest Warrant Relating to the Same Person. Case C-158/21 (Document No. 62021CC0158) 2022, para. 19. X and Y v. Openbaar Ministerie [22 February 2022] Joined Cases C-562/21 PPU and C-563/21 PPU, EU:C:2022:100, para. 19.

115 Opinion of Advocate General Richard De La Tour delivered on 14 July 2022 (n 115) para. 20. The public prosecutor appealed this decision, but the Indictment Chamber of the Brussels Court of Appeal backed it. Opinion of Advocate General Richard De La Tour delivered on 14 July 2022 (n 115) para. 21.

116 Comunicación Poder Judicial (n 44).

of distrust.[117] Adding that Belgian judicial authorities clearly disregarded article 71.3 of the Spanish Constitution from which they wrongly deduced that the place of commission of the offence was what mattered in Spanish law, Llarena criticised the ignorance of the Belgian Court on the Spanish jurisdictional structure and the fact that they completely overlooked the intense debate that took place at national level on this very point.[118] Llarena also noted that although the Belgian judge invoked the lack of competence of the Supreme Court, they then backed their claim by referring to CJEU case law on the independence of courts, hinting at a possibility of persecution, which is a different matter.[119] As for the Court's argument that Puig's fundamental rights would be at risk if he were returned to Spain, Llarena noted that this claim was based on a report from the United Nations Working Group on Arbitrary Detention. He pointed out in this respect that the report did not specifically address Puig's case. Additionally, Llarena argued that the report was not an official document of the United Nations system because the Working Group was established by the Human Rights Council rather than the Human Rights Committee and was thus not created under an international treaty. He finally highlighted that the Working Group issued opinions rather than official reports and that these opinions did not represent the stance of the Human Rights Council or the United Nations as a whole.[120]

As a result, judge Llarena introduced a manifold preliminary ruling question to the CJEU enquiring whether the executing authority was allowed to assess the competence of the issuing judicial authority to try the defendants and if it could refuse the execution of a European arrest warrant on grounds that the requested person's right to a fair trial would be jeopardised due to an error of jurisdiction.[121] Second, in the event the CJEU indeed rules that the executing judicial authority does have power to determine whether the issuing judicial authority is competent to issue a European arrest warrant for the person concerned, Llarena wondered what elements must be taken into consideration to come to a decision on that point.[122] Third, referring to the mechanism for requesting supplementary information provided in the Framework Decision on the European arrest warrant, Llarena considered that the Belgian Court had not made sufficient use of that mechanism to determine the jurisdiction of the Spanish Supreme Court to try the defendants.[123] Fourth, he underlined that

117 Comunicación Poder Judicial (n 44).
118 Comunicación Poder Judicial (n 44).
119 Comunicación Poder Judicial (n 44).
120 Comunicación Poder Judicial (n 44).
121 Opinion of Advocate General Richard De La Tour delivered on 14 July 2022 (n 115) para. 25.
122 Opinion of Advocate General Richard De La Tour delivered on 14 July 2022 (n 115) para. 27.
123 Opinion of Advocate General Richard De La Tour delivered on 14 July 2022 (n 115) para. 30.

Belgium had refused the execution of the European arrest warrant on grounds that its execution would lead to a violation of the defendants' fundamental rights, which is not a ground for refusal expressly provided in the Framework Decision. He noted on this point that the CJEU case law indeed allows the executing authorities to refuse the warrant on those grounds but that this is exceptional and that cooperation remains the rule. He also mentioned the fact that the Brussels Court relied on a report from the Working Group on Arbitrary Detention that did not according to Llarena, constitute objective, reliable, specific, and duly updated information to determine the individual risk of violation of the fundamental rights of the person sought here.[124]

A grand chamber hearing on the case took place in Luxembourg on 5 April 2022, where the European Commission backed the Spanish position. The Commission advanced that, as long as there is no systemic rule-of-law deficiency in the issuing country, surrenders are not conditioned upon a verification of the right to a fair trial of the person sought.[125] Replying to the Commission's argument on the need to establish a systemic deficiency to debate whether individual rights could be violated, Judge Lucia Serena Rossi warned the Commission representatives about the dangers of such a stance.[126] As for members of the Spanish judiciary involved in the Catalan process in Spain, they denounced Belgium's assessment of the ability of the Spanish Supreme Court to ensure Puig's right to a fair trial as being absurd and lacking logic. Gonzalo Boye, the Spain-based lawyer of Catalan exiles, condemned what he viewed as the political persecution towards Catalan leaders.[127] Crucial to the hearing was the question of whether systemic deficiencies needed to be demonstrated (and how they applied to the specific case of individuals targeted by European arrest warrants) or if it was sufficient to show that the particular group of Catalan independence leaders was especially vulnerable to fundamental rights violations in Spain, as argued by the lawyers representing the Catalan exiles.[128]

On 14 July 2022, Advocate General Richard De La Tour issued his opinion on the case in which he strongly favoured cooperation over human rights

124 Opinion of Advocate General Richard De La Tour delivered on 14 July 2022 (n 115) paras. 31–33. Request for a Preliminary Ruling from the Tribunal Supremo (Spain) Lodged on 11 March 2021 – Ministerio Fiscal, Abogacía del Estado, Partido político VOX v. Lluís Puig Gordi, Carles Puigdemont Casamajó, Antoni Comín Oliveres, Clara Ponsatí Obiols, Meritxell Serret Aleu, Marta Rovira Vergés, Anna Gabriel Sabaté, Case C-158/21.

125 Archyde, 'The European Commission Defends Spain at the Hearing in Luxembourg on the Puigdemont Case' (Archyde 2022) <https://www.archyde.com/the-european-commission-defends-spain-at-the-hearing-in-luxembourg-on-the-puigdemont-case/> accessed 2 June 2022.

126 M. Lasalas and M. Piulachs, 'Key Points at ECJ Hearing: Spanish Judicial Deficiencies and Court's Competence' (El Nacional 2022) <https://www.elnacional.cat/en/politics/key-points-european-court-justice-spanish-deficiencies-catalan-exile_737622_102.html> accessed 2 June 2022.

127 Archyde (n 126).

128 Archyde (n 126).

protection. He emphasised that grounds for refusal not specified in the Framework Decision on the European arrest warrant but established in national law cannot be used to justify the non-execution of a warrant. He also underscored the importance of prioritising the effective functioning of the surrender mechanism, which should not be impeded by too many obstacles to it. He noted on this point that the possibility to invoke the lack of competence of the issuing judicial authority could not be derived from article 6(1) of the Framework Decision protecting the fundamental rights of the persons sought.[129] He nevertheless confirmed that risks of violation of the right to a fair trial could – exceptionally only – result in the refusal to execute a European arrest warrant. He recalled, in this respect, the two-step approach developed by the CJEU to determine whether a fear of human rights violations could justify the non-execution of a warrant.[130] In the case at hand, he contended that the requirements of the two-step approach could not be fulfilled and that therefore the human rights argument could not be utilised by Belgian judicial authorities to refuse the surrender of Puig.[131] Finally, with regard to whether issuing judicial authorities could re-issue a European arrest warrant for the same acts and the same person after the executing member state had refused to execute it on grounds contrary to EU law, De La Tour argued that the Framework Decision did not prohibit issuing authorities from re-issuing a European arrest warrant under such circumstances.[132]

The CJEU's ruling overall aligned with De La Tour's opinion on the need to favour cooperation but was more cautious in doing so. Answering the first question of the preliminary ruling request on whether the executing judicial authority could refuse a surrender on grounds that are not explicitly listed in the Framework Decision on the European arrest warrant, the Court reminded that cooperation remained the rule and that refusals to execute European arrest warrants must remain exceptional and must be interpreted strictly.[133] Accordingly, the Court noted that executing authorities could not refuse the execution of a European arrest warrant based on grounds for non-execution emanating from national law only that are not explicitly listed in the Framework Decision.[134] However, the Court also specified that in case the execution of the European arrest warrant would lead to an infringement of fundamental

129 Opinion of Advocate General Richard De La Tour delivered on 14 July 2022 (n 115) paras. 62–76.
130 Opinion of Advocate General Richard De La Tour delivered on 14 July 2022 (n 115) para. 82.
131 Opinion of Advocate General Richard De La Tour delivered on 14 July 2022 (n 115) paras. 82–133.
132 Opinion of Advocate General Richard De La Tour delivered on 14 July 2022 (n 115) paras. 135–138.
133 Lluís Puig Gordi and Others [31 January 2023] Case C-158/21. EU:C:2023:57, paras. 68–74.
134 Lluís Puig Gordi and Others [31 January 2023] Case C-158/21. EU:C:2023:57, para. 79.

rights as enshrined in EU law, the executing authority could refuse to execute the request for surrender.[135]

In response to whether the executing judicial authority could verify if a European arrest warrant had been issued by a judicial authority with the appropriate jurisdiction and refuse to execute it if not, the Court clarified that while executing judicial authorities must ensure that the European arrest warrant requests they receive are issued by a judicial authority as defined by Article 6(1) of the Framework Decision, they are not permitted to assess whether the issuing judicial authority had jurisdiction according to the national rules of the issuing member state.[136] The Court noted that allowing executing judicial authorities to review the competence of issuing judicial authorities to issue European arrest warrants would effectively grant executing authorities the power to review the procedural decisions of the issuing member state. This, the Court stated, would undermine the principle of mutual recognition.[137]

Turning to whether an executing judicial authority may refuse to surrender a person due to concerns that their right to be tried by a court with proper jurisdiction upon their return could be compromised, potentially infringing on their right to a fair trial, the CJEU raised several points. The Court first emphasised the importance of the principles of mutual trust and mutual recognition. These principles entail that executing authorities operate under the assumption that fundamental rights are respected in the issuing state and do not assess whether the issuing authority has adhered to fundamental rights principles as outlined in EU law in the specific case at hand.[138] Having said that, the Court stated that, in case a real risk of violation of the fundamental rights of the person to be surrendered is established, executing judicial authorities can exceptionally refuse the execution of a European arrest warrant.[139] Recalling the two-step approach for determining if a person's fundamental rights are at risk, the Court specifically detailed its application to the right to a fair trial. It emphasised that both steps of this approach must be fulfilled to validly assess the risk of human rights violations if the person subject to the European arrest warrant were to be surrendered. The Court equally noted that, if effective legal remedies are available in the issuing member state to review the jurisdiction of the court that will try the defendant and if these remedies are not undermined by systemic or generalised deficiencies in the judicial system of the issuing country, there is no reason to doubt that the person's right to a fair trial will be respected.[140] The Court reminded in this respect that mutual trust prevails in the application

135 Lluís Puig Gordi and Others [31 January 2023] Case C-158/21. EU:C:2023:57, para. 79.
136 Lluís Puig Gordi and Others [31 January 2023] Case C-158/21. EU:C:2023:57, para. 85.
137 Lluís Puig Gordi and Others [31 January 2023] Case C-158/21. EU:C:2023:57, para. 88.
138 Lluís Puig Gordi and Others [31 January 2023] Case C-158/21. EU:C:2023:57, paras. 93–94.
139 Lluís Puig Gordi and Others [31 January 2023] Case C-158/21. EU:C:2023:57, para. 96.
140 Lluís Puig Gordi and Others [31 January 2023] Case C-158/21. EU:C:2023:57, paras. 97–114.

of the European arrest warrant system and that a review of the risk of human rights violation in the issuing member state must remain exceptional.[141] It finally concluded that if the two-step approach is not conclusive in determining a risk of human rights violation in the event of a person's surrender, a European arrest warrant cannot be refused on the ground that the person might be tried by a court lacking jurisdiction upon their surrender.[142]

Accordingly, to the question of whether a report from the UN Working Group on Arbitrary Detention provides sufficient evidence to refuse the execution of a European arrest warrant on the grounds that the person's fundamental rights may be at risk, the Court stated that while such a report and judgments from the ECtHR might indicate the risks faced by the person sought, they do not, on their own, substantiate claims of systemic deficiencies in the judicial system of the issuing member state. The Court noted, however, that such a report could be used as a supporting element to help determine whether systemic and generalised deficiencies are occurring in the issuing country (step 1 of the two-step approach).[143]

Regarding the Belgian Court's refusal to execute a European arrest warrant on the grounds that the court where the person would be tried lacked jurisdiction – without first seeking supplementary information from the issuing judicial authority – the CJEU reminded the member states of their duty of sincere cooperation and the importance to utilise all available instruments to ensure effective cooperation. It therefore ruled that executing judicial authorities cannot refuse the surrender of a person on the grounds that the person would likely be tried by a court that lacks jurisdiction without having first requested supplementary information from the issuing judicial authority. The Court, however, noted that this request for supplementary information was only justified when the executing judicial authority has objective, reliable, specific, and properly updated information establishing generalised and systemic deficiencies in the functioning of the judicial system in the issuing member state (step 1 of the two-step test mentioned earlier).[144]

The final aspect of the Spanish preliminary ruling concerned the question of whether several successive European arrest warrants could be re-issued for the same person following a refusal by the executing judicial authority to surrender that person. On this point, the Court noted that while the Framework Decision does not preclude an issuing judicial authority from doing so, especially when the first request was denied based on grounds contrary to EU law, two elements should be taken into account before re-issuing a request. The first is that if the

141 Lluís Puig Gordi and Others [31 January 2023] Case C-158/21. EU:C:2023:57, paras. 114–117.

142 Lluís Puig Gordi and Others [31 January 2023] Case C-158/21. EU:C:2023:57, para. 119.

143 Lluís Puig Gordi and Others [31 January 2023] Case C-158/21. EU:C:2023:57, paras. 121–126.

144 Lluís Puig Gordi and Others [31 January 2023] Case C-158/21. EU:C:2023:57, paras. 127–136.

first warrant was denied on grounds that its execution would violate the fundamental rights of the person for whom the warrant has been issued, and that the circumstances in the issuing country have not changed, issuing a second warrant would not be compatible with EU law or the principles of mutual trust and sincere cooperation. The second is that considering that the issuance of a European arrest warrant could lead to the arrest of the person and therefore impinge on its individual freedom, the issuing judicial authority should consider the proportionality of issuing another European arrest warrant, weighing the gravity of the offence to the consequences it would have on the person.[145]

The Court's ruling was rather cautious given the politically charged context of the case. Aligning with its previous case law on the matter, the Court's ruling showed a careful balance between the Court's traditional inclination for cooperation while observing a prudent refrain from pushing too much in the direction of cooperation in cases where allegations of potential human rights violations are raised. With this ruling, the Court thus mostly concurred with the Spanish request for more cooperation on the Catalan case but also allowed room for Belgian judicial authorities to refuse the execution of European arrest warrant requests sent by Spanish judicial authorities in case of serious and substantiated concerns about potential risks of human rights violations.

Looming shadow of political offence exception in this case

In the matter of the surrender of Catalan exiles, there would be a case to argue that, by invoking different arguments, such as the dual criminality requirement or the lack of competence of the Supreme Court to rule over this case, national judges employed a form of 'ghost political offence exception'. What was supposed to be a straightforward and supposedly quasi-automatic surrender escalated, several years later, into multiple waves of European and international extradition warrants, arrests in different EU member states, and several procedures initiated at the CJEU level, yet no surrender. It is thus safe to conclude that the executing authorities in EU member states were uneasy about the prospect of surrendering Catalan leaders back to Spain.

Olivier Peter, the Swiss lawyer of Anna Gabriel, outlined that even though Switzerland still has the possibility to use the political offence exception in extradition proceedings, Swiss authorities often prefer to refuse an extradition based on a procedural vice. He explained:

> You have to give arguments to the state for it to reject the extradition without having to take a stance that will be politically too complicated. Referring to procedural shortcomings therefore offers a dignified and less painful way out for Spain. So, it is clear that we would have taken that

145 Lluís Puig Gordi and Others [31 January 2023] Case C-158/21. EU:C:2023:57, paras. 137–146.

direction [had we received an extradition request]. . . . [T]he strategy is always to offer the judge a way out to acquit the person without having to decide on the question of principle. And it is often this little way out that the Tribunal favours, so we regularly obtain acquittals without having a ruling on the substantive issue. It is something that we systematically find. The judiciary does not want to decide on political questions, on the substance of these cases, but prefers to reach the same outcome without having to adopt embarrassing motivations.[146]

And indeed, even if supposedly neutral, the use of the political offence exemption clause never is, according to Peter. He explained, in this regard, that the use of the clause is easier for certain crimes or against particular countries, precisely because neither its use nor the clause itself is neutral.[147] In situations in which Swiss authorities attempt to avoid adjudicating the merits of a case, Swiss lawyers can occasionally compel the state to act by threatening to pursue political asylum. Peter, indeed, described how, if lawyers introduce a request to get asylum, the state will have to make a decision on the substance of the case. In the case of Anna Gabriel, he reported,

> We said to Switzerland: "If you allow Spain to seize you on the extradition, then we will seize you on the asylum and you will be obliged to formally decide on the justified character or not of the proceeding in Spain".[148]

This shows that even in countries where the political offence exemption clause is still applicable, its use can be problematic and can often involve a behind-the-scenes struggle between lawyers and national authorities. Conversely, when the clause is not invoked, it does not necessarily mean that the rejection is not politically motivated. As explained by Peter, this is evident in instances where a 'dignified exit' opportunity is provided to avoid invoking the political offence exception clause to refuse an extradition request.

Considering the preceding discussion, the question of whether executing judicial authorities in EU member states concealed their refusal to cooperate – due to the political nature of the case – under more acceptable grounds for refusal can certainly be raised, especially in light of the Swiss declarations openly saying that extradition requests for Catalan exiles were likely to be political. The German refusal to surrender Puigdemont for the political charge of the case by purposefully applying an in-depth dual criminality check, its reminder that criminal law should not be used to resolve political issues, the first Belgian refusal to grant extradition due to the absence of a national arrest warrant accompanying the European one, and its later refusal based on the lack of competence of the Spanish Supreme court to issue

146 Interview with Olivier Peter (n 61).
147 Interview with Olivier Peter (n 61).
148 Interview with Olivier Peter (n 61).

a European arrest warrant for Puig, which was a gateway to question the ability of Spanish authorities to provide a fair trial to Catalan separatists – all these actions indicate a clear reluctance among executing authorities in EU member states to send Catalan leaders back due to the political nature of the case and the perceived inability of Spanish authorities to to provide a fair trial to Catalan separatists.

Conclusion

This chapter explored the management of the Catalan crisis at the European level and demonstrated that, despite Spain's extensive efforts over previous decades to reform the EU extradition and terrorism framework to handle crises like this, and despite the diligent efforts of Spanish judicial authorities to return these exiles using the very tools Spain had previously advocated, no EU member state ultimately surrendered them. Lawyers of Catalan exiles made the case of a political trial where the fundamental rights of Catalan exiles, especially the right to a fair trial, were endangered. They also argued that Spanish authorities had judicialised what was essentially a political crisis. They therefore sought to show that Catalan separatist leaders constitute a particularly vulnerable group to judiciary drifts in Spain.

The defence of lawyers seems to have resonated with judges in executing countries who showed great caution and a somewhat veiled distrust towards Spanish judicial authorities. This was, for instance, visible in the rejection of the last European arrest warrant against Puig based on the alleged lack of competence of the Spanish Supreme Court to try Catalan leaders, and concerns that such a trial could undermine their right to a fair trial. In Germany, although the Court granted the surrender of Puigdemont, it did so only for the non-political charge of the case (embezzlement) and refused the surrender for the charge of rebellion. This refusal was based on a stringent dual criminality check, which went beyond EU law requirements, as the Court considered the Catalan crisis to be a political conflict, where criminal law should be applied as restrictively as possible. As for Swiss authorities, they repeatedly invoked the political nature of the crimes and of the prosecutions in public declarations (although they never made a decision on the extradition because the warrant was withdrawn beforehand). This chapter therefore argues that, even though the political offence exception has been abolished in the European Union, executing judicial authorities seem to have applied a form a 'ghost political offence exception' when deciding on the surrender of Catalan leaders in a context of increased caution regarding mutual trust.

Bibliography

Legislation, cases, official publications

European Union

European Parliament, Report on the Implementation of the European Arrest Warrant and the Surrender Procedures between Member States (2019/2207(INI)) Committee on Civil Liberties and Home Affairs, Rapporteur: Javier Zarzalejos RR\1220194EN.docx (PE655.688v02–00) 2020.

European Parliament, Request for Waiver of the Immunity of Antoni Comín i Oliveres. European Parliament Decision of 9 March 2021 on the Request for Waiver of the Immunity of Antoni Comín i Oliveres (2020/2025(IMM)), (P9_TA(2021)0060) 2021.
European Parliament, Request for Waiver of the Immunity of Carles Puigdemont i Casamajó. European Parliament Decision of 9 March 2021 on the Request for Waiver of the Immunity of Carles Puigdemont i Casamajó (2020/2024(IMM)), (P9_TA(2021)0059) 2021.
European Parliament, Request for Waiver of the Immunity of Clara Ponsatí Obiols. European Parliament Decision of 9 March 2021 on the Request for Waiver of the Immunity of Clara Ponsatí Obiols (2020/2031(IMM)), (P9_TA(2021)0061) 2021.
European Parliament Research Service, European Arrest Warrant – Framework for Analysis and Preliminary Findings on its Implementation (PE 642.814) 2020.
General Court of the European Union, The Vice-President of the General Court of the European Union Refuses the New Request for the Suspension of Waiver of the Parliamentary Immunity of Mr Carles Puigdemont i Casamajó, Mr Antoni Comín i Oliveres and Ms Clara Ponsatí i Obiols (Press release no.213/21) 2021.
Joszef Grundza [11 January 2017] Case C-289/15, EU:C:2017:4.
Lluís Puig Gordi and Others [31 January 2023] Case C-158/21. EU:C:2023:57.
Opinion of Advocate General Richard de la Tour Delivered on 14 July 2022. Criminal Proceedings against Lluís Puig Gordi and Others. Request for a Preliminary Ruling from the Tribunal Supremo. Reference for a Preliminary Ruling – Area of Freedom, Security and Justice – Judicial Cooperation in Criminal Matters – European Arrest Warrant – Framework Decision 2002/584/JHA – Surrender Procedures between Member States – Conditions for Execution – Jurisdiction of the Issuing Judicial Authority – Second Paragraph of Article 47 of the Charter of Fundamental Rights of the European Union – Right of Access to a Tribunal Previously Established by Law – Possibility of Issuing a new European Arrest Warrant Relating to the Same Person. Case C-158/21 (Document no. 62021CC0158) 2022.
Order of the Vice-President of the Court of 24 May 2022, Carles Puigdemont i Casamajó and Others v. European Parliament (Appeal – Interim Relief – Institutional Law – Members of the European Parliament – Privileges and Immunities – Waiver of the Parliamentary Immunity of a Member of the Parliament – Prima Facie Case – Impartiality of the Rapporteur When Examining the Request for Waiver of Parliamentary Immunity – Urgency – European Arrest Warrant – Alert on Persons Wanted for Arrest for Surrender Purposes – Exercise of the Mandate of a Member of the Parliament – Balance of Interests) EU:C:2022:413.
Oriol Junqueras Vies [19 December 2019] Case C-502/19. EU:C:2019:1115.
Puigdemont i Casamajó and Others v. Parliament [22 December 2023] C-572/23 P.
Puigdemont i Casamajó et Comín i Oliveres [5 July 2023] Case T 115/20. EU:T:2023:372.
Ramon Tremosa i Balcells (ALDE), Josep-Maria Terricabras (Verts/ALE), Jordi Solé (Verts/ALE), Martina Anderson (GUE/NGL), José Bové (Verts/ALE), Bodil Valero (Verts/ALE), Igor Šoltes (Verts/ALE), Izaskun Bilbao Barandica (ALDE), Josu Juaristi Abaunz (GUE/NGL), Jill Evans (Verts/ALE), António Marinho e Pinto (ALDE), Bart Staes (Verts/ALE), Barbara Spinelli (GUE/NGL), Maria Lidia Senra Rodríguez (GUE/NGL) and Rolandas Paksas (EFDD) 1145474.EN, PE 617.651 Question for Written Answer E-000746/2018 to the Commission. Subject: Misuse of the European Arrest Warrant by Spain [2018].
Regulation (EU, Euratom) 2020/2092 of the European Parliament and of the Council of 16 December 2020 on a General Regime of Conditionality for the Protection of the Union Budget [2020] OJ L 433I.
Request for a Preliminary Ruling from the Tribunal Supremo (Spain) Lodged on 11 March 2021 – Ministerio Fiscal, Abogacía del Estado, Partido político VOX v. Lluís Puig Gordi, Carles Puigdemont Casamajó, Antoni Comín Oliveres, Clara Ponsatí

Obiols, Meritxell Serret Aleu, Marta Rovira Vergés, Anna Gabriel Sabaté, Case C-158/21.

Tribunal de L'Union Européenne, Le Vice-Président du Tribunal de l'Union Européenne Rejette la Demande de Suspension de la Levée de l'Immunité Parlementaire de MM. Carles Puigdemont i Casamajó et Antoni Comín i Oliveres ainsi que de Mme Clara Ponsatí i Obiols (Communiqué de Presse no. 141/21) 2021

Tribunal de L'Union Européenne, Le Vice-Président du Tribunal de l'Union Européenne Suspend Provisoirement la Levée de l'Immunité Parlementaire de MM. Carles Puigdemont i Casamajó et Antoni Comín i Oliveres ainsi que de Mme Clara Ponsatí i Obiols (Communiqué de Presse no. 91/21) 2021.

X and Y v. Openbaar Ministerie [22 February 2022] Joined Cases C-562/21 PPU and C-563/21 PPU, EU:C:2022:100.

Council of Europe

Atutxa Mendiola and others v. Spain, Application no. 41427/14 (ECtHR 13/09/2017).

Spain

La Ley Orgánica 5/1985, de Régimen Electoral General of 19 June 1985 (20 June 1985).

Supreme Court, Judgment No. 459/2019 (14 October 2019).

Books

Willems A., *The Principle of Mutual Trust in EU Criminal Law* (Hart Publishing, Oxford, Dublin 2021).

Journal articles

Bachmaier L., 'European Arrest Warrant, Double Criminality and Mutual Recognition: A Much Debated Case' [2018] *EuCLR.* 152.

Braum S., 'The Carles Puigdemont Case: Europe's Criminal Law in the Crisis of Confidence' [2018] *Ger. Law J.* 1349.

Carrera S., Guild E. and Hernanz N., 'Europe's Most Wanted? Recalibrating Trust in the European Arrest Warrant System' [2013] *CEPS Papers.* 1.

Foffani L., 'The Case Puigdemont: The Stress-Test of the European Arrest Warrant' [2018] *Eur. Crim. Law Rev.* 196.

König J., Meichelbeck P. and Puchta M., 'The Curious Case of Carles Puigdemont – The European Arrest Warrant as an Inadequate Means with Regard to Political Offenses' [2021] *Ger. Law J.* 256.

Lenaerts K., 'La Vie Après L'Avis: Exploring the Principle of Mutual (Yet Not Blind) Trust' [2017] *CMLR.* 805.

Mitsilegas V., 'The Limits of Mutual Trust in Europe's Area of Freedom, Security and Justice: From Automatic Inter-State Cooperation to the Slow Emergence of the Individual' [2012] *YEL.* 319.

Muñoz de Morales Romero M., 'Dual Criminality under Review: On the Puigdemont Case' [2018] *Eur. Crim. Law Rev.* 167, 167–175.

Ruiz Yamuza F.-G., 'CJEU Case Law on Double Criminality. The Grundza-Piotrowski Paradox? Some Notes Regarding the Puigdemont Case' [2019] *ERA Forum.* 465.

Top S. and De Hert P., 'Castano Avoids a Clash Between the ECtHR and the CJEU, but Erodes Soering. Thinking Human Rights Transnationally' [2020] *NJECL*. 52.

Xanthopoulou E., 'Mutual Trust and Rights in EU Criminal Law and Asylum Law: Three Phases of Evolution and the Uncharted Territory beyond Blind Trust' [2018] *CMLR*. 489–509.

Book chapters

Weyembergh A., 'Transverse Report on Judicial Control in Cooperation in Criminal Matters. The Evolution from Traditional Judicial Cooperation to Mutual Recognition' in K. Ligeti (ed), *Toward a Prosecutor for the European Union, A Comparative Analysis* (Volume 1) (Hart Publishing, 2013).

Online resources

Cardiff EDC, 'Case C-502/19, Junqueras Vies' (European Sources Online 2019) <https://www.europeansources.info/record/case-c-502-19-junqueras-vies/> accessed 13 May 2020.

Comunicación Poder Judicial, 'El Instructor de la Causa del "Procés" en el Tribunal Supremo Pide al Parlamento Europeo que Suspenda la Inmunidad de Carles Puigdemont y Antoni Comín y Ratifica la Orden de Detención en Territorio Español. El magistrado Pablo Llarena Señala que la Inmunidad no Sería Aplicable en España al Estar ya Procesados y que no se Requeriría Suplicatorio' (Poder Judicial 2020) <https://www.poderjudicial.es/cgpj/es/Causa-especial-20907-2017/Archivo-de-resoluciones/2020/-El-instructor-de-la-causa-del-proces-en-el-Tribunal-Supremo-pide-al-Parlamento-Europeo-que-suspenda-la-inmunidad-de-Carles-Puigdemont-y-Antoni-Comin-y-ratifica-la-orden-de-detencion-en-territorio-espanol> accessed 22 May 2022.

Comunicación Poder Judicial, 'El Instructor de la Causa del "Procés" en el Tribunal Supremo Resolverá sobre la Euroorden contra Carles Puigdemont Cuando el TJUE se Pronuncie sobre Eventuales Medidas Cautelares' (Poder Judicial 2023) <https://www.poderjudicial.es/cgpj/es/Poder-Judicial/Tribunal-Supremo/Oficina-de-Comunicacion/Archivo-de-notas-de-prensa/El-instructor-de-la-causa-del-proces-en-el-Tribunal-Supremo-resolvera-sobre-la-euroorden-contra-Carles-Puigdemont-cuando-el-TJUE-se-pronuncie-sobre-eventuales-medidas-cautelares> accessed 15 July 2024.

Comunicación Poder Judicial, 'El Instructor de la Causa del Procés en el TS Aplica la Derogación del Delito de Sedición a Carles Puigdemont y Acuerda su Procesamiento por Desobediencia y Malversación. El Magistrado Pablo Llarena Considera que Los Hechos no Encajan en el Delito de Desórdenes Públicos y que la Reforma Legal Ofrece "un Contexto Cercano a la Despenalización"' (Poder Judicial 2023) <https://www.poderjudicial.es/cgpj/es/Poder-Judicial/Tribunal-Supremo/Oficina-de-Comunicacion/Archivo-de-notas-de-prensa/El-instructor-de-la-causa-del-proces-en-el-TS-aplica-la-derogacion-del-delito-de-sedicion-a-Carles-Puigdemont-y-acuerda-su-procesamiento-por-desobediencia-y-malversacion> accessed 15 July 2024.

Comunicación Poder Judicial, 'El Instructor de la Causa del "Procés" Plantea Cuestión Prejudicial al TJUE Sobre la Euroorden' (Poder Judicial 2021) <https://www.poderjudicial.es/cgpj/en/Judiciary/Supreme-Court/Pressroom/Press-Archive/El-instructor-de-la-causa-del-proces-plantea-cuestion-prejudicial-al-TJUE-sobre-la-euroorden> accessed 24 May 2022.

Comunicación Poder Judicial, 'El Juez Confirma al Tribunal Italiano que la Euroorden contra Puigdemont Está Vigente y que no ha Sido Suspendida por el Planteamiento de la Cuestión Prejudicial. El Magistrado del Tribunal Supremo Remite Información Complementaria a Eurojust para Clarificar el Estado de la Causa y Reclamar la Entrega del Detenido a la Justicia Española' (Poder Judicial 2021) <https://www.poderjudicial.es/cgpj/en/Judiciary/Pressroom/News-archive/El-juez-confirma-al-tribunal-italiano-que-la-euroorden-contra-Puigdemont-esta-vigente-y-que-no-ha-sido-suspendida-por-el-planteamiento-de-la-cuestion-prejudicial> accessed 2 June 2022.

Comunicación Poder Judicial, 'El Juez del Tribunal Supremo Pablo Llarena Acuerda la Prisión Provisional Incondicional de Turull, Rull, Romeva, Bassa y Forcadell por Riesgo de Fuga y de Reiteración Delictiva' (Poder Judicial 2018) <https://www.poderjudicial.es/cgpj/en/Judiciary/Pressroom/News-archive/El-juez-del-Tribunal-Supremo-Pablo-Llarena-acuerda-la-prision-provisional-incondicional-de-Turull-Rull-Romeva-Bassa-y-Forcadell> accessed 20 May 2022.

Comunicación Poder Judicial, 'El Juez del Tribunal Supremo Pablo Llarena Emite Euroórdenes contra los Exconsellers Catalanes Comin, Ponsatí y Puig. Las Órdenes Internacionales se han Enviado a Interpol para la Detención a Efectos Extradicionales en el Caso de que Estos Procesados se Localicen en un País que no Pertenezca a la UE' (Poder Judicial 2019) <https://www.poderjudicial.es/cgpj/es/Causa-especial-20907-2017/Ultimas-Noticias/El-juez-del-Tribunal-Supremo-Pablo-Llarena-emite-euroordenes-contra-los-exconsellers-catalanes-Comin-Ponsati-y-Puig> accessed 21 May 2022.

Comunicación Poder Judicial, 'El Juez del Tribunal Supremo Pablo Llarena Rechaza la Entrega de Carles Puigdemont Solo por el Delito de Malversación. El Magistrado Destaca la "Falta de Compromiso" del Tribunal Alemán que Decidió sobre la Euroorden Dictada contra el Expresidente de la Generalitat' (Poder Judicial 2018) <https://www.poderjudicial.es/cgpj/es/Poder-Judicial/Tribunal-Supremo/Noticias-Judiciales/El-juez-del-Tribunal-Supremo-Pablo-Llarena-rechaza-la-entrega-de-Carles-Puigdemont-solo-por-el-delito-de-malversacion> accessed 20 May 2022.

Comunicación Poder Judicial, 'El Juez Llarena Dicta Orden Europea e Internacional de Detención contra Puigdemont por Delitos de Sedición y Malversación. El Auto Señala que la Sala Segunda del Tribunal Supremo ha Dictado hoy la Sentencia que Pone Término al Proceso Respecto de los Acusados Enjuiciados' (Poder Judicial 2019) <https://www.poderjudicial.es/cgpj/es/Causa-especial-20907-2017/Ultimas-Noticias/El-juez-Llarena-dicta-orden-europea-e-internacional-de-detencion-contra-Puigdemont-por-delitos-de-sedicion-y-malversacion> accessed 21 May 2022.

Comunicación Poder Judicial, 'El Juez Llarena Remite un Escrito a Alemania con Información Complementaria para la Entrega de Puigdemont y Otro a Bélgica por Puig, Comin y Serret. El Magistrado Expone que, de Acuerdo a las Reglas de la Orden Europea de Detención (OED), el Estado Requerido Sólo Podría Denegar la Entrega si los Hechos por los que se ha Emitido la Orden de Detención Europea No Son Constitutivos de Ningún Tipo de Infracción Penal en su Territorio' (Poder Judicial 2018) <https://www.poderjudicial.es/cgpj/en/Judiciary/Pressroom/News-archive/El-juez-Llarena-remite-un-escrito-a-Alemania-con-informacion-complementaria-para-la-entrega-de-Puigdemont-y-otro-a-Belgica-por-Puig-Comin-y-Serret> accessed 31 May 2022.

Comunicación Poder Judicial, 'El Magistrado del Tribunal Supremo Pablo Llarena Amplía su Investigación a Artur Mas, Marta Rovira, Anna Gabriel y Otras Tres Personas. El Juez Ha Notificado un Auto en el Que les Comunica la Existencia del Procedimiento y los Derechos que les Asisten' (Poder Judicial 2017) <https://www.poderjudicial.es/cgpj/en/Judiciary/Pressroom/News-archive/El-magistrado-del-Tribunal-Supremo-Pablo-Llarena-amplia-su-investigacion-a-Artur-Mas-Marta-Rovira-Anna-Gabriel-y-otras-tres-personas> accessed 21 May 2022.

Comunicación Poder Judicial, 'El Magistrado del Tribunal Supremo Pablo Llarena Deja sin Efecto las Euro-órdenes contra Puigdemont y los Exconsellers que se Encuentran en Bélgica' (Poder Judicial 2017) <https://www.poderjudicial.es/portal/site/cgpj/menuitem.65d2c4456b6ddb628e635fc1dc432ea0/?vgnextoid=dda146a5fd320610VgnVCM1000006f48ac0aRCRD&vgnextchannel=3f99c38cb605c210VgnVCM100000cb34e20aRCRD&vgnextfmt=default&vgnextlocale=es_ES> accessed 7 April 2020.

Comunicación Poder Judicial, 'El Presidente del TS Remite al del Parlamento Europeo la Solicitud de Suplicatorio de Clara Ponsatí' (Poder Judicial 2020) <https://www.poderjudicial.es/cgpj/en/Judiciary/Supreme-Court/Pressroom/Press-Archive/El-presidente-del-TS-remite-al-del-Parlamento-Europeo-la-solicitud-de-suplicatorio-de-Clara-Ponsati> accessed 22 May 2022.

Comunicación Poder Judicial, 'El Tribunal Supremo Abre Causa Penal por Delito de Terrorismo a Carles Puigdemont y al Diputado Wagensberg en el Caso de "Tsunami Democràtic"' (Poder Judicial 2024) <https://www.poderjudicial.es/cgpj/es/Poder-Judicial/Tribunal-Supremo/Oficina-de-Comunicacion/Archivo-de-notas-de-prensa/El-Tribunal-Supremo-abre-causa-penal-por-delito-de-terrorismo-a-Carles-Puigdemont-y-al-diputado-Wagensberg-en-el-caso-de-Tsunami-Democratic-> accessed 16 July 2024.

Comunicación Poder Judicial, 'El Tribunal Supremo Activa el Trámite para Plantear una Cuestión Prejudicial al TJUE Sobre el Alcance de la Inmunidad en Relación con Oriol Junqueras. La Sala Mantiene la Situación de Prisión del Exvicepresidente de la Generalitat y Deja en Suspenso su Recurso contra la Denegación del Permiso Extraordinario para Acudir a la Junta Electoral Central' (Poder Judicial 2019) <https://www.poderjudicial.es/cgpj/en/Judiciary/Supreme-Court/Pressroom/Press-Archive/El-Tribunal-Supremo-activa-el-tramite-para-plantear-una-cuestion-prejudicial-al-TJUE-sobre-el-alcance-de-la-inmunidad-en-relacion-con-Oriol-Junqueras> accessed 22 May 2022.

Comunicación Poder Judicial, 'El Tribunal Supremo Cita como Investigados a Carles Puigdemont y a Rubén Wagensberg para que Presten Declaración Voluntaria por Videoconferencia el Próximo Mes de Junio' (Poder Judicial 2024) <https://www.poderjudicial.es/cgpj/es/Poder-Judicial/Tribunal-Supremo/Oficina-de-Comunicacion/Archivo-de-notas-de-prensa/El-Tribunal-Supremo-cita-como-investigados-a-Carles-Puigdemont-y-a-Ruben-Wagensberg-para-que-presten-declaracion-voluntaria-por-videoconferencia-el-proximo-mes-de-junio> accessed 16 July 2024.

Comunicación Poder Judicial, 'El Tribunal Supremo Declara no Amnistiado el Delito de Malversación de Caudales Públicos en la Causa del "Procés". El Magistrado Pablo Llarena Mantiene las Órdenes Nacionales de Detención contra Carles Puigdemont, Antoni Comín y Lluís Puig' (Poder Judicial 2024) <https://www.poderjudicial.es/cgpj/es/Poder-Judicial/Tribunal-Supremo/Oficina-de-Comunicacion/Archivo-de-notas-de-prensa/El-Tribunal-Supremo-declara-no-amnistiado-el-delito-de-malversacion-de-caudales-publicos-en-la-causa-del-proces-> accessed 15 July 2024.

Comunicación Poder Judicial, 'El Tribunal Supremo Ratifica la Existencia de Indicios de Delito de Rebelión en la Actuación de los Dirigentes del "Procés" y Rebate los Argumentos del Tribunal Alemán. La Sala Cree que no es Razonable Equiparar lo Ocurrido en Cataluña con las Protestas contra la Ampliación de un Aeropuerto en Frankfurt' (Poder Judicial 2018) <https://www.poderjudicial.es/cgpj/

en/Judiciary/Pressroom/News-archive/El-Tribunal-Supremo-ratifica-la-existencia-de-indicios-de-delito-de-rebelion-en-la-actuacion-de-los-dirigentes-del-proces-y-rebate-los-argumentos-del-tribunal-aleman> accessed 31 May 2022.

Comunicación Poder Judicial, 'La Instructora del Caso "Tsunami Democràtic" en el Tribunal Supremo Acuerda el Archivo de la Causa en la que Investigaba a Puigdemont y Wagensberg. Tras la Decisión de la Audiencia Nacional de Invalidar las Diligencias Acordadas desde Julio de 2021' (Poder Judicial 2024) <https://www.poderjudicial.es/cgpj/fr/Pouvoir-Judiciaire/Tribunal-supreme/Salle-de-presse/Bibliotheque-de-communiques-de-presse/La-instructora-del-caso-Tsunami-Democratic-en-el-Tribunal-Supremo-acuerda-el-archivo-de-la-causa-en-la-que-investigaba-a-Puigdemont-y-Wagensberg> accessed 16 July 2024.

Comunicación Poder Judicial, 'La Juez Lamela Dicta Órdenes Europeas de Detención Contra el Expresidente de la Generalitat Carles Puigdemont y Cuatro Exconsellers Por los Delitos de Rebelión, Sedición, Malversación, Prevaricación y Desobediencia a la Autoridad' (Poder Judicial 2017) <https://www.poderjudicial.es/cgpj/en/Judiciary/National-High-Court/Pressroom/Press-Releases/La-juez-Lamela-dicta-ordenes-europeas-de-detencion-contra-el-expresidente-de-la-Generalitat-Carles-Puigdemont-y-cuatro-exconsellers> accessed 20 May 2022.

CPE-N Commissions de Politique Extérieure, 'Communiqué de Presse – La Protection des Intérêts Économiques Extérieurs de la Suisse à l'Ordre du Jour' (Assemblée fédérale – le Parlement Suisse 2018) <https://www.parlament.ch/press-releases/Pages/mm-apk-n-2018-04-17.aspx> accessed 20 May 2022.

Eurojust, 'Case-Law by the Court of Justice of the European Union on the European Arrest Warrant' (Eurojust 2021) <https://www.eurojust.europa.eu/sites/default/files/assets/2021_12_08_cjeu_case_law_on_eaw.pdf> accessed 19 July 2024.

GRECO, 'Fourth Evaluation Round: Corruption Prevention in Respect of Members of Parliament, Judges and Prosecutors' (Council of Europe 2018) <https://rm.coe.int/fourth-evaluation-round-corruption-prevention-in-respect-of-members-of/1680779c4d> accessed 15 April 2020.

International Trial Watch – Catalan Referendum Case, 'Factual and Legal Assessment by International and National Observers of the Judgment Condemning Catalan Authorities and Social Leaders (SCJ 459/2019)' (International Trial Watch 2019) <https://internationaltrialwatch.org/wp-content/uploads/2019/11/POSICIONAMIENTO_SENTENCIA_12112019-ingles-carta.pdf> accessed 4 May 2020.

Parquet de Bruxelles, 'Communiqué de Presse – Bruxelles – Mandats d'Arrêts Européens Émis par l'Espagne' (Ministère Public 2019) <https://www.om-mp.be/fr/article/communique-presse-bruxelles-mandats-arret-europeens-emis-espagne> accessed 21 May 2022.

Parquet de Bruxelles, 'Communiqué de Presse – Mandats d'Arrêts Européens Émis par l'Espagne' (Ministère Public 2018) <https://www.om-mp.be/fr/article/communique-presse-mandats-arret-europeens-emis-espagne-2> accessed 20 May 2022.

Parquet de Bruxelles, 'Press Release – European Arrest Warrant Issued by Spain' (Ministère Public 2019) <https://www.om-mp.be/fr/node/2254> accessed 21 May 2022.

Press Secretary Frauke Holmer, 'Matter Carles Puigdemont: The Extradition for the Accusation of Embezzlement of Public Funds is Admissible; an Extradition for the Accusation of Rebellion is Inadmissible. Carles Puigdemont Remains Free' (Schleswig-Holsteinisches Oberlandesgericht 2018) <https://www.schleswig-holstein.de/DE/Justiz/OLG/Presse/PI/201806Puigdemontenglisch.html> accessed 10 April 2020.

Scott-Railton J., Campo E., Marczak B., Abdul Razzak B., Anstis S., Böcü G., Solimano S. and Deibert R., 'CatalanGate - Extensive Mercenary Spyware Operation against Catalans Using Pegasus and Candiru' (Citizenlab 2022) <https://citizenlab.

ca/2022/04/catalangate-extensive-mercenary-spyware-operation-against-catalans-using-pegasus-candiru/> accessed 13 May 2022.

United Nations Human Rights Office of the High Commissioner, 'High Commissioner's Global Update of Human Rights Concerns' (United Nations 2018) <https://www.ohchr.org/en/NewsEvents/Pages/DisplayNews.aspx?NewsID=22772&LangID=E> accessed 13 May 2020.

United Nations Working Group on Arbitrary Detention, 'Opiniones Aprobadas por el Grupo de Trabajo Sobre la Detención Arbitraria en su 84o Período de Sesiones (24 de Abril a 3 de Mayo de 2019). Opinión núm. 6/2019, Relativa a Jordi Cuixart I Navarro, Jordi Sánchez I Picanyol y Oriol Junqueras I Vies (España). A/HRC/WGAD/2019/6'(OHCHR2019)<https://www.ohchr.org/Documents/Issues/Detention/Opinions/Session84/A_HRC_WGAD_2019_6.pdf> accessed 24 April 2020.

Urías J., 'Spain Has a Problem with its Judiciary' (Verfassungsblog 2020) <https://verfassungsblog.de/spain-has-a-problem-with-its-judiciary/> accessed 15 April 2020.

Van Elsuwege P., 'Empty Seats in the European Parliament: What about EU Citizenship?' (Verfassungsblog 2019) <https://verfassungsblog.de/empty-seats-in-the-european-parliament-what-about-eu-citizenship/> accessed 14 May 2020.

Weyembergh A., 'The Puigdemont Case Exposes Challenges in the European Arrest Warrant' (CEPS 2017) <https://www.ceps.eu/wp-content/uploads/2017/12/Weyembergh_PuigdemontEAW.pdf> accessed 4 January 2021.

Willems A., 'Understanding Spain's Decision to Revoke the European Arrest Warrant for Carles Puigdemont' (EUROPP blog - LSE 2017) <https://blogs.lse.ac.uk/europpblog/2017/12/12/understanding-spains-decision-to-revoke-the-european-arrest-warrant-for-carles-puigdemont/> accessed 7 April 2020.

Willems A., 'Will Spain's Latest Attempt at Extraditing Carles Pugidemont Succeed' (EUROPP blog - LSE 2019) <https://blogs.lse.ac.uk/europpblog/2019/10/23/will-spains-latest-attempt-to-extradite-carles-puigdemont-succeed/#comments> accessed 25 May 2022

Newspaper articles

ACN Barcelona, 'Wolfgang Schomburg: 'This Was Never a Matter for Criminal Law'' (Catalan News 2018) <https://www.catalannews.com/society-science/item/wolfgang-schomburg-this-was-never-a-matter-for-criminal-law-2> accessed 27 March 2020.

Andersen L., 'Puigdemont's Defence Team Set to Play the "Political Trial" Card' (The Brussels Time 2017) <https://www.brusselstimes.com/all-news/belgium-all-news/44994/puigdemont-s-defence-team-set-to-play-the-political-trial-card/> accessed 27 March 2020.

Archyde, 'The European Commission Defends Spain at the Hearing in Luxembourg on the Puigdemont Case' (Archyde 2022) <https://www.archyde.com/the-european-commission-defends-spain-at-the-hearing-in-luxembourg-on-the-puigdemont-case/> accessed 2 June 2022.

Brooks L., 'Ex-Catalan Minister Vows to Fight "Politically Motivated" Extradition' (The Guardian 2019) <https://www.theguardian.com/world/2019/nov/14/ex-catalan-minister-clara-Ponsatí -vows-to-fight-politically-motivated-extradition> accessed 25 March 2020.

Bunche R., 'Free Movement Threatened if European Arrest Warrant Abused' (EUobserver 2018) <https://euobserver.com/opinion/141498> accessed 25 May 2022.

Carrell S., 'Extradition Case against Catalan MEP Suspended in Scotland' (The Guardian 2020) <https://www.theguardian.com/uk-news/2020/mar/05/clara-Ponsatí-extradition-case-against-catalan-mep-suspended-in-scotland> accessed 15 May 2020.

Harari A., 'La Suisse N'Expulsera pas L'Indépendantiste Catalane Anna Gabriel' (Le Temps 2018) <https://www.letemps.ch/suisse/suisse-nexpulsera-lindependantiste-catalane-anna-gabriel> accessed 17 December 2019.

Heller F., 'Carles Puigdemont Établit son "Quartier Général" Politique en France' (Euractiv 2024) <https://www.euractiv.fr/section/elections/news/puigdemont-sets-up-political-headquarters-in-france/> accessed 16 July 2024.

Jones S. and Rankin J., 'Ex-Catalan Leader Appears Before Belgian Authorities Over Arrest Warrant' (The Guardian 2019) <https://www.theguardian.com/world/2019/oct/18/ex-catalan-leader-carles-puigdemont-belgian-authorities-arrest-warrant> accessed 14 April 2020.

Lasalas M. and Piulachs M., 'Key Points at ECJ Hearing: Spanish Judicial Deficiencies and Court's Competence' (El Nacional 2022) <https://www.elnacional.cat/en/politics/key-points-european-court-justice-spanish-deficiencies-catalan-exile_737622_102.html> accessed 2 June 2022.

McPherson G., 'VIDEO: St Andrews Professor Clara Ponsatí and Lawyer Address Catalonia Supporters Outside Court' (The Courrier 2018) <https://www.thecourier.co.uk/fp/news/politics/scottish-politics/654121/video-st-andrews-professor-clara-Ponsatí-and-lawyer-address-catalonia-supporters-outside-court/> accessed 27 March 2020

Oliveira S., 'Jaume Alonso-Cuevillas' (Catalonia Today 2019) <https://www.cataloniatoday.cat/article/1552272-jaume-alonso-cuevillas.html> accessed 27 March 2020.

Partal T., 'Clara Ponsatí: "We Want to Be the Backbone of the Independence Process"' (VilaWeb 2024) <https://www.vilaweb.cat/noticies/clara-ponsati-we-want-to-be-the-backbone-of-the-independence-process/> accessed 16 July 2024.

Sánchez Iranzo M., 'Why Switzerland Has Again Slammed the Door on Spanish Judge García-Castellón. Switzerland Reiterates that the Democratic Tsunami Demonstrations Are not Terrorism and Refuses to Locate Marta Rovira' (El Nacional 2024) <https://www.elnacional.cat/en/politics/why-switzerland-slams-door-spanish-judge-garcia-castellon_1235613_102.html> accessed 16 July 2024.

SDA-ATS/ac, 'Catalan Crisis: Switzerland to Offer Good Offices but Not Interfere' (Swissinfo 2018) <https://www.swissinfo.ch/eng/politics/separatists-in-exile_catalan-crisis-switzerland-to-offer-good-offices-but-not-interfere-/44068630> accessed 25 May 2022.

Stroobants J.-P., 'En Belgique, la Défence des Ex-Ministres Catalans Dénonce "un Procès Politique" de Madrid' (Le Monde 2017) <https://www.hvlaw.eu/sites/default/files/online/news/presse/Le_Monde_15-11-2017.pdf> accessed 27 March 2020.

Interview

Interview with Christophe Marchand, Lawyer of Antoni Comín and Meritxell Serret (Brussels, 1 October 2018).

Interview with Olivier Peter, Lawyer of Anna Gabriel and Jordi Cuixart (Online, 11 November 2019).

Interview with Paul Bekaert, Lawyer of Carles Puigdemont, Lluis Puig and Clara Ponsatí (when in Belgium) (Online, 1 November 2019).

Interview with Paul Bekaert, Lawyer of Carles Puigdemont, Lluis Puig and Clara Ponsatí (when in Belgium) (Tielt, 29 November 2018).

7 Abolition and use of the political offence exception clause in the European context

The topic of the political offence exception to extradition has largely escaped academic scrutiny in the last decades, overshadowed by the growing focus on terrorism research. However, recent events have rekindled interest in the protection of human rights, particularly in the face of an increasingly robust body of counterterrorism laws. A few examples of incidents indicating deteriorating democratic standards include disinformation campaigns affecting democratic processes, Russia ceasing to be a contracting party to the European Convention on Human Rights, serious warnings issued to Poland and Hungary regarding their adherence to EU values, and the CJEU multiplying rulings emphasising that trust in judicial cooperation within the European Union should not be blind. It is against this backdrop that the Catalan independence crisis took place and that some of its leaders fled in self-imposed exile. This crisis showed that concerns over the respect of fundamental rights, such as the right to a fair trial, spare no one and can affect even countries with strong democratic traditions like Spain. The enthusiasm sparked by the 9/11 attacks for adopting tools increasing cooperation on counterterrorism has now given way to greater caution. It is in this framework that the question of the potential relevance of safeguard mechanisms, such as the one of the political offence exception clause to extradition, has come to the forefront after years of limited interest.

Although research on terrorism has eclipsed the political offence exception to extradition in recent decades, this topic was once the focus of intense academic debate due to the difficulty of conceptualising the notion of political crime. Numerous scholars have attempted to contour a definition of political crimes, with little to no success. Regardless of the impossibility of defining political crimes, however, it has become a standard practice of international law to protect political offenders from extradition, which led to the development of several approaches aiming to determine the political nature of an offence. The Swiss proportionality test has been hailed as the most balanced approach in this respect, as it considers several factors in the determination of the political nature of an offence. Alongside these existing approaches, which aim to offer a positive definition of political crimes, the increasing need to combat terrorism has prompted the adoption of several counterterrorism

DOI: 10.4324/9781003425847-7

instruments that define political offences in a negative manner – by excluding certain crimes from the political offence exception.

This tendency has been observed internationally, and the European legal framework offers a good example of it. The first-ever European multilateral treaty on extradition, the 1957 Convention on Extradition, for instance, anchored the political offence exception to the Council of Europe legal framework on judicial cooperation and offered very generous protection from extradition to political offenders. However, this liberal protection regime has diminished with the successive adoption of counterterrorism conventions that progressively excluded more and more crimes from the scope of the political offence exception. Arguing that members of the Council of Europe form a community of like-minded countries with mutual trust and that the shared values of this community required protection from terrorist attacks, the Council of Europe adopted an increasingly extensive range of conventions and protocols on terrorism. These instruments progressively narrowed the scope of the political offence exception by defining a growing number of crimes as terroristic. Initially, only crimes involving extreme violence were excluded from protection, but over time, the exclusions expanded to include crimes targeting state infrastructures, agents, and symbols more broadly. The definition of terrorist offences was later extended to cover preemptive actions against terrorist crimes. As a result, the protection of political offenders from extradition was significantly reduced in the name of protecting the shared values of the Council of Europe from terrorist attacks endangering them. Despite this reduction, the protection for political offenders from extradition remains applicable to a limited range of residual crimes.

In the European Union, the political offence exception to extradition has been entirely abolished. Spain, in particular, played a pivotal role in advancing the European Union's extradition framework and eliminating the political offence exception to prevent its use in protecting ETA militants in exile. Spanish authorities were equally instrumental in pushing for the abolition of the right to asylum for EU citizens and made significant contributions to developing the EU counterterrorism framework, at the centre of which they put extradition. Initially, Spain faced challenges in rallying other member states to support its counterterrorism agenda, but the 9/11 attacks turned the fight against terrorism from negotiation to evidence. The attacks accelerated the adoption of long-discussed measures, such as the Framework Decision on the European arrest warrant, which nearly automated extradition within the European Union and advanced Spain's goal of enhanced European cooperation on counterterrorism. This Framework Decision was adopted alongside the Framework Decision on combating terrorism, which reversed the initial protection of political offenders by redefining the political intent of crimes as a terroristic intent. The adoption of these measures was justified by the mutual trust among EU member states, which was seen as not only enabling but necessitating the implementation of counterterrorism tools to protect shared values and ideals threatened by terrorism. Today, however, there is a new trend where the need to protect the system's core values occasionally allows for mistrust among member states.

The latter was most visible in the case of Catalan exiles for whom Spain issued European arrest warrants and extradition warrants across Europe. The Catalan independence crisis and the ensuing exile of some of its leaders constitute an exceptionally rich case for the study of the political offence exception in Europe. Indeed, the crimes they committed were political but did not qualify as terrorist despite the fact that the notion of terrorism subsumed most of the crimes formerly protected by political offence exception to extradition. On 1 October 2017, Catalan separatists sought to establish what they considered would be a real democracy in opposition to what they viewed as a postfascist Spanish state. They organised a peaceful referendum in breach of the Spanish legal framework and orders from the Constitutional Court prohibiting them from going ahead with the independence process. The immediate reaction of the reigning PP was to judicialise the crisis and avoid any political negotiations with Catalan separatists. Their view was that there was no case in even discussing the materiality or legitimacy of the Catalan independence project because it was illegal. In the aftermath of the referendum, the strong reaction of the Partido Popular, in terms of both police violence and judicialisation, shocked many observers and fed the argumentation of lawyers of Catalan exiles on the repression of Catalan separatists in Spain. Although the actions of the Catalan exiles were undeniably illegal, the response from Spanish authorities cast doubt on the Spanish system's ability to ensure a fair trial for Catalan separatists. When the Partido Socialista Obrero Español came to power in 2019, they sought to overcome the constitutional crisis generated by the independence process through political dialogue, a change of the criminal code with retroactive effect, pardons, and a law on amnesty. Doing so, they complied with international calls to de-escalate tensions and resolve the crisis on a political level rather than judicially only. Yet, European countries who received extradition requests remained vigilant to Spanish calls to surrender Catalan exiles, as the appropriateness of having the Spanish Supreme Court deal with the matter as well as the ability of the latter to provide a fair trial to Catalan exiles remained questioned.

Despite Spain's efforts to return Catalan leaders smoothly and efficiently, as typically anticipated under the European arrest warrant framework, no Catalan leader was surrendered back to Spain. Notably, Swiss authorities immediately invoked the political offence exception clause when rumours of extradition warrants against Catalan activists in Switzerland started circulating. Olivier Peter, the Swiss lawyer representing Catalan exile Anna Gabriel, noted that while Swiss authorities still have the option to apply the political offence exception clause, they generally prefer to pursue alternative approaches to refuse extraditions. They ideally search for procedural venues to refuse the surrender of political offenders so as to offer a 'dignified exit' opportunity for the country that requested the extradition. This shows that even when national authorities have the possibility to use the political offence exception, they do not always do so in cases involving political crimes. Conversely, when they invoke non-political grounds for refusal, this does not mean that their refusal is not linked to the political nature of the case. The refusals of the judicial authorities of EU member states to surrender Catalan leaders in exile are contemplated in this light in this work. The latest Belgian refusal to surrender Lluis Puig, Catalan politician in exile, on grounds of the lack of authority of the Spanish Supreme Court to rule on the case points to this approach, especially, when the Belgian Court suggested that the alleged lack of authority of the Spanish Supreme Court might pose a risk to Puig's right to a fair trial. Equally, the German Court's decision regarding the extradition of Puigdemont in 2018 reflected a similar stance. While the German Court approved the extradition on charges of embezzlement, it rejected the surrender on the sole political charge of the case, rebellion, applying particularly stringent standards for the dual criminality requirement. The Court justified this strict interpretation by arguing that criminal law should be applied as restrictively as possible in cases of political conflict. In light of this, this work contends that EU executing judicial authorities applied a form of 'ghost political offence exception clause' to the case of Catalan exiles.

What this case more generally highlights is the limit of judicial cooperation in criminal matters in Europe and in the European Union, in particular, where this framework of cooperation is more advanced. Tools enthusiastically adopted in the wake of major events, like the 9/11 attacks, encounter resistance once the urgency surrounding their adoption subsides. The anticipated automaticity of cooperation depends on the willingness of member states to implement it, and the Catalan case showed that cooperation in criminal matters can only go as far as member states' traditions allow. It is safe to assume, in this respect, that the choice of Catalan exiles to go to Belgium was strategic, given Belgium's history of not extraditing Basque separatist exiles to Spain, even when their guilt was established. The Catalan exiles thus exploited existing disparities among EU member states, both in their traditions regarding separatism and in their application of the EU legal framework. Asperities therefore remain in a supposedly fluidified system, specifically when cooperation conflicts with national customs.

In this regard, criminal law and human rights protection represent points of tension that particularly exacerbate the differences in the legal systems of EU member states, as they touch on matters of national sovereignty. While mutual trust and recognition were promoted as alternatives to harmonisation to enhance cooperation in criminal matters within the European Union, the Catalan case showcases how mistrust can still overtake cooperation. In the Catalan case, national judges went to considerable lengths to find reasons to refuse the extradition of exiles, despite what should have been simple cases. Even if these exiles are eventually extradited to Spain, the difficulties faced by the Spanish courts in securing their return will remain a testament to the fact that EU law cannot fully overcome entrenched national reflexes of distrust – or at least extreme caution – in political cases involving criminal law and human rights.

Index

FSC
www.fsc.org
MIX
Papier | Fördert gute Waldnutzung
FSC® C083411

Kolibri 360 GmbH
Ferdinand-Jühlke-Straße 7
99095 Erfurt, Deutschland
produktsicherheit@kolibri360.de